COMPUTER BOOK SERIES FROM IDG

NetWare For Dummies

Cheat Sheet

If you get into a fix and don't want to look up answers, here's a quick look at the commands that take you around NetWare. You type the keystroke in the first column to perform the task in the second column.

W9-BIO-528

Utilities You Don't Want to Forget

SYSCON	Use the most important management command in NetWare versions 2.1x and 3.1x
MONITOR	Get an up-to-date look at your file server
NETADMIN or the NetWare Administrator (NWADMIN)	Replaces the SYSCON, FILER, and SESSION utility if you're using NetWare 4.0
NETUSER	Replace FILER, SYSCON, and SESSION if you're using NetWare 4.0

Lost and Found

These commands tell you where you are and who you are, in case you forget:

MAP	See the mapped drives attached to your login name
SLIST	See a list of servers on the internetwork
USERLIST	Find out who else is working (or playing) on the network
WHOAMI	Find your login name in case you forget
/H, /? or /HELP	You don't know how the command works and you want to find out (works with most commands)

Don't Fumble with Files

CHKDIR	View directory and volume information
CHKVOL	View volume information
FILER	Select directories, change file servers, and add, delete, or modify trustees, attributes, and effective rights; an all-purpose file utility
LISTDIR	List information about subdirectories
NCOPY	Copy files from one place to another
NDIR	See file and directory names
VOLINFO	Look at volume information

NetWare All-Purpose Editing Keys

The following function keys are used in many of the NetWare menu utilities:

F1	See Help screens
F5	Mark an entry to delete items
F6	Mark selections
F7	Cancel changes you have made
F8	Unmark marked selections
F9	Change modes
Alt+F10	Exit from a menu utility

Moving Around the File Server Console

If you're stumped when you use the file server console, remember that two simple keystroke combinations will get you around:

Ctrl+Esc	Bring up the active programs
Alt+Esc	Cycle from session to session

The Rule of the First Letter

NetWare uses the first-letter rule to help you get around its menu utilities: If you enter the first letter of the selection you want, NetWare takes you to the selection. If you have numerous selections that begin with the same letter, try entering the first two letters of the selection and see what happens.

. . . For Dummies: #1 Computer Book Series for Beginners

NetWare For Dummies

Cheat Sheet

If you get into a fix and don't want to look up answers, here's a quick look at the commands that take you around NetWare. You type the keystroke in the first column to perform the task in the second column.

Helpful Keys to Know About

When you're in a command-line utility, remember to use these useful keys (they take you around the menus):

Key	Action
Esc	Exit a program from the main menu, discontinue a process, or return to the previous menu
Ctrl+PgUp	Go to the beginning of a list
Ctrl+PgDn	Go to the end of a list
Yes	"OK, go ahead and confirm or exit"
No	"Nope, don't do what I told you to do"
PgUp	Go to the top of the menu
PgDn	Go to the bottom of the menu
Up	Move to the preceding selection or line
Dn	Move to the next selection or line
Ctrl+left arrow	Move to the beginning of the preceding word
Ctrl+right arrow	Move to the next word
Backspace	The universal key to erase the character to the left of the cursor
Ctrl+Alt+Del	Reboot your workstation if all heck breaks loose
Ins	See a list of options you can select from
Del	Delete an option previously selected
Home	Go to the beginning of the line
End	Go to the end of the line

A Quick Guide to Important NetWare Commands

Command	Description
BROADCAST	Send messages to users if you're the supervisor
CAPTURE	Send information to a printer or save information to a file
CASTOFF	Prevent messages from disrupting the work you are doing
CASTON	Permit messages to get to your workstation
DOWN	Take the file server down (used only by supervisors, if you're smart)
FCONSOLE	Down the file server, get connection information, broadcast messages, view the status of the file server, and see which version of NetWare it's running
FLAG	Change file attributes
GRANT	Give trustee rights to users and groups
LOGIN	Get at the network
LOGOUT	Close your network connection when you're finished for the day
MAKEUSER	Create or delete users
MENU	Create custom menus for your users' applications
NBACKUP	Back up your local drives and file server
NPRINT	Print to a network printer when you're not in an application
PCONSOLE	Create print servers, see information about printing on the network, and control network printing
PRINTCON	Define printer configurations
PRINTDEF	Create printer definitions
PSERVER	Bring up the network print server
RCONSOLE	Manage the server from a remote location
RIGHTS	View a file's or directory's effective rights
SALVAGE	Undelete a file you have erased
SEND	Send a message to another user or group
SESSION	Change file servers, view groups, send messages, select default drives, create search drives, attach to a server, and log out; lots of other functions work through SESSION
SETPASS	Change your password

. . . For Dummies: #1 Computer Book Series for Beginners

NETWARE FOR DUMMIES™

by Ed Tittel and Deni Connor

Foreword by Peter H. Lewis,
computer columnist for the *New York Times*

IDG BOOKS

IDG Books Worldwide, Inc.
An International Data Group Company

San Mateo, California ✦ Indianapolis, Indiana ✦ Boston, Massachusetts

NetWare for Dummies

Published by
IDG Books Worldwide, Inc.
An International Data Group Company
155 Bovet Road, Suite 310
San Mateo, CA 94402

Library of Congress Catalog Card No.: 93-78452

ISBN 1-56884-003-9

Printed in the United States of America

10 9 8 7 6 5 4 3 2 1

Distributed in the United States by IDG Books Worldwide, Inc.

Distributed in Canada by Macmillan of Canada, a Division of Canada Publishing Corporation; by Computer and Technical Books in Miami, Florida for South America and the Caribbean; by Longman Singapore in Singapore, Malaysia, Thailand and Korea; by Toppan Co. Ltd in Japan; by Asia Computerworld in Hong Kong; by Woodslane Pty. Ltd. in Australia and New Zealand; and by transword Publishers Ltd in the U.K. and Europe.

For more information on where to purchase IDG Books outside of the U.S., call Christina Turner at 415-312-0633.

For information on translations and availability in other countries, contact Marc Jeffrey Mikulich, Foreign Rights Manager, at IDG Books Worldwide; FAX NUMBER 415-358-1260.

For sales inquiries and special prices for bulk quantities, write to the address above or call IDG Books Worldwide at 415-312-0650.

 is a trademark of IDG Books Worldwide, Inc.

COMPUTER
BOOK SERIES
FROM IDG

About the Author

Ed Tittel is the author of numerous books about computing and a contributing editor to WindowsUser magazine. He's the co-author (with Bob LeVitus) of three best-selling books: Stupid DOS Tricks, Stupid Windows Tricks, and Stupid Beyond Belief DOS Tricks.

By day, Ed is director of technical communications for Novell, Inc. His job is to control technical content for Novell's corporate trade shows, marketing communications, and presentations. He is also a frequent speaker on LAN-related topics at industry events, and he has been a course developer for Novell in San Jose, where he designed and maintained several introductory LAN training classes.

Ed has been a regular contributor to the computer trade press since 1987, and he has written more than 100 articles for a variety of publications, with a decided emphasis on LAN technology. These publications include Computerworld, InfoWorld, LAN Times, LAN Magazine, The NetWare Advisor, BYTE, MacWeek, Macworld, MacUser, and Computer Shopper. He is also a regular columnist and contributing editor for WindowsUser magazine.

You can contact him at

    512-794-1440
    512-794-1773 (FAX)
    CompuServe ID: 76376,606

Deni Connor is a long-time computer-industry journalist who has specialized in networking since the beginning of time. She is the editor in chief and testing lab manager for NetWare Solutions, an independent magazine for Novell system managers published by Media Publications in Austin, Texas. She is a former technical editor for LAN Times magazine, where she worked for four years. She also has worked as a public relations manager for Thomas-Conrad Corporation.

In addition to the many hundreds of articles Deni has written for the publications already mentioned, she has been a regular contributor to the trade press, including InfoWorld, Data Communications, Corporate Computing, and other publications, in which she sometimes uses the pen name Paul Burch.

You can reach Deni on CompuServe at 75746,2545.

About IDG Books Worldwide

Welcome to the world of IDG Books Worldwide.

IDG Books Worldwide, Inc., is a division of International Data Group, the world's largest publisher of computer-related information and the leading global provider of information services on information technology. IDG publishes over 194 computer publications in 62 countries. Forty million people read one or more IDG publications each month.

If you use personal computers, IDG Books is committed to publishing quality books that meet your needs. We rely on our extensive network of publications, including such leading periodicals as *Macworld*, *InfoWorld*, *PC World*, *Computerworld*, *Publish*, *Network World*, and *SunWorld*, to help us make informed and timely decisions in creating useful computer books that meet your needs.

Every IDG book strives to bring extra value and skill-building instruction to the reader. Our books are written by experts, with the backing of IDG periodicals, and with careful thought devoted to issues such as audience, interior design, use of icons, and illustrations. Our editorial staff is a careful mix of high-tech journalists and experienced book people. Our close contact with the makers of computer products helps ensure accuracy and thorough coverage. Our heavy use of personal computers at every step in production means we can deliver books in the most timely manner.

We are delivering books of high quality at competitive prices on topics customers want. At IDG, we believe in quality, and we have been delivering quality for over 25 years. You'll find no better book on a subject than an IDG book.

John Kilcullen
President and C.E.O.
IDG Books Worldwide, Inc.

IDG Books Worldwide, Inc. is a division of International Data Group. The officers are Patrick J. McGovern, Founder and Board Chairman; Walter Boyd, President. International Data Group's publications include: **ARGENTINA's** Computerworld Argentina, InfoWorld Argentina; **ASIA's** Computerworld Hong Kong, PC World Hong Kong, Computerworld Southeast Asia, PC World Singapore, Computerworld Malaysia, PC World Malaysia; **AUSTRALIA's** Computerworld Australia, Australian PC World, Australian Macworld, Network World, Reseller, IDG Sources; **AUSTRIA's** Computerwelt Oesterreich, PC Test; **BRAZIL's** Computerworld, Mundo IBM, Mundo Unix, PC World, Publish; **BULGARIA's** Computerworld Bulgaria, Ediworld, PC & Mac World Bulgaria; **CANADA's** Direct Access, Graduate Computerworld, InfoCanada, Network World Canada; **CHILE's** Computerworld, Informatica; **COLUMBIA's** Computerworld Columbia; **CZECH REPUBLIC's** Computerworld, Elektronika, PC World; **DENMARK's** CAD/CAM WORLD, Communications World, Computerworld Danmark, LOTUS World, Macintosh Produktkatalog, Macworld Danmark, PC World Danmark, PC World Produktguide, Windows World; **EQUADOR's** PC World; **EGYPT's** Computerworld (CW) Middle East, PC World Middle East; **FINLAND's** MikroPC, Tietoviikko, Tietoverkko; **FRANCE's** Distributique, GOLDEN MAC, InfoPC, Languages & Systems, Le Guide du Monde Informatique, Le Monde Informatique, Telecoms & Reseaux; **GERMANY's** Computerwoche, Computerwoche Focus, Computerwoche Extra, Computerwoche Karriere, Information Management, Macwelt, Netzwelt, PC Welt, PC Woche, Publish, Unit; **HUNGARY's** Alaplap, Computerworld SZT, PC World; **INDIA's** Computers & Communications; **ISRAEL's** Computerworld Israel, PC World Israel; **ITALY's** Computerworld Italia, Lotus Magazine, Macworld Italia, Networking Italia, PC World Italia; **JAPAN's** Computerworld Japan, Macworld Japan, SunWorld Japan, Windows World; **KENYA's** East African Computer News; **KOREA's** Computerworld Korea, Macworld Korea, PC World Korea; **MEXICO's** Compu Edicion, Compu Manufactura, Computacion/Punto de Venta, Computerworld Mexico, MacWorld, Mundo Unix, PC World, Windows; **THE NETHERLAND'S** Computer! Totaal, LAN Magazine, MacWorld; **NEW ZEALAND's** Computer Listings, Computerworld New Zealand, New Zealand PC World; **NIGERIA's** PC World Africa; **NORWAY's** Computerworld Norge, C/World, Lotusworld Norge, Macworld Norge, Networld, PC World Ekspress, PC World Norge, PC World's Product Guide, Publish World, Student Data, Unix World, Windowsworld, IDG Direct Response; **PANAMA's** PC World; **PERU's** Computerworld Peru, PC World; **PEOPLES REPUBLIC OF CHINA's** China Computerworld, PC World China, Electronics International, China Network World; **IDG HIGH TECH BEIJING's** New Product World; **IDG SHENZHEN's** Computer News Digest; **PHILLIPPINES'** Computerworld, PC World; **POLAND's** Computerworld Poland, PC World/Komputer; **PORTUGAL's** Cerebro/PC World, Correio Informatico/Computerworld, MacIn; **ROMANIA's** PC World; **RUSSIA's** Computerworld-Moscow, Mir-PC, Sety; **SLOVENIA's** Monitor Magazine; **SOUTH AFRICA's** Computing S.A.; **SPAIN's** Amiga World, Computerworld Espana, Communicaciones World, Macworld Espana, NeXTWORLD, PC World Espana, Publish, Sunworld; **SWEDEN's** Attack, ComputerSweden, Corporate Computing, Lokala Natverk/LAN, Lotus World, MAC&PC, Macworld, Mikrodatorn, PC World, Publishing & Design (CAP), Datalngenjoren, Maxi Data, Windows World; **SWITZERLAND's** Computerworld Schweiz, Macworld Schweiz, PC & Workstation; **TAIWAN's** Computerworld Taiwan, Global Computer Express, PC World Taiwan; **THAILAND's** Thai Computerworld; **TURKEY's** Computerworld Monitor, Macworld Turkiye, PC World Turkiye; **UNITED KINGDOM's** Lotus Magazine, Macworld, Sunworld; **UNITED STATES'** AmigaWorld, Cable in the Classroom, CD Review, CIO, Computerworld, Desktop Video World, DOS Resource Guide, Electronic News, Federal Computer Week, Federal Integrator, GamePro, IDG Books, InfoWorld, InfoWorld Direct, Laser Event, Macworld, Multimedia World, Network World, NeXTWORLD, PC Games, PC Letter, PC World Publish, Sumeria, SunWorld, SWATPro, Video Event; **VENEZUELA's** Computerworld Venezuela, MicroComputerworld Venezuela; **VIETNAM's** PC World Vietnam

 The text in this book is printed on recycled paper.

Acknowledgments

We have way too many people to thank for this book to get it all right in a short space, so we would like to start out by thanking everybody who helped us that we don't mention by name. Actually, we couldn't have done it without you, even if we can't recall who you are! Thanks, anyway.

Ed Tittel
I want to share my thanks with a large crowd. First off, there's my family: Suzy, Austin, Chelsea, and Dusty — you were there for me when it counted. Thanks! Second, a talented crew of technical people helped me over a variety of humps, large and small. I would like to specifically mention Terry Ahnstedt, Jim Huggans, Iraj Farzaneh, Richard Trocino, Ric Smith, and Eric Robishaw. You guys are the greatest! Third, there's a whole crowd of other folks whose information has helped me over the years, especially the NetWire Sys*Ops — most notably, Mickey Applebaum, Dave Kearns, Les Lovesee, Andy Burbank, Don Crawford, and the rest of the gang. I'd also like to thank the geniuses, sung and unsung, at SuperSet and Novell who made NetWare possible, and my bosses past and present, Terri Holbrooke and Tom Jones, who put up with my weird schedule around book deadlines. And, to put the finishing touch on things, thanks, Mom and Dad, for making all of this possible!

Deni Connor
My thanks to Terry Ahnstedt, who not only provided lots of assistance for this book, moral and otherwise, but who also put up with the LAN outgrowing our office and snaking its way across the hallway into the living room and terminating in the dining room. My thanks and considerable respect also go to Mark Anderson, Ed Liebing, and Dave Kearns, who agreed with me that a book of this nature was worth working on, and who taught me almost everything I know about LANs. And of course, like Ed, there are two people, and only two people, who made this all possible — my parents.

Ed and Deni owe an incalculable debt to our NetWare (Lite and otherwise) guru, Earl Follis, without whom this book would have been impossible. We need to thank his wife, Kaye, and his pigs, for letting us take so much of their prime time away from them. We hope it was worth it! We'd also like to thank Susan Price, sole proprietoress of Susan Price and Associates, who did the killer graphics for the book. Last, we want to thank the editorial staff at IDG books, especially Becky Whitney, our main contact and favorite copy editor of all time; Chuck Hutchinson, proofreader extraordinaire; Janna Custer, the lady who made it all happen; Jeremy Judson, the developmental editor; and the other editorial folks, including Mary Bednarek, Megg Bonar, Tricia Reynolds, Dorothy Aylward, and of course, David Solomon, the man with the golden touch!

Please feel free to contact either of us, care of IDG books, at 155 Bovet Road, Suite 310, San Mateo, CA 94402. If you like CompuServe, Ed's ID is 76376,606 and Deni's husband's ID (Terry Ahnstedt) is 75146,2545. Drop us a line sometime!

The publisher would like to give special thanks to Patrick J. McGovern, without whom this book would not have been possible.

Credits

Publisher
David Solomon

Managing Editor
Mary Bednarek

Acquisitions Editor
Janna Custer

Project Editors
Jeremy Judson
Rebecca Whitney

Editorial Assistants
Pamela Mourouzis
Patricia R. Reynolds

Technical Reviewer
Dennis Cohen

Production Manager
Beth J. Baker

Production Coordinator
Cindy L. Phipps

Production Staff
Valery Bourke
Mary Breidenbach
Drew R. Moore
Tony Augsburger

Proofreader
Charles A. Hutchinson

Indexer
Sherry Massey

Book Design
University Graphics

Say What You Think!

Listen up, all you readers of IDG's international bestsellers: the one — the only — absolutely world-famous *...For Dummies* books! It's time for you to take advantage of a new, direct pipeline to the authors and editors of IDG Books Worldwide.

In between putting the finishing touches on the next round of *...For Dummies* books, the authors and editors of IDG Books Worldwide like to sit around and mull over what their readers have to say. And we know that you readers always say what you think.

So here's your chance. We'd really like your input for future printings and editions of this book — and ideas for future *...For Dummies* titles as well. Tell us what you liked (and didn't like) about this book. How about the chapters you found most useful — or most funny? And since we know you're not a bit shy, what about the chapters you think can be improved?

Just to show you how much we appreciate your input, we'll add you to our Dummies Database/Fan Club and keep you up to date on the latest *...For Dummies* books, news, cartoons, calendars, and more!

Please send your name, address, and phone number, as well as your comments, questions, and suggestions, to our very own *...For Dummies* coordinator at the following address:

...For Dummies Coordinator
IDG Books Worldwide
3250 North Post Road, Suite 140
Indianapolis, IN 46226

(Yes, Virginia, there really is a *...For Dummies* coordinator. We are not making this up.)

Please mention the name of this book in your comments.

Thanks for your input!

Contents at a Glance

Cartoons at a Glance

Table of Contents

Chapter 21: Keyboard Practice:
NetWare's Command-Line Utilities

Foreword

*R*elax, you're not a dummy. You're smart enough to have considered purchasing this book, after all. Obviously, you're an intelligent person who simply wants some simple, practical, no-nonsense guidance on how to use Novell NetWare.

Dummy? No, indeed. What you are, instead, is an innocent dupe of space aliens who are trying to take over Earth through local-area networking technology.

This book can save you.

It can now be revealed that sometime in the early 1980s, a scouting party of aliens from PlaNet Novell crash-landed in the Utah desert, where they established a central command post (a "hub," in their language) and began plotting the takeover of Earth. Their plan, code-named "NetWar," went through several revisions — Plan A, Plan B, etc. — before arriving at its current form, Plan E.

Net War E, cleverly renamed NetWare, has a deviously simple goal: to sow confusion and frustration among otherwise intelligent humans, in advance of the invasion, by forcing them to deal with the complexities of networked computers.

NetWare has succeeded in becoming the most common software for allowing two or more physically connected computers to exchange information. More than half of all the personal computers used in businesses and schools are now connected by local-area networks, and NetWare networks are even beginning to appear in your neighborhood.

Tens of thousands of otherwise normal humans have been enslaved as "network managers," with the seemingly impossible mandate to install, maintain, and otherwise keep the NetWare networks humming. Others have been driven crazy by the task.

You may be one of them, or perhaps a loved one.

You've seen what NetWare does to people: they have the glassy eyes and plastic pocket protectors, or, in the worst cases, they shout networking acronyms at inappropriate times:

> You: "Pardon me, sir, what time is it?"

> NetWare victim: "Whoami? Login! Purge! Nver!"

But these aliens did not count on Ed Tittel. I have known Mr. Tittel for many years and have come to rely on his refreshing ability to explain complex systems — ranging from networking protocols to obscure poker games — in simple, understandable terms. He's the only guy I know who can explain the differences between NetWare 2.*x* and 3.*x* while smiling.

His calm, gentle, and often humorous approach to the mysteries of NetWare have been reassuring and informative, and suddenly the threat of local-area networking does not seem so sinister as before.

NetWare can be a powerful tool for sharing information and tapping in to the true power of personal computers. It doesn't have to be hard, as Mr. Tittel demonstrates, and you don't have to have an advanced engineering degree from the University of Mars to set up an effective and reliable network.

And you don't have to be a dummy.

Peter H. Lewis
New York Times

Introduction

*W*elcome to *NetWare For Dummies*, the book that helps anybody who might be unfamiliar with Novell NetWare or with networks in general — even someone who might already be PC-literate — find him way into and around this mysterious world. Networks are the coming thing, or so the pundits say, and we all will have to use them one day, sooner or later.

Even though a few experienced individuals out there may already be familiar with NetWare and networks, an awful lot more of us are not just unfamiliar, but downright scared, of networking technology. To those who may be worried about the prospect of facing new and daunting technologies, we say "Never fear." Using a network is not beyond anyone's intelligence or abilities — it's mostly a matter of putting things in terms mere mortals can understand that's the problem.

This book talks about using NetWare and networks in everyday — and often irreverent — terms. Nothing is too wonderful to be made fun of, nor nothing too mysterious to put into basic English. This book focuses on you and your needs. In this book, you will find everything you need to know about NetWare and networking to be able to find your way around without having to know lots of arcane jargon and without having a Ph.D. in computer science. Plus, we want you to enjoy yourself — if networking really is the coming thing, it's important to be able to get the most out of it. We sincerely want to help!

About This Book

This book is designed so that you can pick it up at any point and begin reading — like a reference. Each one of the first 23 chapters covers a specific topic about networking or NetWare — networking basics, the various flavors of NetWare, setting up and using networked drives and printers, running networked applications (such as electronic mail), and the like. Each chapter is broken up into self-sufficient collections of information, all related to the major theme of the chapter. The chapter on LAN technology, for example, contains collections of information like this:

- The concept of a network service and why it's important
- How independent computers can share network services as peers, called peer-to-peer networking

✔ The rules of etiquette involved in sharing things with fellow users on a network, or how to be a good network client

✔ Learning how to find and use network services because asking for them isn't the same as getting them!

✔ The concept of a network server, along with a discussion of what servers are for and how they get used

✔ How to avoid overkill when you work with a network, or which tools are available and which ones make sense to use and when

You don't have to memorize things from this book. Each section is designed to supply the information you need, to make it easy to learn and use. On some occasions, you will want to work directly from the text to make sure that you get things right, but we do our best to warn you when that's happening. In most cases, you can go straight from the book and get right down to work.

How to Use This Book

This book works like a reference. Start with the topic you want to learn more about; look it up in the table of contents or in the index to get started. The table of contents supplies chapter and section titles and page numbers. The index supplies topics and page numbers. Turn to the index entry you select to find the related information you need. You can use the table of contents to identify areas of interest or broad topics; the index works best to pinpoint single concepts, individual topics, or particular NetWare capabilities, tools, or commands.

After you have found what you're looking for, you can quickly close the book and go through the task you have set for yourself — without having to grapple with anything else. Of course, if you want to learn additional information about your selected topic, or about something entirely different, you can check many of the cross-references used throughout this book or just continue reading from wherever you get started. We think that it would be a good idea to read Part I, "Introducing Local-Area Networks (LANs)," if you have never worked on a network; otherwise, just dig in!

When you need to key in something, you see the text you need to key in as follows:

```
TYPE THIS LINE
```

In this example, you're expected to type **TYPE THIS LINE** at the keyboard and then to press the Enter key. Because typing stuff can get confusing, we always try to describe what it is you're typing and why you need to type it.

When we describe a message or other information that you should see on your screen, we present it as follows:

```
This is an on-screen message
```

This book occasionally suggests that you consult the NetWare manuals for additional information. In most cases, though, you can find everything you need to know about a particular topic right here — except for some of the extremely bizarre and little-used details that abound in NetWare and information about applications that run with or on top of NetWare. If there's a topic we don't cover for those reasons, we suggest that you look for a book on that subject in the ...*For Dummies* series, published by IDG Books Worldwide. We also provide information so that you can get help when you need it, even if you choose not to investigate other ...*For Dummies* titles.

If you really want to learn all the nitty-gritty details about networks and NetWare, you need more information than you can find in this book. In addition to making yourself familiar with the voluminous manuals or on-line information that Novell typically furnishes with its products, we recommend that you look into the training classes on NetWare that are available, and that you consult the networking section of your local bookstore. Better yet, try a university bookstore or one that specializes in technical subjects. Some great tutorials and classes exist, as well as books and magazine articles that can expand your understanding. We cannot recommend anything offhand because nobody's offered us a kickback here!

What You Don't Need to Read

Computers swim in boatloads of technical information, much of it gibberish to the uninitiated. To better protect you from the uglier details, we have enclosed the most technical stuff in sidebars that are clearly marked as technical information. In most cases, you really don't have to read it. Sometimes, it's just a complex explanation of things we have already told you — it's aimed at those of you who have to know why or why not, or how a left-handed frammistat really works. Reading that information may teach you something substantial about networking or NetWare, but that's not our real goal here: We want you to be able to get on with your life and work, without having to get bogged down in too many details.

Who Are You, Anyway?

We're going to go out on a limb and make some potentially foolish assumptions about you, our gentle reader. You have a computer and a network — and probably some NetWare, or you are at least thinking about getting some — and you need to use it to *do* something. You know what you need to do, and you may even be able to do it, if somebody can just show you how (hopefully somebody more knowledgeable than yourself). Our goal in this book is to decrease your need for such a person, but we don't recommend telling him that out loud — at least not any time soon!

How This Book Is Organized

This book is broken into four major parts, each of which is divided into chapters. Every chapter covers a major topic and is divided into sections, which discuss particular issues or concerns about the topic. That's how things in this book are organized, but how you read it is your choice. Pick a topic, a chapter, a section — whatever strikes your fancy or fits your needs — and start reading. Any related information is cross-referenced in the text, to help guide you through the entire book.

Here are the parts and what they contain:

Part I: Introducing Local-Area Networks (LANs)

This part contains networking basics, including fundamentals of technology, operation, usage, and etiquette. If you're not familiar with networks, this section comes in really handy. If you're already an old hand, it's optional. Look here for discussions about a great deal of networking terminology, such as client, server, NIC, topology, and much more.

Part II: Gimme a Light — a NetWare Lite

This part covers Novell's peer-to-peer networking product known as NetWare Lite, including information about the basics of using the program, its requirements, its tools and capabilities, administering a Lite network, and deciding whether Lite is what you want, or less than what you really need.

Part III: Networking with NetWare

This part covers Novell's client-server network operating systems, known to one and all as NetWare, ranging from early versions to the more powerful and capable versions available today. This part starts with a road map to help you figure out which one you have and what to do with it. This part then talks about rules for running NetWare, the NetWare file system, network security, printing, messaging and electronic mail, backing up and restoring networked data, and lots more. In this part, you can find most of the real meat of the book, especially for those of you who already have NetWare and who want to become more familiar with it right away.

Part IV: The Part of Tens

This part serves in the grand tradition of the ...For Dummies books — namely, it provides lists of information, which we hope will mostly be unnecessary, plus tips and suggestions, all organized into short and convenient chapters. This supplemental information is supposed to be helpful and is supplied at no additional charge.

Icons Used in This Book

The icons used in this book point you to important (and not-so-important) topics discussed in this book.

This icon lets you know that you're about to get swamped in technical details. We include this information because we love it, not because we think that you absolutely have to master it in order to use networking or NetWare. If you're aspiring to apprentice nerd status, you probably will want to read it; if you're already a nerd, you will want to write us letters about stuff we left out or other information we should put in.

This icon usually signals that helpful advice is at hand, or provides some insight that we hope will make networking or NetWare more interesting or easier to use. For example, when you are adding a new piece of equipment to your computer, make sure that you unplug it before cracking open the case!

Oh gosh, we're getting older — we can't recall what this one means. Maybe you should check one out and see whether it's worth your time!

This one means what it says — that you need to be careful with the information it covers. Nine times out of ten, it's warning you not to do something that can have particularly nasty or painful consequences, as in "Have you ever played Bet Your Job?"

This icon lets you know that you're about to learn the background or history relevant to a particular subject. Read it only if you care about the past; if your problems are in the present, skip it and get to the *real* dirt!

This icon refers you to another area in the book that more fully describes the topic being discussed.

Where to Go from Here

With this book at hand, you will be ready to go out and wrestle with networking, and be ready to take on even the most advanced version of NetWare. Find a subject, turn to its page, and you'll be ready to rock 'n' roll! Also, feel free to mark up this book, fill in the blanks, dog-ear the pages, and do anything that might make a serious librarian queasy. The important thing is to make good use of this book, and to enjoy yourself doing it!

Part I

Introducing Local-Area Networks (LANs)

The 5th Wave   By Rich Tennant

In this part...

You can get acquainted in this part with the basics of local-area networks, or LANs. We present the raw essentials here: such important ideas as how computers communicate with each other, why it's a good idea, and what makes it all happen. We also deal, of course, with such vital topics as proper network etiquette, the hardware and software that make up a LAN, and networking terms no one has ever bothered to explain (but that everyone assumes you already know). We even perform the dance of the seven veils, as we reinterpret a standard but ho-hum model for the way networking really works.

We present each chapter's material in small, easy-to-understand sections. And, if information is really technical (mostly worth skipping, in other words), it is clearly marked or isolated in a sidebar.

Chapter 1

A Network Is Just Like Tin Cans and String — Only Better!

● ●

In This Chapter

▶ Looking at a network

▶ Making a network work

▶ Talking trash: what computers say to each other

▶ Playing network trivia: the state of the art

▶ Touring a typical network

▶ Traveling on the network: how programs work

▶ Sharing resources on a network

▶ Networking applications

● ●

*I*f you have ever built a tin-can-and-string telephone, you know more about networking than you think you do. If not, we can't help you to recover your lost childhood, but we can make some basic points about networking anyway. If you're feeling nostalgic or adventurous, you can even try to build one today. Go ahead — go for it.

TECHNICAL STUFF

Primitive communications or nostalgia trip?

The way the tin-can-and-string telephone works is that two cans are attached by a string. One kid yells into the open end of one tin can, and the other kid holds the open end of his tin can around his ear and strains to hear what the other kid bellows. The two secrets to building a good tin-can-and-string telephone are shown in this list:

1. Make the knots at the end of the string big enough to plug the small holes the string gets threaded through.

2. Stretch the string taut between the yeller (the sender) and the yellee (the receiver).

The key ingredients are that someone talks while the other person listens, and the string between the cans is capable of transmitting the sound. In addition to being much more reliable, an electronic network is much more efficient and much more precise. No yelling is required, although it does seem to help sometimes, especially when things get weird.

From an electronic perspective, a networked PC has an awful lot in common with a telephone handset or a household intercom system. Extending the tin-can-and-string metaphor, a network requires the ability to listen or to talk over a connection between at least two machines. Although computerized networks may seem much more mysterious than this basic idea, that's what they all boil down to, sooner or later. When computer networks aren't working, they boil down to even less than that.

Now that we hopefully have demystified some of the magic of networking PCs, you can relax and enjoy this chapter, which provides a gentle introduction to networking. You will learn basic ideas in this chapter, which is a primer for the rest of the book.

What Is a Network?

What is this networking stuff about, anyway? Why is everyone so excited about it? What is a network interface? Why do I have to worry about which kind of network I'm using? All these topics are important to networking, and you will want to understand the pieces and parts to be better equipped to deal with connecting your computer to a network.

A *network* is a collection of at least two computers that are linked together so that they can communicate with each other. Most networks are based around some kind of cable that's used to link computers together — typically, copper wire of some sort — through a connection that permits the computer to talk (and listen) to the wire. More than just hardware is involved, though. Cables and connections are essential to networking; without computer software to use them, however, they're purely decorative.

A really simple-minded view of networking has these three fundamental requirements:

- **Connections:** Include the physical pieces of gear needed to hook up a computer to the network and the wires or other materials — known as the networking *medium* — used to carry messages from one computer to another, or among multiple computers. Because the gear that hooks up a computer to a network acts as an intermediary between the computer and the network, that gear is called the *network interface* (for PCs, attaching to the network requires an add-in board called a *network interface card,* or *NIC*). Without physical connections, computers are isolated from the network and have no means to communicate with it.

- **Communications:** Establish the rules for how computers talk to each other, or what things mean. Because one computer can — and often does — run radically different software than another one might, this requirement states that computers must be capable of speaking a "shared

NOTE

Networking prehistory (you can skip this background material)

Networks were invented back when computers were really big — most computers then filled very large rooms. Computers were also really, really expensive — most of them cost more than a thousand times the average worker's annual salary. Because computers were such scarce and fabulously costly beasts, they weren't expected to be widely available or easy to access.

The U.S. government got a number of companies involved in building networks so that they could spread the use of Uncle Sam's fabulously expensive machines among different groups of users.

Even though the scope, cost, and size of networking has changed radically since those pioneering days, the key concept of sharing remains one of the best justifications for networking. Networking makes it possible to share things that may still be scarce or expensive. A single printer may not cost much, but when you begin to calculate the cost of putting one on every desk, it adds up quickly. Electronically speaking, networking is still the preferred method of bringing together people and resources.

language" to be able to communicate successfully with each other. Without shared communications, computers are incapable of exchanging information with each other and they remain isolated.

✔ **Services:** Define the things computers can talk about with each other. Put differently, services are the things that computers can *do* for each other, including sending or receiving files, sending or receiving messages, looking up information, and talking to printers. Without services, computers cannot understand requests, or formulate replies, to what other computers may ask for or provide. Again, without the capability to *do* things for each other, computers still remain isolated.

What Makes a Network Work?

The three fundamentals of networking — connections, communications, and services — must come together in order for a network to function. But what really makes a network work?

First, the connections have to work so that any computer can talk or listen to the wire (or other medium) that provides the highway over which signals can move between computers. Without a connection, nothing happens. Think of a network as a telephone at the phone store, sitting on a shelf. It's perfectly capable of working, after you hook it up to the phone system; without a connection, however, it cannot do anything. If it did ring, who would answer it?

,econd, the communications have to work so that, when one computer talks (sends a message), the others can listen to what that computer is saying and, hopefully, even understand what is being said. Without communications, nothing meaningful happens. The phone system analogy is illustrative here. Put yourself in a place where you don't understand the local language, and no one speaks yours either. You can try to talk to other telephone users, including the operator, but because you cannot understand what anyone is saying (and she can't understand you), you cannot have any kind of conversation.

Third, the computers have to be able to work together so that one can ask for things the other can deliver, and vice versa. Without a shared set of services, neither computer can do anything for the other. Without a shared set of services, nothing can happen. It's similar to trying to buy tires at a flower shop, or flowers at a tire store. Even though everyone knows what flowers and tires are, what you want isn't what they have.

Networking depends on being able to talk (having a working connection), being able to understand what other speakers are saying (sharing communications), and having something useful to say or do as a consequence of speaking (sharing services). It probably sounds simple, and it should, but making sure that all those components are doing what they're supposed to can be a difficult experience.

In short, all these different components must work properly in order for a network to be usable. As you become familiar with networks, you will realize that no one really notices when things are working OK; as soon as something goes wrong, however, everyone notices that things aren't working.

When Computers Talk to Each Other, What Do They Say?

When we look at what computers do to communicate with each other, the analogy to a telephone conversation breaks down somewhat. The basic principles are still there, however — unless you're talking to a teenager, and then all bets are off. Breaking down a typical conversation, as shown in Table 1-1, shows some striking similarities between the ways humans talk to humans and computers talk to computers.

Table 1-1   How Humans and Computers Converse

Human conversation	Computer conversation
Hello, this is Bob.	Computer states name and address of sender.
Is Mary there?	Computer states name and address of receiver.
Can I speak to her, please?	Computer asks for and sets up connection, and establishes access to receiver.
Mary, do you want to buy some insurance?	Computer requests or offers services.
Mary, I can offer you a whole-life plan for only $100 a year?	Computer makes specific request or provides specific service.
Thanks for your time.	Computer closes service.
Good-bye.	Computer breaks connection.

On the surface, the human and computer conversations aren't all that different — the basic pieces of each exchange are pretty much equivalent. When you look at the actual contents of the pieces, of course, you quickly realize that humans communicate with sounds that have specific but very flexible meanings, and that computers communicate with electronic bit patterns (for now, let's ignore the way they are shipped over the medium) that have specific and highly inflexible interpretations.

The answer to the question about what computers say is that they spend a small amount of time establishing a connection so that they can talk, the bulk of their time exchanging information about a specific service or request, and a small amount of time breaking the connection so that others can use the network. This process sidesteps the nitty-gritty details but captures the stages of communications.

The devil is in the details

Most of what computers do when they communicate is pass very specific electronic messages between themselves. Looking at communications from a gross level helps you to understand the basics of what's going on, although most people will never know — and do not care — about exactly what's happening. This statement is as true for the networking guru as it is for the average person. Most concerns about networking, no matter how technical, are related to getting things working and letting the details take care of themselves.

What's Normal? A Look at Network Industry Trends

Now that you have looked at how networks work and what computers say to each other when they're communicating, it's time to look at a typical network. Because of the range of networks out in the world, the incredible variation in network sizes, and the wide differences among the users who participate, this is an exercise in abstraction. In other words, the information about what's typical is based on industry statistics (and you know what statistics are worth).

It is estimated also that NetWare of one kind or another is in use on some 40 percent of these networks, or by 40 percent of the total number of users. This figure fits Novell's claims, from early 1993, that it has sold more than 2 million copies of regular NetWare and more than 700,000 copies of NetWare Lite. It also fits the company's claims that somewhere between 15 and 30 million individuals use some kind of NetWare regularly.

If the numbers don't lie — or at least don't misrepresent the truth too much — most networks now are fairly small and simple. The trend, however, is toward ever-increasing size and complexity. The number of individual networks per company, including all sizes of businesses, is up from a modest 0.78 in 1988 to a more aggressive 1.31 in 1992, and it continues to grow. When you consider that 95 percent of all businesses fall on the "small" end of the continuum, this figure makes for some pretty large and complicated networks in the remaining 5 percent. This 5 percent has most of the networks in daily use, but it means that small business is where you may expect to see the biggest growth as we push into the 21st century.

Three kinds of data: lies, damned lies, and statistics

Even though lots of networks are in use — by most industry estimates, between 3.5 and 5 million networks are in use worldwide, with more than 60 percent of them running in the United States alone — the total number of users per individual network averages between a modest 8 and an equally modest 15 users. By all accounts, this estimate puts the total number of network users worldwide between 28 and 75 million individuals (source: Meta Group, 1993). The basic point is that many networks are out there, with many users taking advantage of their capabilities.

Here's the picture that emerges from the numbers:

- ✔ The average network handles a small number of users, that is, from 8 to 15.

- ✔ The average network uses a small amount of dedicated networking equipment, including one server, one or two printers, and a small amount of other gear to get things working.

- ✔ Most networks are too small to justify hiring dedicated networking specialists, which means that average folks — like you — end up being responsible for running the bulk of those networks.

It's an interesting world to find yourself in, and an increasingly common one. Because you're reading this book, you probably are pretty well described by these statistics, or you may be networking on a smaller scale. If you're not, taking a look at the networking in your immediate vicinity should still fit this model. As you will learn later, large, aggregated networks usually break down into collections of small, individual networks. When it comes to understanding what's going on, your own, immediate neighborhood is always the most important one to know well.

A Tour of the Facilities

If you take a tour of a statistically average network, you generally find several classes of equipment and a variety of different kinds of software in use. If you make an inventory of these pieces and parts as you take the tour, you can use the inventory to try to figure out what's out there, what the pieces and parts are for, and what they do. Ready or not, let's do it.

First stop: Your desktop

Part of the great beauty of networking comes from taking the perspective that what you do at your desk — and we hope, for your sake, that your activities are best described as "productive work" — is extended by merely adding a network. From that point of view, adding networking to your bag of tricks gets you to resources and other things that otherwise may be unavailable to you, or at least much less affordable. Taking this view doesn't require a giant leap of faith — just stretching the boundaries of your desktop.

For convenience, call the computer you work at every day your *desktop machine* or, simply, your *desktop*. One of the key goals of networking is to take all the desktops in use in an organization and hook them together so that they can communicate with each other and share resources such as large disk drives, expensive laser or color printers, access to a CD-ROM, or whatever else users may need to do their job.

In a networked environment, it's normal to find a user-to-desktop ratio that's close to one-to-one. Put another way, every user has access to, if not exclusive possession of, a desktop computer attached to the network. Because desktops are typically the source of requests for resources and services, it's reasonable to call a desktop machine a *client on the network* or, simply, a *client*. Calling it a desktop focuses on its role in supporting an individual, typically working at a desk; calling it a client focuses on its connectedness to the network. Whatever you call it, it's still the same thing — the machine you sit in front of when you're working.

Second stop: Services come from servers

As you already have learned, without access to a shared set of services, or without a shared set of requests for information or service — and replies to match those requests — networking is a sterile exercise. Because networks aren't useful unless you can *do* something with them, access to services is a critical component of networking.

You go to a server to get a resource or to get something done. When you want to access a networked printer, it's safe to assume that a print server is lurking somewhere in the background to handle your print job. When you want to save or retrieve files from a networked drive, it's safe to assume that a file server also is lurking somewhere in the background. The same thing is true for most networked services, including such things as electronic mail, database management systems, and so on. For every service, there's a server that can handle what's necessary in order to deliver that service. Sometimes one server may provide many services; at other times, a server may be dedicated to only a particular service.

So, even though a service may not be handled exclusively by a single computer that provides only that capability — and this is seldom the case these days — it's useful to think of the computers that provide services as *servers*. A server's job is to listen for requests for its particular services and to satisfy all the legal requests it receives across the network. You will spend a great deal of time considering this idea as you read the rest of this book.

Third stop: The ties that bind it all together (the "glue")

In an era of Clintonomics, it has become fashionable to talk about "the infrastructure." This infrastructure is the system of roads, bridges, highways, and other modes of transportation that link our country into a working whole. From a networking standpoint, the pieces of equipment that hook computers into a network, the wires or other media that make up the network, and the specialized pieces of hardware and software used to control a network make up its particular infrastructure.

By the same token, it's reasonable to call this collection of connections, cables, interfaces, and other paraphernalia the "glue" because it is what ties the computers together into a working network. But, just as highways are useless without cars and trucks moving across them, networks are useless without computers to send and receive traffic across their links and pathways.

At this level, you may begin to worry about which kind of wiring to use — or which kinds of wireless technologies, if applicable. You also may be concerned about the kind of networking you're doing, the software that does it, and the pieces that make it all fit together. Because networking is invisible when it works as it's supposed to, it's also one of the easiest components of the computing puzzle to overlook, even if it is the most common source of problems.

Figure 1-1 is a simple diagram of the typical network that was just discussed. Notice that desktops outnumber servers and that the infrastructure must be everywhere in order to connect all the pieces and parts.

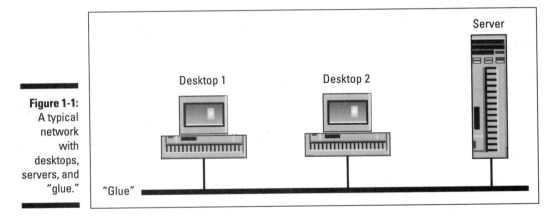

Figure 1-1:
A typical network with desktops, servers, and "glue."

How Programs Use the Network

The critical ingredients for using a network include the necessary hardware to make a physical connection, at least one other computer out on the network to communicate with, and a shared set of services that represent what the network can do for you. With all these requirements, what actually has to happen so that your computer can use the network? The answer is that your computer must know how to ask for services from the network and know precisely what to request.

Asking for services doesn't mean asking for favors

Knowing how to ask for network services means being able to tell the difference between what's local to and immediately available from your own computer, and what's available from the network. Determining this difference is the key to handling networks properly, and it depends on some specialized software to handle this job.

Sometimes, a program that keeps track of what you own and control on your own machine versus what's available across the network is used to discriminate between local requests and network requests. Because this piece of software takes requests for service and redirects any request that cannot be delivered by your own computer to a service provider (also known as a server) on the network, it's called — surprisingly enough — a *redirector*. Using a redirector is a pretty common way to handle network access from a desktop.

The local computer's main control program usually is called its *operating system* because it's the program that lets the computer operate and run the programs you're really interested in using to get things done. This control program sometimes gets a special augmentation or uses a modified version to incorporate "network intelligence" with an understanding of what's happening locally on the desktop. This augmentation is sometimes called a *shell program* or, simply, a *shell*. The shell handles all service requests, and rather than pass along things that aren't local to the network, the way a redirector does, it separates what's networked from what's not and hands things off accordingly. It too is a pretty common way to handle network access from a desktop.

It's becoming increasingly common for computer operating systems to have networking built in. Rather than bolt on a redirector or a shell to add networking intelligence, the operating system program already understands networking and includes it as a member of the set of functions it provides. As networking has become more commonplace, network support seems to be gaining a foothold in computer operating systems. This is the way the Macintosh, UNIX, and Windows NT provide networking capability.

Whatever the operating system, or the kind of network access it needs, the point is that a set of network services gets defined and a way to talk and listen to the network becomes available. Now you will want to figure out how to use this capability.

What's on the services menu?

For a computer to use network services, it must know how to ask for them, but knowing what to ask for is equally important. In most cases, your applications supply the knowledge about which network services are available, either through information supplied by the redirector or the shell or by intelligence built right in to the applications. Electronic-mail and remote-control applications are good examples of programs built to use networking capabilities directly.

Sometimes, all that's needed in order to add network know-how to your computer is to augment local applications or commands to make them network-aware: Extending directory listings or other DOS file-handling commands (DIR, TYPE, DELETE, and COPY, for example) to talk to networked drives is a classic illustration, as are other basic commands, such as printing and sharing data files.

Working through a specific command or a particular kind of program also means that you're working with a well-developed understanding of what you want the network to do. This understanding helps users interact with the network, and it also helps the people who write the programs you use to do what you expect them to.

Whether you treat the network as a basic part of your desktop or look at it as an extension of your local world, you can interact well with it only as long as you know exactly what you're trying to do. This statement may sound incredibly basic, but the crucial aspect of defining a common service is to work from a shared and explicit understanding of what that service is and what it does. Nothing less will do.

Whether this process happens is a function of the networking software and how it's set up. Even though all flavors of NetWare in this book can notify you when a print job is finished, they don't do so unless you set things up that way. (Don't worry — there's much more information about this subject in Chapter 18).

This discussion doesn't really capture all the nuances of how programs talk to the network, but it does capture the basics: knowing about a service, requesting that service, providing the information to handle the request (in this case, the file to be printed), and waiting for a reply (the optional notification that the file has printed successfully).

Every model and make of printer is a little different from all the other models and makes. To make the stuff coming from the printer look like what's on your screen — or to format it the way it's supposed to look, anyway — a spreadsheet program must translate the information you're trying to print from its internal format to an external format aimed at the printer you're printing to, or at least to a standard format, such as PostScript, that the printer understands. Sounds complicated, right? Well, it is. But that's what makes computing fun!

How networking works is...magic!

When a program is running — a spreadsheet, for example — and you want to print a copy to a networked printer, the sequence of actions works something like this:

1. Request print services from the spreadsheet.

2. Program formats the spreadsheet and then builds a print file for the printer.

3. The spreadsheet program sends the file to the printer.

4. The local networking software (whether it's a redirector, shell, or built-in operating system extension) recognizes that the chosen printer isn't local and ships the print file to a print server somewhere else on the network. It knows how to get to the print server and how to ship it the required print file.

5. The print file gets copied across the network to a holding tank for the chosen printer, where it gets in line behind any print files that may have arrived ahead of it that have not yet been printed.

6. The print file gets printed when its turn comes.

7. In this optional step, the user may get notified when the file has finished printing (so that you don't have to wait around the printer for your stuff to come out).

Sharing Resources Is Where It's At!

The preceding example provides a good picture of how network resources get used — by asking for them and by providing the right information so that services can be supplied. Because many users can send files to be printed on the printer in the hypothetical example just presented, it's also a classic illustration of how resources get shared. Sharing is the key to networking. After you have mastered this idea, everything else makes more sense.

The secret to sharing is making sure that everyone gets a shot at what needs to be shared. For the printer discussed in the preceding example, sharing access to the printer requires a "stand-in-line" mechanism so that print files can hang around until it's their turn to get printed; it also provides a dandy mechanism for keeping track of who goes next. This kind of waiting in line is called "first come, first served" because whoever gets in line first gets first crack at the printer. Other services may take a different approach to fulfilling requests, but they all have to have some way to keep track of who has asked for what, and in what order, so that they can handle requests from multiple users in some kind of reasonable way. Isn't that what sharing's all about?

The most important job a server performs is keeping track of all the requests for service it receives, controlling access to its resources, and delivering on valid requests as soon as it possibly can. The mechanisms that make that delivery possible also make sharing possible. Ain't it grand?

Chapter 2
Linking Up Your Network, or Lost in the Wires

In This Chapter

▶ Making connections that work
▶ Identifying common cable types
▶ Wrestling with the wires to come out on top
▶ Cabling up: Network wiring schemes
▶ Introducing the Big Four network technologies, plus one

Chapter 1 described networking as requiring three fundamental components: connections, communications, and services. Here, you look deep within the connections that tie networks together to see how they behave.

Connections are the wires or other media that move electronic signals from computer to computer, along with the interfaces that hook up the computers to the media.

Because wires on networks behave much like pipes do for plumbing, this chapter looks at the pipes that move data around. Hopefully, you will be better able to understand how things work, and why they sometimes don't work, on your real networks if we follow the metaphorical pipes around to see where they go and what they do!

The Tangled Web: Making Connections Work

Without a working connection, there's no way for information to get from one machine to another. This requirement is the most fundamental for networking, and it's also the most common source of problems and failures.

For many people, the secret to success in the business world can be summed up in one word: "connections." To explain how that fits in more precisely with an understanding of the cause for most network problems, it's what you probably would call "loose connections."

You know Alice in accounting, right? She — and her desk chair — ricochet around her office like a crazed projectile as she answers the ceaseless stream of questions from upper management about payables and receivables. She's always racing from one set of files to another, compiling the meaningless statistics that keep the fat cats happy. So what if she runs over the cables that stick out of the back of her PC every now and then. They still look OK, don't they? Don't they?

It really doesn't matter how they look — it only matters how they conduct electricity (or light waves, or whatever) when the network is running. And, as for who cares about the condition or integrity of her network cables, the answer might very well be "everyone." For several kinds of networks, failure of one cable means failure of the whole networking shebang. It's a truism that a well-run network fades into the background, and it's equally true that a broken network throbs worse than a finger slammed in a car door. If you don't believe us — break your network on purpose and see what happens.

As contrived as this scenario may seem, it doesn't even come close to capturing all the wacky ways that "loose connections" can come back to bite you — or at least, your network. The truth-is-stranger-than-fiction department of wiring problems includes notable items such as these:

- "I needed something to tie up a package."
- "What do you mean, I can't unhook my computer from these wires whenever I want to?"
- "Oh, I borrowed that cable to hook up my VCR."
- "I didn't even know we had a network!"
- "The electrician" (or the plumber, the A/C guy, or whomever) "said that these wires weren't important and, anyway, they were in his way."

We hope that you're beginning to get the idea. If not, here it is again — no wires (or no medium) means no network. Break the wires (or damage the medium) and you break the network. Got it?

Common Cable Types

Before we can get into much detail about how wires can be arranged and how networks can use them, we have to tell you a little about what kinds of wires are typically used in a network.

Three basic kinds of cable typically get used in networks these days:

- ✔ Twisted-pair
- ✔ Coaxial cable
- ✔ Fiber-optic cable

Twisted-pair wiring

Twisted-pair wiring lives up to its name, as depicted in Figure 2-1. Twisted-pair's greatest strength is also its greatest weakness because TP, as it's called, is also the type of cabling used for telephone systems. This means that TP is everywhere. It also means that the temptation is nearly irresistible to use telephone wiring for LANs as well as for telephones. Although recycling unused telephone wiring has the appeal of saving money — believe it or not, the biggest single expense item for most new networks is cabling costs — and works perfectly well for today's voice-grade phone lines, it doesn't always work that well for networks.

Recycling is a wonderful idea, and saving money resonates with preserving the bottom line. Nevertheless, it's a wise move to have your TP wiring system tested before blithely assuming that it will do the job for your LAN. It's much more expensive to have to rebuild a network than it is to build one right in the

Look, Ma — no wires!

Just to make things more confusing, it's also possible to omit wiring entirely when you are building a network or connecting pieces of a network. This concept is called — surprise! — wireless networking. It typically uses some kind of broadcast frequency that ranges from infrared for short-range or special-purpose connections to radio frequencies for spread-spectrum devices all the way up to microwaves for high-speed LAN-to-LAN links.

Soon, cellular telephone modems and battery-powered laptop computers may even create the foundations for so-called virtual networks, in which everyone can move around and yet remain connected to each other. Today, wireless networking is too expensive to be a reasonable choice, but it's definitely coming. When it happens, you will never be able to get away from the office! We can hardly wait. You probably can't either.

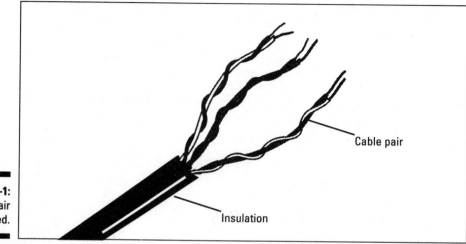

Cable pair

Insulation

Figure 2-1:
Twisted-pair
revealed.

first place. So, if you're thinking about reusing already installed TP wiring for your LAN, make sure that you avail yourself of the services of a cable-testing technician who can tell you whether that's a wise move or a pipe dream.

TP comes in two flavors: shielded and unshielded, sometimes abbreviated as STP for shielded twisted-pair and UTP for unshielded twisted-pair. The difference between the two, of course, is that one has a foil or wire braid wrap around the individual wires that are twisted around each other in pairs, and the other does not.

UTP is the main kind of cable used for telephone systems, but STP offers better conductivity and insulation, and generally better fits the needs of an office environment. STP also costs more than UTP — it has more stuff in it. If you can choose which cable to buy, go for STP; if not, test what you have before using it — you may be able to make a case for STP.

No network is bad news!

What's worse than no network at all? A network that doesn't — or cannot ever — work is much worse than no network. Take heed of our advice to test your already installed TP wiring before trying to build a network around it. An ounce of testing is worth a pound of later expense. It may also be worth your job.

For better or worse, TP is the wiring system of choice for bringing network connections to people's desktops. Recent advances in networking technology make TP safe and usable, if the wiring is up to snuff. That is the reason that older wiring can be such a pain.

The upside of TP is that the wiring is cheap, it's easy to install if new cable is needed, and existing telephone equipment can be used for networking as well as for telephone needs. If you work for a company that's big enough to care about these things, you're probably already using TP.

One downside of TP is that it requires specialized hardware, called *hubs,* to connect more than two computers, which adds costs to the construction of a network. Another downside is that it forces telephone techies and computer nerds to — gasp! — work together regularly. If you think that computer nerds are weird, wait until you meet the phone pholks! The final negative is that TP can handle only short distances between the hub and the desks it must reach. The real number varies with the cable used, but a good rule of thumb for maximum TP reach is 75 feet from hub to desktop, and that ain't as the crow flies — it's as the cable runs.

Coaxial cable

Coaxial cable consists of a two-element cable: A center conductor is wrapped by an insulator, which is wrapped by an outer conductor that is typically a wire braid, which is covered by still more insulation. Coaxial cable, or *coax,* as it prefers to be known, is used for cable TV. Even if you don't think that you know what it is, you probably can relate to cable TV. If not, check out Figure 2-2 — it shows all the different parts.

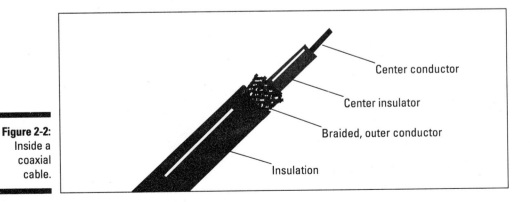

Figure 2-2:
Inside a
coaxial
cable.

Center conductor

Center insulator

Braided, outer conductor

Insulation

Coaxial cable can handle many signals across a broad range of frequencies. Look at it this way: Each TV channel eats a fair amount of spectrum, and a single coax cable can carry as many as 200 channels and more these days. So, it's no sweat to use coax for networking, either.

The downside of coaxial cable is that it's thick and relatively stiff, especially in comparison to TP. It also requires expensive, specialized connectors and well-trained, knowledgeable installers to handle it. If you have ever tried to make your own cables run between your TV and VCR, you may begin to relate to one of our "wire stories" earlier in this chapter. Even though coax is much stronger than TP, it is also much more difficult to repair if it does break.

The upside of coaxial is that it's very resistant to electrical and magnetic interference, which can be a problem in some office buildings. Coax can also be used to build networks that span much larger areas than TP can cover. Again, the maximum length per cable varies with the kind of cable in use, but it ranges from 500 to 1,500 feet. Many network designs use both TP and coax, with TP used on a per-floor basis to run wires out to individual desktops and with coax used to wire together multiple floors. Who says that you can't have the best of both worlds?

For very small networks, coax is worth considering because you can buy prefabricated cables of varying lengths. You can easily hook up a network, and you can change things around equally easily when you have to. We're writing this book on a LAN that's been cabled together with something called Thinwire Ethernet (a.k.a. 10Base2). Its biggest attraction is that you can go to the electronics store and buy everything you need to cable up a small network for about $30 per workstation (not including each computer's network interface).

Fiber-optic cable

Unlike its copper cousins, there's not much that's metallic about *fiber-optic cable*. Figure 2-3 shows that the anatomy of fiber-optic cable closely resembles that of coax. Take our word for it, though: Only the drawings look similar, not the cables.

Fiber-optic is much more flexible than typical coaxial is (but you still must handle it carefully, especially the glass-based variety). Fiber-optic cable runs can also be pretty long, ranging from 1½ to 20 miles per cable, depending on which kind of cable and which kind of network is in use.

On the plus side, fiber-optic cable is immune to environmental interference, short of a black hole wandering nearby. If a black hole does happen by the neighborhood, we would bet anything that problems with your fiber-optic cable will be very low on your priority list anyway.

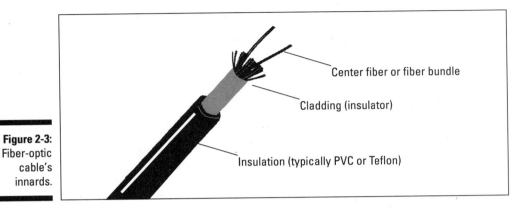

Center fiber or fiber bundle

Cladding (insulator)

Figure 2-3:
Fiber-optic
cable's
innards.

Insulation (typically PVC or Teflon)

Fiber's biggest advantage is the amount of information it can carry, called the *bandwidth*. Fiber-optic typically can handle thousands of times more data than copper cable can. If you're planning for the future, fiber's the only way to go.

On the downside, fiber is more expensive than copper. Even though the cable costs aren't that different, installation costs for fiber are much higher. The reason is that each end of a fiber must be polished to achieve maximum light transmission, and the best polishing is still done one cable at a time, by a human technician.

Because of the sensitivity and precision necessary to achieve the best results, experienced fiber-optic installers are scarce, and their labor charges come at a premium. Installation costs are the main reason that fiber still costs twice as much as copper — or more. The interface costs also are still high, at about the same ratio as installation costs. If you add it all up and aren't prepared to amortize it over the long run, fiber isn't worth it.

Never, never, never hire a cable installer who cannot provide multiple references for a fiber-optic installation job. Always check those references, too. It's not what the installer says that counts — it's what paid-up customers think that makes the difference. Don't spend your money to be someone's guinea pig. It can cost you more than you would ever want to know — or spend.

Cabling Tips for Do-It-Yourselfers

If you're going to mess around with wiring, either to extend an existing LAN or to build an entirely new one, here are a few things you should attend to as you go about your business:

TECHNICAL STUFF

Fiber, you light up my life!

Fiber-optic cables are built around conductive elements that move light, not electricity. For most fiber-optic cables, the conductive element is most likely a form of special glass fiber rather than copper or some other conductive metal. Even though plastic-based fiber-optic cable is available today, it's not as light-conductive as glass, and it cannot cover the long distances that glass can. This property means, among other things, that you must be careful when you handle fiber-optic cable — a sharp bend or an overly tight stretch makes the glass fibers act the same way as any other overstressed piece of glass might. Mistreat it too much, and it breaks.

✔ Observe local, state, and federal building codes. If you're planning to run cable, some of it will probably be in the ceiling. If that area is used also for A/C ventilation (it's called plenum airspace or plenum air return), building codes require you to use nontoxic, nonflammable cables — Teflon-coated cable — in these areas. It costs more, but it doesn't release toxic fumes, as plain plastic coatings will, if the place ever catches on fire. Plus, it's the law!

✔ The make-versus-build argument is worth reviewing for copper cable, but not for fiber. If you decide to build your own copper cables, buy the best cable and connectors you can afford. Then buy a professional crimping tool, whether you can afford one or not. These tools rarely go for less than $100 a pop, and they require special insets, called dies, for each specific cable and connector diameter. Although a cheap crimping tool — and you can find them for as little as $20 — screws up your work every time, a good one brings home the bacon.

✔ When it comes to TP, buy the best cable you can get. Use STP if you can possibly justify it. Better quality means better conduction for TP of any kind and, because it's marginal stuff to begin with, it's smart to hedge your bets and go with the best possible cable.

✔ If you have to lay cable in any amount, large or small, make sure that you check the building's electrical plans before getting started, especially if you are using TP cable. More than one LAN installation has been botched by running cable right next to large motors or transformers (elevators usually have big samples of each genre, right near the shaft) that then interfere with transmissions forever after. An ounce of planning is worth lots of expensive cure.

✔ If you plan to lay any cable yourself, be prepared for slow, dirty, back-breaking work. Check your budget again. If you have to be a do-it-yourselfer, spend at least enough money to get an experienced installer to review your installation plan and help you get started. This job is best left to professionals, and experience is a dear teacher.

> ✔ Above all, plan ahead and stay upbeat when things get weird — and they
> always do. If you know what you need to do and are confident about what
> you can accomplish, you will know when to move ahead and when to ask
> for help. These are truly words to live by, and not just for installing cable.
> Good luck!

Now that you have looked at the wiring itself, the next step is to examine how
wiring typically gets laid out.

It's Not a Wiring Layout — It's a Topology!

Mathematicians love to create fancy words for abstruse ideas and other
mysterious stuff. The term used to describe wiring layouts comes from their
sick minds. Any arrangement of lines can be called a *topology*, and that's what
network-savvy folks call the different kinds of networking schemes. The *star* and
bus discussed here are short for *star topology* and *bus topology*. Likewise, a *ring
topology* refers to a wiring pattern laid out in a circular manner. Isn't that special?

There are many ways, in fact, in which network wiring can be laid out. Figure 2-4
shows the two most common layouts — the star and the bus.

Stars get in your eyes

A star consists of separate wires that run from a central point (the hub, 'cause
it's in the middle) to devices — typically, computers — on the other end of
each wire. A bus consists of a single cable to which all the computers on a
network, or a piece of a network, get attached. If you break a wire in a star, it
affects only the link that's broken; if you break a wire on a bus, it affects
everything connected to it. It's true that wire breaks are more catastrophic on a
bus than in a star, but if your machine is the one that's affected by the break,
you won't care which kind of layout you have.

In a star topology, the hub at the center of the star acts as a relay for computers
attached to its arms. The process works like this:

1. The sending computer sends a chunk of information — let's call it a
   message — across the wire to the hub.

2. The hub resends the message to the destination computer, if it's attached
   to the same hub, or to another hub if it's not.

3. The hub to which the destination computer is attached resends the
   message to the destination computer.

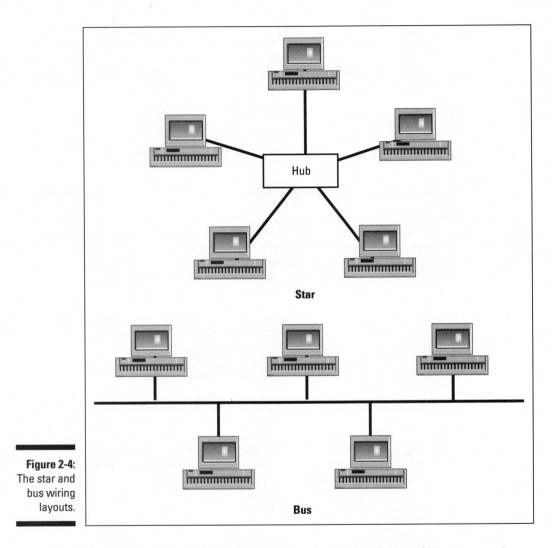

Figure 2-4:
The star and
bus wiring
layouts.

On a large network, the middle step may be repeated several times as you jump from the hub to which the sender is attached, across hubs between the sender's and receiver's hubs, until you reach the receiver's hub and then, finally, the destination computer.

You're either on the bus or off the bus!

On a bus topology, every computer on the wire sees every message that gets sent. If sender and receiver are on the same wire, messages get delivered very quickly. If sender and receiver are not on the same wire, a special message-forward computer has to route the message from the sender's wire to the receiver's wire, which consists of copying the message as sent and then retransmitting it over another wire.

Just as you might have to forward a message through multiple hubs in a star topology, you can forward a message through multiple message-forwarding computers, called *routers,* on a bus topology.

Running rings around the network

While we're on the subject of topology, here's another one for you: the ring topology. Real rings seldom get built because they're too prone to failure; the idea of a ring often gets implemented, however, over a bus or a star, or in the form of a redundant ring with multiple cables and pathways to improve the odds that it will keep running. It sounds strange, but mapping a ring onto a star or a bus is the way some networking technologies work, including ARCNET (bus and star) and token ring (star).

What makes a ring attractive is that it keeps track of who gets to send a message by circulating an electronic "permission form" around and around the network. This form keeps workstations from trying to send messages at the same time and can greatly improve network availability for everyone. The idea is that you must wait until the permission form comes around to your computer before it can send a message. Everyone then must wait the same amount of time to send a message, on average, and it enables networks to be used very fully before they start slowing down.

Brand X Basics: The Kinds of Networks

Although literally hundreds of different kinds of networks are out there for sale, the kinds of networks can be broken into five different categories. You can distinguish these kinds from one another by answering the following questions:

- What kind of technology does the network use?
- How does the network work?
- What are the network's technical pros and cons?
- What kinds of media does it support?
- How business-friendly (cost, availability, reliability, and that sort of thing) is this network?

These basic concerns are discussed in this section, and the mystery candidates then are compared and contrasted. Then we make some admittedly biased recommendations.

Introducing the Contestants

When you start talking about kinds of networks, you're talking about the name for and type of networking technology the network hardware is built around.

It's important to distinguish between a network topology and a network technology.

The *topology* identifies a network's wiring scheme. It describes how communications move around and among the computers and other devices that send and receive information across a network.

The *technology* identifies how the network behaves. It describes the network's electrical characteristics, the type of signaling it uses, what the connectors look like, how the interfaces work, and everything else necessary to build a working environment. Topology deals with network layout; technology deals with how the network operates. Put another way, a topology describes a wiring layout, and a technology is what you buy to make it work.

For the purposes of this book, there are four different network technologies (but that's a gross oversimplification, as you will see in a minute):

- ✔ Ethernet
- ✔ Token ring
- ✔ ARCNET
- ✔ Fiber Distributed Data Interface (FDDI)
- ✔ Other

Acronym-o-phobes beware!

Acronyms provide a useful form of shorthand. Referring to something by its initials, such as FDDI rather than Fiber Distributed Data Interface, is a way of life in the computing industry in general, and in the networking industry in particular. If the idea of swimming in a bowl of alphabet soup makes you queasy, maybe networking isn't the right thing for you.

The point we're trying to make is that we introduce and use networking acronyms throughout this book. This is not deliberate torture — it's just the way things are done in the networking world.

We tried to beat them and failed, so we have joined them. We try to make joining up as simple and painless a process for you as we possibly can. Hang in there!

If you get lost, or forget what something means, we do our best to make sure that all the acronyms we use in this book appear in the glossary at the back of the book. Think of it as reading a novel by Dostoyevski, where you have to make a list of all the characters' names to keep track of a cast of thousands.

Counted 'em yet? Five, not four! The first four technologies are the important ones, and there's enough left over in the "other" category that it's worth mentioning as a networking grab bag.

Entertaining Ethernet

As networking technologies go, Ethernet has been around longer than most — since the mid-to-late 1970s. It was the brainchild of Digital Equipment Corporation (DEC), Intel, and Xerox — which is why the old-fashioned, 15-pin D plugs for thick-wire Ethernet are still called DIX connectors — but it has long since passed into commodity status. Ethernet is a well-known, widely used, and readily available networking technology.

Description

Ethernet is known as a carrier-sense, multiple-access, collision-detection networking scheme. The following sidebar explains what this stuff means, in as close to everyday English as the subject allows.

The easiest way to think about how Ethernet works can be stated as "Listen before sending, listen while sending, quit if garbage happens, and if it does, try again later."

Strengths and weaknesses

Ethernet's strengths are many: It's robust and reliable, and comes in a broad and affordable range of flavors. Its weaknesses are lack of speed and collisions. For emerging high-volume applications such as real-time video or multimedia — you have those on your desktop, right? — Ethernet's speed is on the slow end. For the same kind of applications — lots of volume typically means lots of use — or, for networks that are heavily trafficked by more familiar applications, Ethernet does not perform well.

Three-plus flavors are available

Ethernet comes in all the basic flavors you would want, which means that it can run over all the major cabling types and works in both bus and star topologies.

The major cabling types are twisted-pair, coaxial cable (thin and thick), and fiber-optic cable. Ethernet devices to mix and match these cable types are readily available, which means that you can use Ethernet to build networks of just about any size or for even the most hostile environments using Ethernet. For more details, you can check out the section "Common Cable Types," earlier in this chapter.

Think of Ethernet as bumper cars for networks

The acronym that describes Ethernet is CSMA/CD, which stands for *carrier sense, multiple access/collision detect*. For those who are unfamiliar with this terminology, echoes are the auditory equivalent of a collision, and a collision means that you must repeat everything we have just said. The following list provides a definition for each term in this acronym:

- **Carrier sense:** Everyone attached to the network is always listening to the wire, and no one's allowed to send while someone else is already sending. When a message is moving across the wire, an electrical signal called a carrier is used, so listening to the wire lets you know when it's busy because you can *sense* that signal.

- **Multiple access:** Anyone attached to the network can send a message whenever he wants, as long as no carrier is being sensed. Because this statement means that multiple senders can begin at roughly the same time — when things are quiet — it's called *multiple access.*

- **Collision detect:** If two or more senders begin sending at roughly the same time, sooner or later their messages run into each other on the wire, which is called a *collision.* Collisions are easy to recognize because they always produce a garbage signal that bears no resemblance to a valid message. Ethernet hardware includes circuitry that can recognize this garbage quickly, which causes senders to stop sending immediately and forces each one to wait a random amount of time before listening to the wire (in case it's already busy) and trying to send again.

The business side

In spite of its age, Ethernet remains the most widespread and popular networking technology. Twisted-pair leads the pack for new Ethernet cabling choices, but there's still lots of coax out there. Fiber-based Ethernet is typically limited to connecting campus environments, where long distances and electrical-interference issues are greatest; it's also used in elevator shafts to connect multiple floors in a single building. (Remember what we said about elevators shafting your networks?)

The main reasons for Ethernet's continuing use are shown in this list:

- **Affordability.** Cabling is cheap, and interfaces range from less than $100 for desktops to less than $400 for servers. Ethernet isn't the cheapest of all available networking technologies, but it's close.

- **Many choices.** Ethernet supports all the cabling types, it offers lots of gear for building hybrid cabling setups, and many manufacturers offer Ethernet-based hardware. If you have a specialized need for networking gear, chances are that an Ethernet variant is on someone's drawing board, if it's not on a retailer's shelves.

✔ **Experience.** Because Ethernet has been around for so long, Ethernet-savvy people are easy to find. It means that many training courses, books, and other resources are out there to help you or your colleagues become more knowledgeable as well.

✔ **Continuing innovation.** At 10 Mbps, Ethernet isn't the fastest networking technology — not by a long shot. But vendors are out there who make special high-speed network switches for Ethernet, and there's even a proposal on the table for a new version of "fast Ethernet" that would increase its speed by a factor of 10 (to 100 Mbps). That speed should help Ethernet survive the climb to the next level of networking, where far-out things such as real-time video and multimedia will become commonplace.

Let's talk token ring

Token ring hasn't been around as long as Ethernet and ARCNET have, at least not in commercial form, but it has gained a substantial foothold in the market-place. Token ring, based on technology that was refined and originally marketed by IBM, is more commonly found in places where IBM is entrenched rather than in other kinds of computing environments

Description

Token ring is known as *token-passing* technology, and it should be understood as a collection of individual point-to-point links that happen to form a circulating pattern. *Point-to-point* means that one device is hooked to another; for token ring, that typically describes a computer attached to a hub, which itself may be attached to other hubs or computers.

The nice things about token ring are that it's fair to everyone who participates and that it guarantees that it cannot be overwhelmed by traffic. It's fair because it constantly passes an electronic permission slip, called a *token,* around the network. Any computer that wants to broadcast must wait until it has possession of the token to do so, and the token doesn't get released until the message has been delivered (or until it's obvious that it cannot be delivered). Everyone gets a regular shot at using the token, so token ring is equally fair to all computers on the network.

The easiest way to think about how token ring works can be stated as "Wait for a token; when the token comes by, if you want to send a message, tack it on to the token; when the token comes around again, strip off your message and send the token on."

Strengths and weaknesses

Token ring's strengths are its fairness and its guaranteed delivery capabilities. What these boil down to, operationally speaking, is that token ring works predictably and reliably, even when it is loaded to the max. Token ring is available in two speeds: The lower (and older) version runs at 40 percent of the purported speed of Ethernet but really runs only slightly slower because of Ethernet's incapability to use its full capacity. The higher (and newer) version runs at 160 percent of Ethernet's purported speed, but it really runs much faster because it can use multiple tokens and because it can run as fast as it says it can.

So, if token ring is so great, why does anyone buy anything else? Token ring's weaknesses have more to do with inflexibility and expense than with technical reasons, but its main downside is its requirement for expensive hub-like devices, called *media access units* (MAUs), and its requirements to run double strands of cable from computer to hub (one for the outbound trip and the other for the return trip). These requirements add to the expense and reduce the maximum distance between computer and hub. Token ring is also more complicated and uses fancier connectors than either Ethernet or ARCNET does.

Three-plus flavors are available

Even though token-ring implementations for TP, coax, and fiber are all available, TP is by far the most common implementation, and it's the most likely medium for tying desktops to hubs. Fiber is the cable of choice for spanning longer distances, and only limited amounts of coax get used for token-ring networking. Because of individual cable-length limitations and maximum ring-size limitations, cabling a token-ring network takes more planning and number-crunching than does cabling either ARCNET or Ethernet.

The business side

From a cost-benefit perspective, there's not enough upside in the reliability, fairness, and guaranteed performance of token ring to offset its higher costs. Token ring now costs between 160 to 200 percent more than Ethernet without necessarily conveying significant performance or reliability advantages. Although one school of network thought proclaims, "Token ring: Don't do it," we're not willing to go that far. If someone is giving the stuff away, or if that's what you're told to use, go ahead and use it. It won't kill you, and it works just fine. It's just not the technology of choice for starter networks.

Arguing ARCNET

Datapoint Corporation, of San Antonio, Texas, originated ARCNET, which stands for Attached Resource Computer NETwork. ARCNET is in use in more than 10 million computers worldwide, but that number is not as large as it could have been. Whereas both groups that fomented Ethernet and token ring pushed for their technologies to become engineering standards (and lost control over those technologies in the process), Datapoint tried to maintain exclusive control over ARCNET to take better financial advantage of it. The irony is that, by letting go, the other companies benefited far more than did Datapoint, which elected to hold on to its own technology. If it had not been for Datapoint playing its technology cards a little too closely to its vest, the complexion of the computer industry might be radically different today.

Description

ARCNET is called a *token-bus technology*. In this technology, the wires act like a bus — everything gets broadcast to everyone at more or less the same time — but a token-passing scheme is used to circulate the electronic permission slip that controls when a computer is permitted to transmit information.

Just as token-ring implementations typically map a ring topology onto a star configuration, ARCNET typically maps itself onto a star. ARCNET also supports coax buses, TP daisy chains (in which each machine hooks to each of its neighbors on a separate cable), and a variety of other configurations. From a cabling standpoint, ARCNET is the most forgiving and flexible of all the networking technologies covered in this section.

Strengths and weaknesses

ARCNET's upsides are cost, flexibility, and ease of use. Of all the major commercially available technologies, ARCNET is the cheapest. You can find Ethernet interfaces in the range from less than $100 to $400, and you can find equivalent ARCNET interfaces in the range from less than $50 to $250. It's easy to purchase prefabricated ARCNET cables and other components and put together a home-baked, hybrid network that will still be robust and reliable. It's also easy to mix and match components and cable types without having to plan all the details in advance. Finally, ARCNET offers the longest cable-length restrictions, from 300 to 2,000 feet per segment, and an equally capacious 20,000 feet (which can be doubled and redoubled at the cost of slowing things down) for total network span.

The primary downside is a function of the technology's age: a "speed limit" of 2.5 Mbps, only one-fourth of Ethernet's official rating and roughly one-half to one-seventh of token ring's. ARCNET still works very well for basic business applications, such as word processing and spreadsheet use; it bogs down, however, for the more demanding applications that loom on today's business horizons — multimedia, real-time video, and whatever else the futurists can dream up as the next big thing.

Three-plus flavors are available

As with Ethernet and token ring, ARCNET is available for TP, coax, and fiber-optic, with plenty of hubs that link together any two or all three of these wiring types. ARCNET's flexibility and electrically forgiving nature make it ideal for small networks or for networks that have to keep moving around a lot.

The business side

From a business perspective, ARCNET is every bit as much a commodity as is Ethernet. Despite its bandwidth limitations, ARCNET is just as "fair" as token ring, and it also guarantees delivery. ARCNET is the cheapest of all the technologies discussed in this section, and that doesn't look like it's due to change any time soon. Because ARCNET appears stuck in its current design — Datapoint tried to propagate a design for a 20-Mbps version called ARCNET-Plus, but it never went anywhere — it doesn't have as much room to grow into the 21st century as do the other alternatives that are discussed.

Here's how you should approach ARCNET:

- ✔ If you already have it, keep using it. It's even OK to add more, but add it judiciously.

- ✔ If you have to go absolutely bottom dollar, ARCNET is as low as you can go without pulling out the tin cans and string.

- ✔ If you're not forced to go with ARCNET, choose Ethernet or token ring (or something even faster). ARCNET is not the right place to start out anymore.

Fabulous FDDI

As networking technologies go, FDDI is about as fast as you can get and still be able to buy the stuff at your nearby high-technology store. The Fiber Distributed Data Interface was designed in the mid-1980s — at least 10 years after the options already covered in this chapter — to provide a high-speed, fiber-based, token-passing network. A successor, named FDDI-II, has already been designed that adds support for video, image, and voice data to conventional network traffic. You don't have to worry about this distinction, though. Both versions are lumped together and are just called FDDI.

One of the authors of this book pronounces FDDI using the letters — "eff dee dee eye"; the other one pronounces it "fiddy" — which rhymes with "giddy" or "Liddy" (as in G. Gordon, of Watergate fame). We don't care how you pronounce it, but it's safest to use the letters for clarity. (Can you guess which author wrote this tip?)

Description

FDDI was originally designed with the idea of tying together multiple networks, as a kind of superhighway for network data. Its data rate is a speedy 100 Mbps, which ranges from 40 times faster than ARCNET to 8.5 times faster than fast token ring. Figure 2-5 covers all these numbers for you, in a way we think is easy to understand. It's also a pretty good indicator of how all the technologies discussed here stack up against each other.

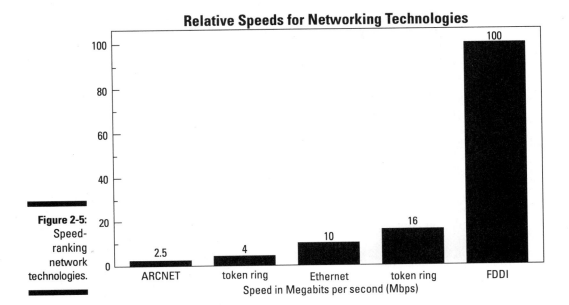

Relative Speeds for Networking Technologies

Figure 2-5:
Speed-
ranking
network
technologies.

Speed in Megabits per second (Mbps)

One of FDDI's best uses today is as a networking *backbone*. Just as your backbone ties the rest of your body together and carries all the important neural information throughout your body, a network backbone provides a special-purpose, high-speed link for tying lots of networks together. All FDDI networks aren't backbones, though, nor is every backbone an FDDI network. The two go together quite well because that's one of the things FDDI was made to do!

FDDI is another token-passing technology. FDDI cabling uses a real ring topology, but it consists of two rings — one transmits messages clockwise; the other, counterclockwise. If either ring breaks, the other ring automatically functions as a backup. If both rings get cut at the same place — look out for the guy with a backhoe! — the two rings can be spliced together to form a ring about twice the length but still capable of functioning.

Although FDDI functions well as a network that services other networks, it is also available for use as a LAN technology to hook computers together for high-speed connections. It's far more typical as a backbone technology today, but its LAN applications keep growing. We expect that this will change over time, however, as applications get more demanding and the technology gets cheaper.

Strengths and weaknesses

Certainly, FDDI's biggest advantage is speed — and lots of it. But there's still more to like about FDDI. It supports rings as much as 200 kilometers in circumference (that's *124 miles*, or thereabouts, for you nonmetric types). FDDI also supports as many as 1,000 devices on a single cable segment, which also is considerably more than any of the other technologies discussed here. Speed, distance, and coverage — what more could anyone want?

On the downside, FDDI requires fiber-optic cable for runs of any length. Even though there's a CDDI (*C* stands for copper, but otherwise it's the same as FDDI), it doesn't support cable runs of longer than 75 feet, and CDDI isn't widely available yet.

Cost is another negative. FDDI uses fiber for expensive installation and higher-cost cables, and FDDI interfaces range from a low of $1,000 to as high as $7,000 to $8,000 per computer. Even on the low end of that range, that's more than many consumers want to pay for a computer, let alone a network interface. Expect that figure to change soon, though. Recently, the bottom end of the FDDI interface market was $1,800 or so. As the technology gets cheaper, FDDI looks better and better.

Two flavors: High in fiber and copper

FDDI is the fiber version; CDDI, the copper version. Currently, the copper side of the family is purely a coax technology, but an STP version is in the works. (A UTP version is unlikely to show up any time soon, but you never know.) Not much hub and other connectivity gear is available yet, but that too is changing almost daily. Because of the expense, you will end up shopping carefully, anyway.

The business side

For widespread use, FDDI is still a little ahead of the business curve. Not many operations are willing to bite the bullet to the tune of running fiber everywhere and spending upward of a grand per networked desktop. Plenty of companies are working toward FDDI, though, and several of them have deployed FDDI backbones.

What else is there?

If you have to ask, you're probably wondering why this book doesn't mention your networking technology. It's a sorry thing to bear sad tidings, but, if you're not using one of the four technologies already covered — Ethernet, token ring, ARCNET, or FDDI — networking is going to be harder for you than for most folks. Sorry.

The sad thing is that literally hundreds of other kinds of networks are out there. If *A* is for AppleTalk, and *Z* is for zero-slot LANs, there's something for all the other letters of the alphabet, too.

Using exotic networking technologies can be a problem for NetWare too. If you're involved with an exotic networking technology, you should find out whether NetWare works with it before you spend any money on the software. The good news is that NetWare runs over more kinds of strange stuff than does any other network software, including network technology dinosaurs like Corvus OmniNet, Allen-Bradley broadband, and IBM's PC-LAN. The bad news is that you will have to do some research to find out whether your stuff is on the supported list. The worst news is that you will have to work harder to do basic stuff that the more commercial technologies take for granted, and you may have to forgo more exotic options, such as LAN-attached printers.

The best way to find out what's what is to get up on CompuServe and ask the collective wisdom on NetWire: "Does my QuackNet work with NetWare?" (For instructions on using CompuServe and NetWire, see Appendix C.) Chances are, you will get the right answer within a day. If you don't have access to CompuServe, ask around. With more than 30 million users worldwide, you shouldn't have to look far to find someone who can help you. Good luck.

The Polls Are In!

If you have to make a choice for a new networking technology today, with no constraints, go for FDDI. It's the only widely available technology that has significant room for growth. If budget is a concern or your needs are modest, Ethernet should be your first choice. Token ring is worth considering only for new networks if an IBM mainframe or mini operating system is somewhere in the picture, or if other considerations — such as company policy — dictate it. ARCNET is a bottom-feeder's choice for new networks today. But hey, if money is the main object, it can be the difference between networking or not.

"WE SORT OF HAVE OUR OWN WAY OF PREDICTING NETWORK PROBLEMS".

Chapter 3
Message in a Bottle:
Mastering the Art of Protocols

In This Chapter

▶ How does this work?

▶ Protocols let computers speak

▶ Moving messages

hapter 1 described networking as requiring three fundamental components, called connections, communications, and services. Here, you leave behind the connections — the wires and interfaces — and climb inside the network to look at its communications, or how messages moving across the network are fielded by their senders and receivers. From the proper perspective, everything in life is a football game, right?

Communications are based on a shared set of rules about how to exchange information and about what things mean at the most rudimentary levels — such as what's the convention used to represent digital data, or what's a one and what's a zero? Communications also specify the formats of and meanings for network addresses and other necessary information. Communications don't tell you, however, about that football-shaped box on your desk, or why it's ticking. Maybe someone wants to tell you something.

Rather than play network football, though, and go out for the bomb, in this chapter you continue your look at the network plumbing. This time, rather than look at the pipes and connections that tie the network together, you look at what's moving through the pipes — the messages that computers send to each other. This examination should help you better understand how computers communicate — and why they sometimes don't — on your real network.

How Do Computers Really Communicate with Each Other?

Chapter 1 compared a computer conversation to a human conversation. In that chapter, Table 1-1 illustrated that any kinds of communication, whether between humans or computers, have much in common. This is true, at even more than a superficial level, but, hey — we all know that computers use ones and zeroes and that humans use words to communicate.

In addition to the things humans and computers have in common as communicators, there's much that's really different about the ways people talk to each other, and the ways that computers talk to each other. Understanding the differences will help you to understand networking better, too.

Do what I mean, not what I say!

When they're communicating, human beings are always interpreting things and misunderstanding things. What one person says is not always what the other person hears. Humans can also rely on shared understandings and assumptions when we communicate — like knowing what's being talked about at any time, so that a relatively empty phrase such as "How 'bout da Bears?" means something specific to a couple of Chicago Bears' fans — they don't have to go into much detail. That is possible because humans are good communicators, and because all of us have a common frame of reference to draw on at any time to help supply meaning when the total substance of a conversation may be implied rather than explicitly stated.

Computers, on the other hand, can only do exactly what they're told to do — neither more nor less. For computers to communicate, for any information to be delivered, every little bit of information to be exchanged between sender and receiver must be supplied, not implied. For computers to communicate, they must start out with complete agreement about the following issues (the first-person pronoun *I* is used to state questions from a particular computer's point of view):

  ✔ What's my address? How do I find it out? How do I find out other computers' addresses?

  ✔ How do I signal another computer that I'm ready to send a message? That I'm ready to receive a message? That I'm busy? That I can wait if it's busy?

This is really just the tip of a cold, technological iceberg. It must be completely mapped out and then implemented in software before computers can communicate with each other.

All the answers to those questions must be known and understood for computers to be capable of communicating. In fact, the collection of all these answers forms the basis of a set of rules about how computers can communicate; they can then use those rules to handle the networking part of their activity.

Rules...in a knife fight?

Building a complete set of communications rules is time-consuming, persnickety, and completely boring to most normal people. In the early days of the computer industry, individual companies or groups would decide that they wanted to do something (such as networking), and they would put a group of programmers to work building programs to do just that. Over time, this process led to many different ways of doing things (such as networking), none of which would work with anything the talented programmers over at some other companies were doing.

In the early days, incompatibilities like these were not a big deal (or so it seemed). As networking became more widespread, however, it was natural for the people who bought computers from companies A and Z to say "Well, gee, if my company A computers can talk to each other, and my company Z computers can talk to each other, why can't the As talk to the Zs and vice versa?"

Why not, indeed?

Uncle Sam played an important role in bringing order to this emerging trend toward network chaos. He tried to get his computers — from companies A through Z — to talk to each other and learned that he had a compatibility problem — in spades! What emerged from this fracas was a consensus that a set of rules was absolutely necessary for networking. Even more important, the industry learned that networking was difficult, if not impossible, when everyone didn't share the same set of rules.

We would like it if this story had a happy ending, one that went like this: "Today, there's only one set of networking rules, which everyone is using wisely and well." Too bad that that's not true. Even though the chaos has been reduced, there's still plenty of it to go around, and vendors are always trying to get an edge by inventing communication rules as they go.

Protocols Let Computers Speak the Languages of Love

It's starting to get clumsy to call these protocols "sets of networking rules." They're usually called *networking protocols* or *networking standards,* or even *standard networking protocols.* You get the drift.

In diplomacy, *protocol* refers to the rules for behavior that let representatives from sovereign governments communicate with each other in a way calculated to keep things peaceful, or at least under control. That is why diplomats refer to heated screaming matches as "frank and earnest discussions" or to insoluble disagreements as "exploratory dialogue." Double-talk aside, the word *protocol* captures very nicely the flavor of what these sets of rules have to do for networks, and that's why it gets used.

Raising the standards....

What makes any discussion of networking rules interesting is that both the vendors and the standards groups call their stuff a "standard." Some of the vendors expel a lot of hot air talking about the difference between *de facto* and *de jure* standards. De facto means, "It ain't official, but a lot of people use it, so we can call it a standard if we want"; de jure means, "It's a standard because XYZ (a standards-setting group) has declared it to be so and has published this foot-high stack of documentation to prove it."

Part of the heat behind the discussion of what's standard and what's not is a control issue. Purists of all stripes—including academicians, researchers, techno-weenies, and others — flatly assert that only a standards-setting group can be "objective and fair," and that only they can appreciate the chore of selecting the very best that technology has to offer by putting it in their standard to make the world a better place for all of us to live in.

The other source of the heat is the vendors who try to build products and get them out the door as fast as they can. Although the objectivity and fairness and leading-edge character of many standards are not in dispute, making standards happen involves groups of individuals who must agree on what's in them. And reaching agreement takes time. In the meantime, technology keeps evolving and nothing goes stale faster than leading-edge technology. Vendors, in their desperation to keep up with the market and their customers' demands, struggle mightily to get their products out the door. "Of course we have to be in control of our technology," they say. "It's the only way we can keep up!"

Whether networking technologies are standards or not, or de facto or de jure, doesn't matter. The real action is where the markets are. The funny thing about the vendor versus standard-group debate is that vendors must be involved on both sides because they cannot afford to miss any of the technology boats that sail from port. Some vendors have been astute enough to publish their "standards" and to give customers and industry people sufficient documentation and input to keep things working and keep up with technology. Some standards bodies have been bold enough to realize that a standard is a good thing only when it's implemented in large quantities, and they have given vendors opportunities to deal with the real-world concerns of getting products to market. There are winners in both camps, and those sets of rules are the ones that get used the most.

The key to a networking protocol is that any two computers that want to communicate must have in common an identical protocol. The protocol defines the language, the structure, and the rules for communicating that the computers will use to exchange information.

How suite it is!

Even though this book is about NetWare and focuses most of its attention on Novell's NetWare-related protocols, it would be an injustice to you not to admit that Novell's protocols are just one member of a large cast. The interesting thing about Novell's protocols is that more computers use them to communicate every day than does any other protocol that's out there. Maybe it's because they were built to enable PCs and other desktop computers to communicate and because there are more PCs out there than there are any other kind of computer.

One last remark on protocols: They rarely, if ever, occur in the singular. Most networking protocols consist of a named collection of specific message formats and rules for interaction rather than a single set of formats and rules. For that reason, protocols are also called *protocol suites,* not because they like to lounge around on matched collections of furniture, but because they travel in packs.

A protocol's work is never done

OK, fine. So now you know that your computer cannot talk to another computer without sharing a common protocol. Where does this protocol stuff come from? Put differently, who decides which protocols get used?

Protocols span the range of networking capability all the way from software to hardware. The programs which run on your computer that let you access the network must use a protocol to interact with it. This protocol continues all the way down to the edge of the hardware, where the computer says "send this message" to talk to the network, or "give me the message" when the hardware tells it that there's something to look at.

The answer to where the protocol stuff comes from is "a little from here and a little from there." For example, most protocols don't care which kind of network they're talking through. They don't even notice, in most cases, if they're talking through an ARCNET, Ethernet, or token-ring network. The reason is that part of the software which provides network capability comes from a piece of software called a *device driver,* and part of it comes from other sources.

You install the device driver on a computer to tell it exactly how to talk to the network interface in your machine. If you're lucky, you use a network machine such as a Macintosh. If not, you must locate and install a device driver for your network interface so that your computer can talk to it, and so that it can talk to the network. "Bigger fleas have littler fleas" is what it all comes down to.

Some applications may know how to communicate directly with a network through a special kind of software interface. Applications with this kind of network savvy used to be pretty rare, but they're becoming more and more common as networks become more and more widespread. Other applications may use standard computer system access and end up talking through the network without necessarily being aware that the network is being accessed.

The key to accessing the network from applications, or from a computer's operating system, is a collection of software that implements the protocol suite being used. The operating system is a program, like DOS on a PC, that keeps the computer running and capable of doing the jobs you ask it to do.

All or part of the network access software, down to the device driver, may be supplied by the application vendor, if an application is network-savvy. All or part of this software may be supplied by a system vendor, if the operating system is network-savvy.

For NetWare, Novell supplies software for most of its desktop clients. Of the desktops that NetWare services, UNIX and Macintosh make use of their own networking software, whereas DOS, Windows, OS/2, and Windows NT make use of networking software that Novell supplies for those machines along with NetWare. This is where the protocol stuff comes from. For a picture of these possible software relationships, look at Figure 3-1. It shows that software components to communicate over the network, called a shell or redirector, are needed. The figure also shows that additional software to use the network interface, called the interface driver, provides the link between programs and hardware.

Moving Messages, or the LAN Must Go Through!

So now you know that a protocol suite lets computers share a set of common rules for communications, and you know that the protocol handles the moving of information between the hardware on the computer that interfaces to the network and the applications you run on your machine. The next question is, what happens between the applications and the hardware while the protocols do their thing?

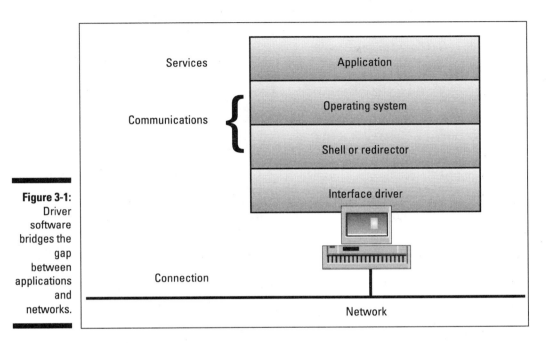

Figure 3-1:
Driver
software
bridges the
gap
between
applications
and
networks.

The Dance of the Seven Layers

Much of what happens between applications and hardware consists of taking messages, breaking them down, and stuffing them into envelopes as you move farther from the application and closer to the hardware. It works the other way too — moving from hardware to applications, where the protocols would unpack envelopes and stick individual pieces together to build a complete (and hopefully, meaningful) message.

A post office analogy works well here. You might think that the post office handles mail, but what it really handles is envelopes, packages, or whatever — things that have addresses on them with sufficient postage to pay their way. How does a letter get delivered? It goes something like this:

1. You address a letter and drop it at a mail pickup.

2. The mail carrier on whose route the pickup is located gets the letter.

3. The mail carrier delivers the mail to the local post office.

4. The mail sorters check the ZIP code and route the letter.

5. The letter gets shipped to the post office that services the destination on the address.

6. The mail sorters check the street address and route it to the mail carrier who covers that address.

7. The mail carrier delivers the letter to the address.

8. The recipient gets the letter.

The key ingredients for successful mail delivery are timely pickup, short transit time, and correct delivery. The factors that most influence transit time and delivery (other than the mind-numbing effects of a federal bureaucracy) are correct identification of and routing to the mailing address.

The crucial similarity between networking protocols and the postal service lies in recognizing addresses, routing messages from senders to receivers, and providing delivery. The main difference is that the postal service doesn't care what's in the envelopes or packages you send (within reason) — as long as they meet size, weight, and material restrictions. Networking protocols, on the other hand, spend most of their time dealing with envelopes of varying sizes and kinds.

Another example helps to explain this process. Imagine that you want to copy a file across the network from your computer to another computer somewhere across the wire. It's a sizable file, about 1MB (megabyte), and because it's the spreadsheet covering your sales forecast for the next quarter, you want it to get there quickly and correctly.

If you were using the post office, you could copy the file to a floppy and mail it to the recipient, but that would take at least a day, and that's not fast enough. Over the network, it gets there in less than a minute. While the file is moving from your machine across the network to the other machine, there's a lot going on that you cannot see.

Actually, size considerations — the biggest chunk of data you're allowed to move across the network — is only one reason the envelope game gets played. Handling addresses is another reason. In the postal service example, the pickup post office cared only about the destination ZIP code, but the delivering mail carrier worried about the street address. In the same vein, one protocol might care only about the name of the computer the file needs to be shipped to; at a lower level, however, it would have to know not just that computer's address, but also where to direct the chunks of data moving from sender to receiver so that the file can be reassembled on delivery.

Taking things apart to deliver them accurately and efficiently is what the protocol software spends most of its time doing when you're sending something somewhere from your computer. When you're receiving something, the computer spends its time stripping off packaging information and putting things back together. Notice that sender and receiver keep talking to each other along the way to monitor the accuracy and effectiveness of their communications and to determine if and when delivery is complete. Protocols also do a lot of keeping track of the quality and usability of network links.

Chapter 4

Who's Out There? Round Up the Usual Suspects!

In This Chapter

▶ Identifying common NetWare protocols and fellow travelers

▶ Introducing IPX

▶ Toasting TCP/IP: Score one for the government

▶ Applying AppleTalk: Bringing Macs into the fold

▶ Mixing multiple stacks

▶ Recognizing and categorizing your protocols

*I*n this chapter, you're still learning about the way computers communicate over networks, but this time you learn how to recognize which kinds of communications you're dealing with. You also learn which kinds of protocols go with which operating systems or with specific applications. By the time you finish, you should be ready to figure out what you have been using all this time, or what you will be using soon.

For networking, a *network protocol* is a set of rules that govern the way computers can communicate with each other. For computers to be capable of communicating, they must have a protocol in common.

Network protocols are usually organized into groups of capabilities that handle everything from sending and receiving messages from the network interface — talking to the hardware — to enabling applications to use the network to do their thing — talking to the software. Because protocols travel in packs, they're generically referred to as *protocol families*. Because this process involves stacking multiple layers of functionality, and because software often goes with each layer, when the software that supports a particular network protocol gets loaded on a computer, it's usually called a *protocol stack*.

In this chapter, you meet the most popular protocol stacks for the NetWare environment. You learn how to tell them apart and what they're most commonly used for. In the process, you also will learn a little more about how networks work and what kinds of built-in functionality help to keep things that way.

Just as diplomatic protocols help grease the wheels of diplomacy, network protocols help keep your networks running. If you get to know the players, you may even be able to help things along.

Welcome to the Rogues' Gallery

In dealing with the protocols commonly encountered in the NetWare environment, you are expected to rattle off strange-sounding collections of letters (and sometimes even numbers) with aplomb. You are expected also to know which acronyms belong together and, in some cases, to understand how these pieces fit together.

In setting up and troubleshooting a NetWare network, it is helpful to understand the kinds of jobs that various protocols do and to be able to make an educated guess about the kinds of problems each one is subject to. When things get weird, you have to be acquainted with this rogues' gallery of protocols so that you can recognize who the perpetrators might be.

Warning: Entering the acronym zone!

Not many protocol families aren't completely populated by members made up of abbreviations. You will encounter more strange alphabetic combinations, and even a few odd-looking combinations of letters and numbers, than you ever suspected could exist.

Meet the basic NetWare protocols

Novell's basic protocols are called IPX, for Internetwork Packet eXchange, and SPX, for Sequenced Packet eXchange. Surprisingly, IPX and SPX are the most widely used networking protocols in the world, with more than 25 million regular users. This number also happens to represent the size of NetWare's estimated user population, so there's a close identification between these protocols and NetWare itself. This section presents just an introduction, though. IPX is used with NetWare on DOS, Windows, OS/2, and some versions of UNIX, with Macintosh and Windows NT versions in the works as this book is being written.

The government protocols

No, this isn't a set of rules for doing business with foreign heads of state. It's the outgrowth of Department of Defense funding for networks, which began in the early 1970s, to tie together government computers. These protocols are more commonly referred to either as DOD (Department of Defense) protocols because the DOD requires that all computers they purchase be capable of running them, or as Internet protocols because they're required in order to use the quasigovernmental Internet.

The real name of this protocol suite is TCP/IP, which stands for two of its members, the Transmission Control Protocol and the Internet Protocol. Because the Internet is composed of more than 30,000 sites worldwide, and TCP/IP claims more than 15 million users, it's another major player in the protocol game. TCP/IP has deep roots in the UNIX community, and it also is widely used to link together different kinds of computers, including a plethora of free or inexpensive implementations for PCs and Macintoshes.

Other faces in the gallery

Lots of other protocols are out there on networks all over the world, but you are most likely to find the ones discussed in this section on NetWare networks or in the operations that use NetWare:

- **AppleTalk:** The name of the set of protocols developed by Apple Computer, whose Macintosh was one of the first mass-market computers to offer built-in networking capabilities. In most cases, where there's a Mac, there's also AppleTalk.

- **ISO/OSI:** Not a cruel technician's idea of a nifty palindrome. It stands for the International Standards Organization's Open Systems Interconnect family of networking protocols. Though highly touted as the successor to TCP/IP and the next big "networking thing," OSI has yet to live up to its promise.

  Because most governments, including Uncle Sam, require systems to be OSI-compliant, a good bit of it is still out there in industry, government, business, and academia. Like TCP/IP, ISO/OSI is available for a broad range of systems, from PCs to supercomputers.

- **SNA:** Systems Network Architecture is IBM's basic protocol suite. Where there's a mainframe or an AS/400, you also typically find SNA. Because SNA was one of the pioneering protocols, companies that invested heavily in mainframe technology in the 1960s and 1970s typically also invested in building large-scale SNA networks.

Numerically, there are more SNA networks than any other kind, but because it's old, cumbersome, and expensive, the number is dropping. That's also why IBM's newer operating systems, like OS/2 and AIX, offer other protocols in addition to links to SNA. This topic is a special, esoteric networking one, and you aren't confronted with much more of it in this book.

✔ **NetBIOS:** NetBIOS, or Networked Basic Input-Output System, was designed by IBM as a networked extension to PC BIOS. NetBIOS is a higher-level protocol that runs on top of many lower-level protocols, including IPX and TCP/IP, as well as others. Even though it's pretty old, it's easy to program with and consequently is used in many different networked applications on a broad range of computers and operating systems.

✔ **NetBEUI:** The NetBIOS Extended User Interface was designed as a second-generation protocol especially to support NetBIOS-based communications. You can call NetBIOS and NetBEUI a matched set, and that's what Microsoft and IBM use for their networking products.

You might find NetWare networks that use NetBIOS, but not NetBEUI, or you might find hybrid networks that use both IPX and NetBEUI, along with NetBIOS. It all depends on what's installed. Because NetBIOS is not explicitly part of NetWare, though, we don't deal with it in much more detail in this book.

The world has hundreds of protocol families, each with its own collection of acronyms and its own special outlook on the world. Hopefully, you won't have to get to know each of them intimately, but believe us — they're out there, along with a host of other, even more exotic ones we didn't bother to mention in this chapter.

Natively NetWare: IPX/SPX

NetWare's roots began to grow in the late 1970s and early 1980s, when networking was still in its early childhood.

NetWare's protocols are based on a set developed at Xerox, called the Xerox Networking System and abbreviated as XNS. Many XNS-derived protocols are in the world today, proving again that Xerox is great at delivering ideas that other people end up delivering as products.

NetWare's protocol family is called IPX, which is short for Internetwork Packet eXchange. It's also sometimes called IPX/SPX, where SPX stands for Sequenced Packet eXchange. These two protocols are the foundation on which the rest of NetWare's protocols are built.

IPX and SPX handle the basic job of moving packets around NetWare networks and are the workhorses of everyday networking. This list shows three other important NetWare protocols you will encounter on your NetWare networks:

Connection-handling helps classify protocols

IPX is a connectionless protocol, and SPX is connection-oriented. What does this mean? Why should you care?

Chapter 3 established that the most important job of a lower-level protocol — and both IPX and SPX qualify — is to break up application information of an arbitrary size into digestible, same-size chunks for sending and to put those chunks back together into their original form when they are receiving. These chunks, called *packets*, form the basic message unit for information moving across a network.

Connectionless protocols work the same as mailing letters with the postal service: You drop off a letter and expect it to get delivered. You may or may not find out whether it doesn't get where it's supposed to go — unless it's a bill — but you typically don't care that much, either. IPX provides no guarantee on delivery, and packets can arrive in any order, which may differ from the order in which they're sent.

Connection-oriented protocols use a *handshake* to start communications, and they more closely resemble a conversation. Connection-oriented protocols act more similar to the process of sending a registered letter, in which information about its delivery, such as who signed for it, is returned to the sender. SPX packets are sequenced so that they arrive in proper order; SPX is more reliable and not only notices when delivery fails but also can request redelivery or send error notices to applications when successful delivery is impossible.

IPX and other connectionless protocols are considered lightweight. They're typically fast and don't require much overhead. SPX and other connection-oriented protocols offer higher reliability. They run more slowly than connectionless protocols because they have to keep track of what has been sent and received and because there's more record-keeping information built in to each packet that gets sent (such as keeping track of sequence numbers and deliveries).

✔ **NCP (NetWare Core Protocols):** The service protocols for NetWare. For virtually every service NetWare can provide, an NCP is used to let users send requests for that service — to begin the process of delivering in response to their requests. The kinds of services provided by the NetWare NCPs range from file transfer to directory services lookups.

✔ **RIP (Routing Information Protocol):** A broadcast protocol (meaning that it is addressed to everyone who's listening on a network) that gets used one time per minute by every IPX router on a network to declare what it knows about how to get around on the network. (For NetWare 3.11 or higher-numbered versions, any server can be a router.)

Routers exchange RIP packets to keep the common knowledge of how a collection of individual networks — called an *internetwork* — is laid out. This information is used to move packets around, which is why the servers that do it are called routers.

Talk it up!

Because RIP and SAP are "chatty protocols" — they send a fair amount of traffic at very regular, frequent intervals — IPX has gotten the reputation of being a high-overhead protocol family.

Being high in overhead is not so bad for local-area networks, in which bandwidth is cheap and there's lots of it to go around. For wide-area networks, however, it makes IPX much less effi-

cient than it might be. Novell is in the process of fixing this problem by developing a new routing protocol, the NetWare Link-State Protocol (NLSP), and by building methods to control both the way SAP and RIP behave. NLSP also helps IPX limit its broadcast behavior (so that it can be kept off wide-area links, for example).

✔ **SAP (Service Advertisement Protocol):** Advertises the services available on the network. Like RIP, SAP is a broadcast protocol and each server sends out its collection of SAPs one time per minute in versions of NetWare before 4.0. NetWare 4.0 and higher-numbered versions use directory services to deliver and advertise services, so the only services that must be advertised in that environment are the directory services themselves.

IPX/SPX is Novell's property, which is why it's called *proprietary* technology. Even though it has undisputed control, Novell has been very open about sharing IPX specifications and technologies. This openness has much to do with why Novell is the number-one networking vendor. In the minds of some users, however, there is still a stigma attached to proprietary technologies of any kind. For that reason, Novell is working on a version of NetWare that eschews IPX/SPX in favor of our next contestant, TCP/IP.

Score One for the Uncle: TCP/IP's a Winner!

With roots in the defense community, you would expect a certain martial air of performance and reliability to characterize TCP/IP. And you would be right!

TCP/IP originally was developed because of the government's penchant for buying at least one of everything known to man, including one of every kind of computer system imaginable. Because most early networking development done by vendors assumed that all the machines being networked were theirs, this practice left the government's hodge-podge out in the cold.

Also, these computers were scattered all over the country, and beyond — some in such truly remote spots as Thule, Greenland — where no one goes unless he absolutely has to! So, from the ground up, TCP/IP was designed to link up different systems and to be capable of working as well over wide-area connections as over local-area ones. This design helps to explain TCP/IP's enduring appeal.

TCP/IP is in the hands of a governing body called the Internet Activities Board (IAB). This consortium of government, academic, and research and development (R&D) types take very seriously their custodianship of the rules and regulations governing TCP/IP formats and interfaces. Because it's governed by a not-for-profit group and does not "belong" to any particular company, TCP/IP is regarded as a standard protocol.

TCP/IP includes a set of high-level, basic services, along with the protocols that move messages around the network. These services include a universal *terminal emulator* called Telnet (a terminal emulator lets one computer pretend that it's a terminal attached to another computer over the network — in grand government tradition, it's capable of taking any smart computer and turning it into a dumb one). They also include a file-transfer program named FTP (for File Transfer Protocol), which can copy files between any two TCP/IP-equipped computers.

A set of military specifications governs the basic requirements for acceptable implementations of TCP/IP, and these specifications include requirements for Telnet and FTP support. These specifications have the advantage of letting users assume that basic services will be available from TCP/IP-capable machines, as well as a common language for networked communication.

Two of the protocols in the TCP/IP gave the protocol suite its name. TCP stands for Transmission Control Protocol and is a guaranteed-delivery, reliable protocol (much like SPX) that is widely used. IP, which stands for Internet Protocol, provides the basic packet structure used to move all messages in a TCP/IP environment.

Even though TCP/IP has been around since the late '70s, it continues to grow and to be more widely deployed as a networking protocol. Despite its age, continued innovations and an open-minded governing body have kept it usable and effective.

TCP/IP is probably the most widely used and best known large-scale networking protocol in use today. Despite many premature predictions of its demise among protocol pundits, TCP/IP is chugging happily along and promises to be around well into the 21st century.

Applying AppleTalk: Making the Mac Connection

Like IPX/SPX, AppleTalk is a proprietary protocol stack. The property of Apple Computer, it is considered the most likely way to network Macintoshes. Even though IPX and TCP/IP implementations for the Mac are available, AppleTalk is the most frequently used Macintosh networking protocol simply because it's built in to the Macintosh environment and is incredibly easy to use. AppleTalk defines a model for plug-and-play networking that any implementation would benefit from following. We wish that more protocols had tried as hard to be as easy as this one is.

AppleTalk has a lot going for it, especially in terms of ease of use. However, friendliness and performance tend to be at somewhat opposite poles of the spectrum. Novell's NetWare for Macintosh has consistently been the top-performing AppleTalk File Server platform since 1989, when it was first introduced, despite being based on a PC platform.

But Wait — There's More!

We can go on in this vein almost indefinitely, but by now you should have the idea that every protocol suite includes a cast of characters, each of which has its own special job in making networking happen. You have read about most of the common concerns, which include moving packets across the network (packet or datagram delivery), connectionless versus connection-oriented communications, address handling, network management, service advertisement, routing, and service protocols of all kinds.

A close look at any protocol suite typically displays some, if not all, of these capabilities. After you grasp the idea that packet delivery, routing services, address handling, and the rest are part of what it means to supply a workable network, things should start making at least a perverted kind of sense. Don't worry if the acronyms are unfamiliar or the terminology is strange; the main thing is to concentrate on learning how protocols help to connect programs and services to the network. If you know about those concepts, you know all that's important.

Hybrid Vigor: Mixing Protocols

In some situations, you may need to use more than one kind of network from a single computer. Although this process can require some contortions, depending on the network interface and drivers in use, it is typically very doable. The key is to understand whether the machine has to be capable of interacting with both networks at will, or whether it's always one *or* the other, as opposed to one *and* the other.

IPX/SPX and TCP/IP, for instance, can — and do — run successfully together on PCs every day. Novell's LAN Workplace offers drivers and installation tools to easily mix and match the two environments so that users can use both networks in a single DOS command, such as transferring a file from a NetWare networked drive to a TCP/IP computer using the File Transfer Protocol (FTP).

Likewise, Macintoshes can run AppleTalk and TCP/IP quite easily, and UNIX is capable of running as many protocol stacks as necessary to provide the right range of network services. This means that a UNIX machine's protocol collection can include TCP/IP, OSI, and IPX, or perhaps even more, for truly diverse networking environments.

The key is to obtain network interface drivers that can switch between one protocol stack and another as needed. Some drivers are not that flexible and would require the computer to be restarted to switch from one stack to another on the same interface; or it might even require two interfaces to be installed on the same network to provide simultaneous support for two stacks. This problem is most acute for DOS and Windows because those environments cannot change their configurations on the fly. Most other operating systems and platforms, including Macintosh, OS/2, Windows NT, and UNIX, are designed to be more flexible and forgiving.

No matter which type of operating system or machine you're using, one consequence of using multiple stacks is constant: The more protocols you use, the more resources they consume. Each stack has a certain memory requirement, and every one you add increases the overhead needed to run your system. Again, multiple stacks weigh heaviest on DOS and Windows, but it's a fact of life that working with multiple network protocols imposes greater overhead than working with only one, no matter which platform they run on.

Reading Between the Lines: How to Tell What's What

The details differ from machine to machine, but there are two basic methods for determining which protocols you're using and the versions of the software that's running them.

Method 1: Inspect your screen

In the first methods, you watch carefully for a message to be displayed on your screen when your machine starts up. Typically, as software gets loaded, it writes information about what it is and how it's doing; if you're observant, in many cases, the machine tells you exactly what you need to know.

For a PC running NetWare 3.11, the bootup messages related to networking look like this:

```
Novell Link Support Layer  V1.00 (900530)
(C) Copyright 1990 Novell, Inc.  All Rights Reserved.

Novell NE2000 Ethernet MLID  v1.10 (901129)
(C) Copyright 1990 Novell, Inc.  All Rights Reserved.

Int 5, Port 300, Node Address 1C8842F0E
Max Frame 1514 bytes, Line Speed 10 Mbps
Board 1, Frame ETHERNET_802.3
Novell IPX Protocol  V1.00 (900530)
(C) Copyright 1990 Novell, Inc.  All Rights Reserved.

IPX protocol bound to NE2000 MLID Board #1.
NetWare V3.22 - Workstation Shell (910731)
(C) Copyright 1991 Novell, Inc.  All Rights Reserved.
```

A great deal of useful information is displayed on this screen, but for now (you see this same screen again later in this book), the important items are the version numbers for the Novell and NetWare items — the Link Support Layer, the Ethernet MLID, the IPX Protocol, and the Workstation Shell.

All these version numbers uniquely identify the software pieces and can help you to determine whether what you have is what you need. The answer to that question typically comes from your NetWare manual, or by asking someone who's more familiar with the current state of NetWare than you are (this question is asked frequently on CompuServe's NetWire, for example).

Method 2: Inspect your machine

If your computer doesn't tell you what it's doing, network-wise, you must find another way to figure things out. The second method is not as easy as the first because it takes some research work, but it can be much more educational. (Who knows what else you will find out there while you're looking for the network stuff?)

Inspection of all your networking-related driver and protocol files is the only way to figure out what your computer is using (or trying to use) to access the network. On a DOS or Windows PC, you can guide this process by reading through the configuration files — typically, you can find the names of the files you're after in AUTOEXEC.BAT — and looking for network stuff. On a Macintosh, you have to examine your Network Extensions and Control Panels to check for things with Network in their names (or AppleTalk-sounding stuff, such as EtherTalk and TokenTalk). On a UNIX machine, you have to look at the device drivers, which usually live in a directory called /etc/bin, and see what's there.

What to do with what you learn

Whether you write down what the computer says on bootup or go digging for information on your machine, this information usually suffices to identify what's what to the knowledgeable. Your next step then can be to go find someone knowledgeable and ask for help!

Remember — if you don't know where to look for assistance, you can always call the people who sold you the machine or the vendor with whose operating system it runs. Network software information is generally so common that there are lots of ways to skin this particular cat. If you learn that what you have is not so hot, or could be newer, these same people usually can steer you to a source for the latest and greatest drivers.

The network interface vendor can also be an invaluable source for this information, and is usually the owner, if not the author, of the drivers for its gear. Persistence pays off and should help you to make sure that your protocol stacks are the right vintage for your particular environment.

The 5th Wave By Rich Tennant

"I DON'T THINK OUR NEWEST NETWORK CONFIGURATION IS GOING TO WORK. ALL OF OUR TRANSMISSIONS FROM OHIO SEEM TO BE COMING IN OVER MY ELECTRIC PENCIL SHARPENER."

Chapter 5
NICs and Knocks:
How to Understand Network
Interface Cards

In This Chapter

▶ What's in a network interface card?

▶ Catching the right bus — ISA, EISA, or MCA?

▶ Plugging in

▶ Avoiding trouble: Do your homework

▶ Dealing with doublespeak: How to read a manual

▶ Configuring NICs to put them to work

▶ Troubleshooting your NIC installation

▶ Cabling up to the NIC

▶ In the driver's seat: Installing your drivers

▶ Is it working?

*A*t this point, you have learned the basics of connections and communications. Now, you're finally ready to tackle the joys and sorrows of installing network interfaces. This discussion throws you back into dealing with connections, but now that you know what they can do for you, you should be better equipped to get things working.

If you have an IBM PC or a PC clone, you probably will want to read this chapter because it's where we discuss how to install network interfaces for such machines. If you're running a Macintosh or something else that's not a PC or a clone, you can skip this chapter with impunity!

NIC is an acronym for *n*etwork *i*nterface *c*ard. Most NICs are built to plug in to computers and provide the essential link between the wire (the medium of communication) and the computer (the sender and receiver of communications).

What's in an NIC?

A typical NIC, as its name suggests, is an add-in card configured to fit your computer. The role of an NIC in your PC is to work both sides of the network connection:

✔ The NIC's capability to plug in to the computer's bus lets the NIC talk to the CPU and lets the CPU talk to it. This capability makes the connection between the computer and the NIC possible.

✔ The NIC's accommodation for a network connection to the network typically involves an external connector that lets the network medium be hooked up. Hooking up with a cable of some kind is what makes the connection between the NIC and the network possible.

Figure 5-1 shows a schematic diagram of a typical NIC and illustrates its bus connector and the media interface.

Bus connectors vary according to the kind of bus on your computer, and media connectors vary according to the networking technology and cabling type you're using. Learning how to recognize what you have helps you to select the right kind of NIC for your machine and also helps you to get it properly connected to your network.

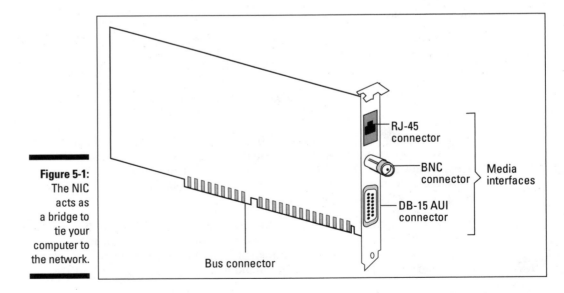

Figure 5-1:
The NIC
acts as
a bridge to
tie your
computer to
the network.

RJ-45
connector

BNC
connector

Media
interfaces

DB-15 AUI
connector

Bus connector

Not all NICs come in the form of cards that plug inside your computer, though. For laptops, portables, and other machines that may not be built to accommodate standard internal interfaces, you may have to attach an external network interface instead. Even though these interfaces aren't cards, they do the same job as other, more conventional NICs and are often called NICs as well. Figure 5-2 shows an external interface, called a *parallel-port connector,* that can attach to a computer's parallel port.

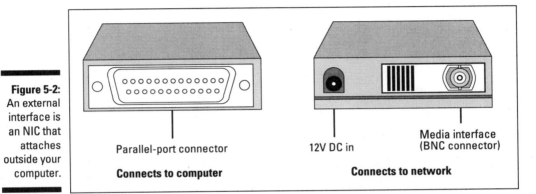

Figure 5-2: An external interface is an NIC that attaches outside your computer.

Parallel-port connector

Connects to computer

12V DC in

Media interface (BNC connector)

Connects to network

Which Bus Do You Have to Catch — ISA, EISA, or MCA?

If your computer is a PC, you have to match its NIC to the type of internal bus connections your machine needs. If it's not a PC, the only decision you have to make is whether to go with an NIC or an external interface. Either way, you don't have to grapple with the subtleties that would-be networked PCs have to master. If that's the case, feel free to skip the rest of this section.

The business end of an NIC that plugs in to the computer is called an *edge connector.* By looking at your computer's bus, you should be able to recognize which kind of interfaces it can handle. Likewise, by looking at an NIC, you should be able to tell for which kind of bus it was designed.

Figure 5-3 depicts the three types of buses this section investigates and shows their respective edge connectors alongside each one.

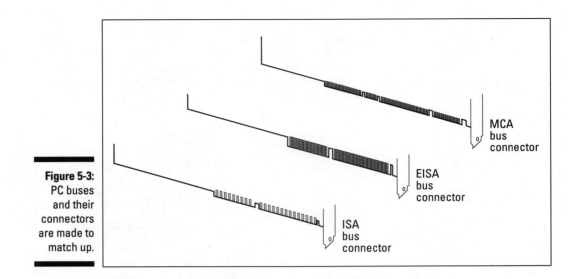

Figure 5-3:
PC buses
and their
connectors
are made to
match up.

MCA
bus
connector

EISA
bus
connector

ISA
bus
connector

ISA and EISA are related

The term ISA, which stands for Industry Standard Architecture, is used to describe the bus that most PCs have used since IBM introduced the PC AT back in 1985. ISA is still the most common PC bus, and it most likely will be the one you use to plug in to your NIC.

EISA, or Extended ISA, is an attempt to extend the capabilities of the ISA bus. EISA is *backward-compatible* with ISA, which means that you can plug in ISA cards to an EISA bus and they work just fine. EISA cards use a different edge connector from ISA cards, even though they both can plug in to an EISA slot.

The difference between ISA and EISA is based on the two changes made to ISA to extend its capabilities that created EISA:

- ✔ ISA uses a 16-bit *data path,* and EISA uses a 32-bit data path. To put it in English, an ISA interface can move only half as much data across the bus between the NIC and the CPU as an EISA interface.

  Widening the bus has two benefits: It enables an EISA interface to move more data in the same amount of time and does a better job of matching modern CPUs, which are built for 32-bit data paths themselves. The PC AT CPU is an Intel 80286, which uses a 16-bit data path; if you have an 80386 or higher-numbered processor, it uses a 32-bit data path.

✔ EISA is capable of running much faster than does ISA. ISA's bus speed is based around the clock speed of the original IBM PC AT, which was introduced at 4.77 MHz and later upped to 8 MHz. EISA, on the other hand, is capable of running as fast as 33 MHz. EISA, therefore, not only can move more data than ISA but also move it from four to seven times faster.

Under these circumstances, why would anyone use ISA? The answer is that speed and performance always have a price. In this case, it means that EISA computers cost at least $200 more than their ISA cousins, and the EISA interfaces cost around twice as much as their ISA counterparts. (It's easy, for example, to find $100 ISA Ethernet NICs, but $200 is about as low as you can go for an EISA Ethernet equivalent.)

We think that EISA is a good idea, but it's overkill for most networks in use today. Unless you're sure that the machine which needs an NIC will be a high-volume network consumer, don't bother installing an EISA NIC, even if your machine can accommodate one. What constitutes high-volume? The following elements can justify the use of EISA NICs:

✔ A network server

✔ A high-speed networking technology (faster than fast token ring, that is)

✔ A dead certainty that your machine will be the focus of lots of network traffic (using high-volume database applications or a computer-aided design package, for example)

If these things are what you're dealing with, spending the extra money pays off in improved performance (or acceptable performance, anyway). If not, save your money.

MCA: A better idea?

MCA, which stands for MicroChannel Architecture, is also the brainchild of IBM. Like EISA, MCA is a 32-bit bus, with most of the same advantages: higher speed and a broader data path. If you have an MCA computer, you have no choice but to buy MCA NICs to go with it. Its main advantage is that, in most cases, you can plug in your NIC and it handles its own configuration from there. You pay for this privilege, however.

Closing the gate after the livestock has run off

Around 1986, IBM realized that it had lost control over the PC marketplace by letting the whole world get access to the specifications for PCs and their buses, disk drives, and so on. Although this loss of control was a terrific boon to consumers because it resulted in rock-bottom prices, IBM's PC division felt that it was losing out because it couldn't compete against all the garage-based, fly-by-night outfits that were walking off with the bulk of the PC business—and the bulk of people's money too.

In an effort to regain control of the leading edge of the PC market, IBM introduced its Personal System 2 (PS/2) line. The company touted it as the next generation of PC computing and sold it heavily through its internal sales force and dealers. Even though PS/2s cost a bunch more than conventional PCs, IBM did pretty well with this product family, especially within corporate America, which had long been used to doing business with IBM.

One of the significant advantages of the PS/2 family of computers was its inclusion of a hot, new 32-bit bus called the MicroChannel Architecture. Unlike EISA, it was completely different in size and connector design from the old PC AT bus. IBM's idea was that consumers should throw away their old PCs and buy these great new ones. And, while they were at it, they should throw away all their old interfaces and buy new ones for them too!

Because IBM didn't invite vendors to participate in the PS/2 bonanza the way it did with the original PC family, vendors didn't come out in droves to support this new architecture. To this day, the PS/2 family and MCA are not nearly as popular, or as widely supported, as are ISA and EISA. They're also still at least 40 percent more expensive than their counterparts. Maybe that's one reason that IBM is hurtin' these days!

Avoid Trouble: Get Off to a Good Start

Before you start mucking around inside your PC, you should do a few things to get ready. Because messing with the system is one of the few things that can kill a computer deader than a doornail, taking some preventive steps can keep you out of trouble. These preventive steps may also get you back to work more quickly.

Please recognize, too, that you may end up back where you started. There are two ways your NIC installation maneuvers can turn out. If you're lucky, your brand-spanking-new NIC will be safely ensconced in your PC, doing exactly what it's supposed to be doing. If you're not, it will be back in its original packaging, ready to be replaced with what you now have learned that you *really* need! If at first, you don't succeed, you have no choice but to try again....

Unplugged: It's not just an MTV thing

Electricity is your friend, but you don't conduct it very well on a personal level. *Never, never, never* open a machine that's plugged in to a wall socket. This mistake can get you fried, or it can create all sorts of creative opportunities for you to fry your equipment. Neither alternative is a good one, so remember to unplug before you open the case. The easiest way is to start by detaching the power cord from the case. While you're at it, it's a good idea to unplug all the other cables from the back of the computer too.

Getting back to where you began

Assuming that nothing gets fried, what's the worst thing that can possibly happen if you install something new? You can turn on the computer — or try to — to a big, resounding nothing. Zero — zip — nada! If it's really bad, you may end up having to send the computer to the shop so that a real professional can fix it. Most commonly, if you take out the new stuff (and reverse any software changes you may have made to go along with it), you will be back where you started.

Software changes, you ask? These changes lead to a crucial preemptive step you should always take before getting down to your hardware: *Always* back up any system that will be fiddled with, before you start fiddling. Backing up has two vital benefits. First, assuming that the worst case happens — a computer that's DOA — you can install your backup on another, similarly configured machine and keep working until your original machine returns. Second, if the new installation doesn't work for any reason, you can use the backup to quickly restore the machine to the pristine state it enjoyed before you mucked with it. Backups take time, and the temptation is always to ignore this safety tip, but ignore it *at your peril.*

Figure out what you're dealing with

PCs can seem like minefields, or at least like strange, exotic beasts, when it comes to adding yet another interface to an already jam-packed machine. If you don't have an inventory of what's already installed, and configuration information to go along with it, take the time to figure out what's in there before you start trying to change things. This step makes quick work of doing an installation and might head off configuration confusion before it has a chance to happen.

Microsoft includes with Windows a peachy utility called the Microsoft Diagnostics (also known as MSD.EXE, which gets installed in the root Windows directory). If you run this utility from DOS, it tells you useful things about your PC's configuration that steer you toward the clear spots needed to install an NIC.

Use a tool, or your own research, to build a list of what's installed and the settings for each item. This step documents what's on the system and keeps you from trying to occupy settings that are already taken.

Be ready for trouble

Although it's not guaranteed that things will get weird when you install an NIC, it's well-known that they sometimes do. This statement is especially true for machines that already have lots of stuff in them. Potential problems can range from conflicts in which two interfaces can occupy only overlapping settings — which means that one of them has to go — to not knowing what changes need to be made in order to get things to fit together.

Therefore, gather all the manuals about your system that you can find. Hunt down the manuals for your PC and for each and every interface installed in it. And, for good luck — or at least, good use — try to find a general-purpose PC book for all-around reference. We recommend *PCs For Dummies* (Dan Gookin and Andy Rathbone, IDG Books 1992) or *PC Secrets* (Caroline M. Halliday, IDG Books 1992).

Give yourself room to maneuver

Even if it takes more effort and extra time, clear off some space for yourself to work. Be sure to bring some small paper cups, clean ashtrays, or other small containers to put screws and connectors in, and, if you're really going to take things apart, label what goes where. This system eliminates guesswork and can let you get back to work rather than tear out your hair. Also, bring the right tools for the job. Most computer stores will happily sell you general-purpose toolkits for $50 to $100 that contain everything you might need when you install stuff in a computer. They come in handy little zip-up cases and should go with you whenever it's time to open up a computer and fiddle with its innards.

Know the lay of your LAN

If you are installing an NIC, you eventually will want to connect it to your network. Part of the configuration drill is to know the names and addresses of the servers, users, and networks around you. Make sure that you read the installation requirements before you get started and then run down any the network-related details you will have to supply during the installation process. This step heads off the need to stop halfway through an installation procedure to research the information and lets you knock it off in one swell foop.

All in all, the idea is to invest in the ounce of prevention that helps to avoid expensive, time-consuming chores.

It's All in the Cards: Beware the Golden Fingers

When you read the manuals provided by offshore manufacturers, you have unparalleled opportunities to encounter bizarre brands of written English. Although the technically correct term for the part of an NIC that plugs in to a bus slot is an "edge connector," we like a nameless Taiwanese company's description of that part: golden fingers. Even though they're really brass-colored and not truly golden, they're what plugs in to the computer and makes NICs work.

Even if the fingers are brass and not gold, when you plug an NIC into an empty bus slot, make sure that it is firmly seated and fully connected. In other words, make sure that the edge connector is hidden from view and that the network interface on the side of the card is well positioned in the cutout on the back of your PC case.

Normally, you also should screw the metal tab into place, by using the screw that attached the placeholder before you removed it to insert your NIC. To help you visualize what we're talking about, Figure 5-4 shows the placeholder with the screw hole.

You should remember two things about placeholders:

✔ Be careful when you're messing with the little screw that holds them in place. Dropping one can lead to all kinds of crazy contortions to recover them. If you drop one, pick up the PC case and rock it gently back and forth — you can usually get the screw to show itself more readily that way.

✔ Be sure to put the placeholder in a toolbox or spare-parts drawer so that you can find it again. If you ever have to remove the NIC (or any other interface), you will want to be able to close the case again. Some cases use odd-size placeholders, so being able to find the right one when you need it beats the pants off trying to scare one up.

Figure 5-4:
Empty slots are closed off by place-holders, which keep dust and dirt out of your PC case.

Dealing with Doublespeak: How to Read a Manual

The first rule of installing NICs is to skip ahead in the installation manual until you find a picture of the NIC, with all the important stuff highlighted. With a well-thought-out manual, this step can save you the bother of reading the whole thing. Even for the more usual manuals — which often are boring and hard to follow — it can help you to figure out what you really need to know more quickly than starting at the beginning does. Our suggestion: Go for the pictures!

The second rule in installing NICs is to understand exactly what you have to do to make the installation work. If you have peered at the pictures and have puzzled through the text and still aren't sure what to do, make a call to the NIC vendor's technical-support hotline and ask them to explain it to you. This step has the benefit of letting you check up on your drivers at the same time and can shortcut the learning process. The wonderful folks at tech support deal with confused people every day, and they can steer you clear of the pitfalls better than anyone else can. The help is worth it, even if you have to pay for a long-distance call.

NIC Configuration

Configuring an NIC requires making all the right hardware selections and choosing the right software settings, to make sure that the NIC can work in your PC. You must therefore deal with a number of different kinds of settings and make sure that the right information gets supplied to the software drivers that make your NIC and PC work together in perfect harmony. Become familiar with all five subsections in this section to understand what's involved.

NICcus interruptus: Setting interrupts

Because activity on the network can happen at any time, an NIC must be capable of signaling the CPU whenever a message arrives so that incoming data can be received. Likewise, the CPU has to talk to the NIC to tell it when outgoing traffic must be handled.

The most common method for handling this type of activity is to reserve an *interrupt line* for the NIC's exclusive use. PCs offer 16 interrupt request addresses, called IRQs, that are numbered 0 through 15. Interfaces use them to signal activity. Each NIC requires that one of a particular restricted range of IRQs be selected for its use, and no two interfaces are typically allowed to share a common IRQ.

Hopefully, this discussion helps to explain why mapping out your existing configuration is a good idea. Your mission here, like it or not, is to find an unused IRQ the NIC can accept. If none is available, other stuff must be reconfigured to free up an IRQ it can use (which is why we told you to get out *all* the manuals!).

Setting IRQs generally requires setting *DIP switches* (DIP stands for *d*ual *i*n-line *p*ackage) or moving *jumpers* to select the right IRQ number for the NIC to use.

DIPsy doodles

Figure 5-5 shows a typical DIP switch. Most DIP switches, which are really banks of individual switches, show you which way is On and which way is Off. If you can't tell and the manual doesn't help, don't delay — call the tech-support department right away. They know the answer and will save you unneeded guessing and experimentation.

Jumper jeepers!

Jumper blocks consist of two rows of adjacent pins that are connected with itty-bitty connectors called *jumpers* (see Figure 5-6). The pins typically are numbered, and sliding the jumper over both pins turns that jumper on. To turn off a numbered pin set, remove the jumper from both pins and slide it over one of the two pins so that it sticks out from the pin block. Typically, when you are setting IRQs with jumpers, you see one jumper inserted for an entire block of pins, and the pin set you jump with it selects your chosen IRQ. In that case, make sure that the jumper covers both pins in the set. Otherwise, you have nothing selected and it probably won't work.

Doing defaults

Before you worry about DIP switches or jumpers, first check the manual to find out where the factory set the IRQ. If this particular IRQ, called the *default setting,* is not in use, you can stick with the default and not do anything. We like it when this happens!

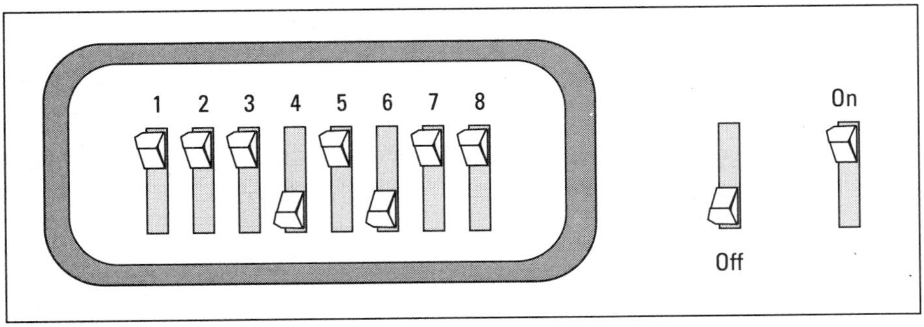

Figure 5-5: DIP switches and jumper blocks control NIC settings.

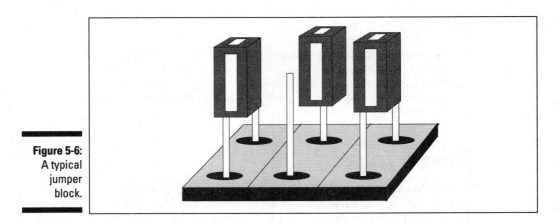

Figure 5-6:
A typical jumper block.

The right port in a storm: The I/O port address

Each card in a system has its own unique I/O port address, where certain addresses are reserved for some interfaces, especially video cards. NICs aren't quite that picky and usually can get an I/O port address assigned from a reserved range of addresses. This particular address most likely is handled by a DIP switch on most NICs because a pretty broad range of potential settings usually is available.

An I/O port gets set up to let the computer read from or write to memory that belongs to an interface. When an interrupt gets signaled, it tells the computer to read from the I/O port address, indicating incoming data. When the computer wants to send data, it signals the NIC to get ready to receive and writes to that address. What happens is that the information written to or read from that address gets copied across the bus between the NIC and the computer's brain, or CPU (central processing unit).

Possible I/O port addresses for NICs commonly range from 2E0h to 380h, and the most usual default port I/O address is 300h; 300h is a typical default for lots of interfaces, though, so you still have to do your configuration homework before you can choose to stick with that address.

Computer addresses are often computed in base 16, also called *hexadecimal.* The lowercase *h* after the number tells you that it's hexadecimal, as shown in the following example:

```
2E0h = 2*16² + 14*16 + 0 = 736 (decimal)
```

In hexadecimal, letters *A* through *F* are used to stand for 10 through 15 because 10 hex equals 16 decimal, and six more digits are needed to get from 9 to 10 in hex.

Getting direct with memory: Setting the DMA

Some older NICs use a technique called *direct-memory access* (*DMA*) for moving information between the NIC and the CPU. This technique allows for fast copying of information from the computer's memory to the NIC, and vice versa. As equipment and computers have gotten faster, this technique has become less necessary.

DMA works by matching up two areas of memory, one on the computer and the other on the NIC. Writing to the memory area on the computer automatically causes that data to get copied to the NIC, and vice versa. *Setting a DMA address* means to find an unoccupied DMA memory block to assign to your NIC. Again, your earlier research on what's taken helps you to avoid conflicts. Just pick an unoccupied block and make the right NIC settings, and you are on your way. If conflict exists, you must figure out a way to resolve it. Remember to check your defaults here too.

Running the NIC address bases: The MemBase setting

NICs contain their own RAM to provide working space for information coming on and off the network. This RAM is called *buffer space* because it provides room for incoming and outgoing data to be stored. This buffer space must be assigned an equivalent region in the PC's memory and, for DOS and Windows, usually is located in the high memory area between 640K and 1024K, which is reserved for such uses.

Just like the IRQs and DMA, this setting must be unique. You must watch out for potential address conflicts and steer around them, and you usually use jumpers to set the base memory address (also known as MemBase) for your NIC. Common settings for network cards include C000h, D000h, and D800h.

In the Driver's Seat: Loading NIC Drivers

After the hardware is in place, it's time to deal with the software. If you have purchased your NIC recently — and it hasn't been sitting on a distributor's shelf somewhere since the last Ice Age — the drivers on the disk that comes with it may actually be worth something.

If you're lucky, you can load the disk, run an installation program, and maybe supply a few values here and there, and then you are ready to roll. If you're not lucky — and we rank this up there with the probability of winning small in the lottery — you must chase down new drivers and use them instead.

Our advice: Win or lose, always check to determine the latest and greatest drivers for your NICs before you begin the installation process. Ask for help in this order:

1. From the outfit that sold you the card.

2. From the vendor that built the card.

3. From NetWire, on CompuServe. Look in the NOVB forum, under your networking technology (sections 9 through 12) or in Workstation Shells (section 14). For more information about NetWire and CompuServe, see Appendix E.

If the NIC vendor doesn't automate driver installation for you, you may have to manually edit configuration files, such as AUTOEXEC.BAT and CONFIG.SYS. If you're running Windows, you may also have to edit SYSTEM.INI to insert the correct .DRV (driver) reference. Again, if you're in doubt, get some help.

Cabling Up to the NIC

OK, the software is installed and the hardware is plugged in. All that's left is to cable the NIC to the network. For modular technologies such as twisted-pair ARCNET, Ethernet, or token ring, that means plugging in the modular connector on the LAN cable to the receptacle on the NIC. For other technologies, it means hooking up a T-connector or a transceiver cable from the LAN to your NIC. Whichever option you must use, make sure that your connection is tight and well seated and that the NIC has stayed put in its slot. Now you're ready to fire it up and see what happens.

Looking for Trouble in All the Right Places

You have worked your way through the maze of potentially conflicting addresses and you have set your NIC to steer clear of all the shoals. The software has been installed, and everything should work, right? Well, sometimes it does (hooray!) and sometimes it doesn't (boo, hiss!). When things don't work, you find out in one of three ways:

1. **Your PC doesn't boot.** This one is pretty obvious. If it happens, you will know; when it does, it's time to start undoing what you have just done. First, restore the system to the way it was before you started fiddling (you *do* have a backup, right?) If it works, you know that the NIC is the problem. Time to get some help from one of the recommended sources. If it still doesn't work when you're back at square one, you have bigger problems. Time to call in a service tech.

2. **Your PC boots, but it doesn't load the drivers.** The most common causes of failure to load drivers are shown in this list:

   a. **Loose connections.** Check to make sure that the wire is tight and properly seated on the NIC, and make sure that it's plugged in to something on the other end!

   b. **Installation problems.** Make sure that the drivers are in the right directory and that the directory is referenced directly in your bootup files or defined in your DOS PATH. If the computer can't see the drivers, it can't use 'em!

   c. **Conflict!** It might just be that you missed something and have introduced a configuration conflict. Try all your other stuff; if something else also has quit working, it's a dead giveaway. Time to go back to square one and recheck all system settings. Something, somewhere, is fishy, so be extra careful.

   The good news here is that the problem is most likely a loose connection or a configuration boo-boo. If it's not one of those, it's time to get serious and figure out what's causing the problem.

3. **You try to use the network and it doesn't respond.** This more subtle variant of the preceding problem usually has one or more of the same causes. An extra element of mystery exists here, though, because it can be a conflict with another application you have installed and not a driver problem. Only by working through a careful process of elimination can you find your way to an answer. All we can say is — good luck, think hard, and take lots of breaks. You *will* figure it out. If you have to, ask for help.

Ready to Rock 'n' Roll?

After you have made it over the hump and can talk to the network, you're ready to get to work. Or, if you're learning the ropes as a network administrator, you will have the pleasure of letting someone else get to work. Either way, you have the satisfaction of pushing the networking wave another workstation ahead.

Chapter 6
Any Good LAN Has a Pedigree

In This Chapter

▶ What's on a map? Why bother?

▶ Formalizing your network map

▶ Building a network inventory

▶ Keeping track of what's what

▶ Recording additions to your LAN keeps you on top

▶ Planning for changes means staying in charge

*A*fter you begin working around networks on a regular basis, you begin to get the hang of how things work in general. By now, you have been exposed to most of the basic principles of networking, and you probably have a pretty good idea about how things are supposed to work, if not how they *do* work.

As you will quickly realize, however, when you spend time around networks, what you *think* about them isn't nearly as important as what you *know* about them. It doesn't even matter if you have to wrestle with networks regularly because that's your job, or if it's just something you mess with so that you can get your real job done. Either way, there's nothing like a network map to help you keep track of what's out there on the network, and to let you know where you might find things if you need to.

What's on a Network Map? Why Should You Bother?

What we recommend that you do requires more than just a map, which might simply indicate where items are located. A map that clearly marks where each item is situated is just a handy, visual way of organizing the following information:

It's a map, and an inventory, and a database, and a....

By now, the idea should be clear: A network map is a way to track and organize detailed information about what's on your network. It's a combination inventory, configuration database, and catch-all for other useful bits of trivia. It should also tell you where your network cables are and, if it's a really good map, how long each cable section is and where to find cable ends. In short, this annotated map is a container for just about everything you should know about a network and just about everything anyone would need to know about your network if anything ever happened to you.

- ✔ A list of all the computers on your network, with supporting documentation
- ✔ A list of all the networking equipment — including such things as routers, hubs, and servers — with supporting documentation
- ✔ A list of all the printers and other specialized equipment on the network, with supporting documentation
- ✔ Lines to indicate where network cable runs, and where junctions, taps, and other items are located

Formalizing Your Network Map

Because a network map is such an important and powerful tool, we think that you should go out and make one right away. Be prepared to spend some time at it because it incorporates a great deal of information that's probably scattered all over the place.

Building this kind of map is a worthwhile investment, though, and pays for itself many times over if you take this assignment seriously. At worst, you probably will learn more than you ever want to know about your network; at best, you will get acquainted with your network and may even find some things that can benefit from some time and attention.

Where should you start?

If you can get hold of a set of architectural drawings or engineering plans for your building, you can take them to almost any architectural supply house and have copies made. The most common copying technology uses an ammonia-based reproduction system called a blue-line; even large-size plans can be copied for less than $20 apiece. You can mark up copies and use them as your base map.

If you cannot locate plans, sketch out a room-by-room layout of your working area and mark where machines are located, with approximate locations for cable runs and so on. If your cable was installed by a professional cabling outfit, you probably can get a copy of its cabling plans, which should also work nicely as a master layout for your network map.

What should you record?

Anything that merits attention or costs money is worth recording on your map. You probably don't need to take it to a level of detail that includes each connector, nor is it necessary to know the exact length of every cable (approximate lengths to within a yard or so are OK). But you should indicate every major cable run, every computer, and every other piece of gear attached to the network.

You probably won't be able to write all this information directly on the map, but you should key this information to a machine or cable name and store the details on your computer in a file with the same name. Or, if you prefer a different scheme, pick one and use it religiously. Write up some brief notes that describe how your scheme works — again, the idea is for someone else to be able to take over without necessarily being able to talk it over with you. The important thing is for you to build a map and to key the rest of your network information to it.

Keeping Track: Building a Network Inventory

The information you're gathering to support your network map is nothing more than a detailed inventory of what's out there. Unfortunately, as you will quickly realize, this is a large volume of information. One way to proceed is to build a file template (or to print hard copies of that template) that you fill out for each item. In this way, you make sure to collect consistent information and you even can enlist the aid of your co-workers and get them to help you complete the inventory.

This list shows what your inventory should include:

For each computer on the network:

✔ The hardware configuration, including a list of all interfaces and their configuration settings, and information about the RAM and drives that are installed and the make and model of the keyboard, display, and so on.

Keeping track of equipment is something that accounting departments typically take responsibility for, so you will want to check out your capital asset inventory (if you have one). This inventory should give you a place to get all the serial numbers and other identification for hardware on the network. If somebody doesn't already have this information, go ahead and collect it. It's valuable. If you can find out who sold you the equipment, write that down too.

✔ The software configuration, which should include listings of configuration files, the operating system and version installed, and a list of programs and versions also installed on the machine.

✔ The network configuration, including the make and model of NIC and a list of driver files with names, version numbers, dates, and sizes (editing a DOS DIR or similar directory listing should do the trick nicely).

For other equipment (such as hubs, routers, and printers):

✔ Note the manufacturer, model, make, and serial number. If the equipment incorporates memory modules or disk drives, get the information about them too. If the equipment uses software, get a rundown on it like the one you will compile for computers. In fact, the computer template works well for other equipment too.

For the cable plant, compile a listing of all the cable segments. Give each one a name or a number, and key its information to that identifier. You should record the type and make of cable, its length, and the locations of its ends and other significant connections.

✔ Make a list of all the vendors who have worked on your network, or its machines, with names and phone numbers. This list can be a source of information about what's what and a valuable resource for technical support. Over time, you will want to add the names and phone numbers of tech-support individuals who prove to be knowledgeable and helpful.

What has been described in this list is a database of everything you need to know about your network. If you're database-savvy, you might even want to consider building an honest-to-gosh computer database to hold this information; if you're not, the file- or paper-based approaches already described should be fine. Whatever method you use, take that inventory and make it complete.

Keeping Up with Ch-Ch-Ch-Changes

One thing is certain about networks: They keep changing. Your map is only as good as the information it contains, and it's only useful if the information is an accurate reflection of what's out there in the real world.

It's important to allocate time to stay up to date and to make updating the map and its database a priority whenever things change. Because others may have to use the map, anything you do to the network must be included; because you will need to use it, too, anything anyone else does to the network must be in there also.

Look at it this way: It's much less work to look at a map than it is to walk around and look at things. If the map is correct, you don't have to go anywhere to look things up. If it's out of date, you better start walking — and writing down what you see.

Get Ready for the Real Thing

If you have money to spend, you can find software products that help maintain your map for you. Novell's Network Management System (NMS) includes the capability to merge a logical, electronic map of your network that it finds for itself with a set of scanned-in site plans. NMS also includes electronic links to just the kind of database described earlier in this chapter, which can accommodate the information we have recommended that you collect. Unfortunately, you still have to collect the data that goes in the database, but all the infrastructure you ever want comes predefined. Of course, at a list price of nearly $5,000 for NMS, you expect Cadillac treatment.

Other alternatives for network inventory are available from third parties. These alternatives are not always network-management products per se, but they cost much less — typically, from $300 to $500 per file server. We recommend looking at LAN Directory, from Frye Computer Systems, Heaven Nodes!, from dtech, or LAN Auditor, from Horizons Technology. All these products offer great database support for doing network inventories. If you have a network of any size, they are well worth the investment.

Stay Current, or Get Lost!

After you have made the investment in building a network map and the database that goes with it, you have to make an ongoing commitment to keep things up to date. After all, it's not just a one-night stand you have going here — it's a real relationship, and any good relationship requires maintenance.

The moral of the story is to stay current, or you will wind up getting lost following a map that leads to where things used to be. This is today, so make sure that your map and your database reflect what's out there now. Don't just sit there — check it out!

Chapter 7
Beyond Installation: Living Off Your LAN

In This Chapter
- Maintenance: Paying now versus praying later
- Upping the ante: Upgrades, uprevs, and one-upmanship
- Getting help when you need it
- Building a routine
- Noticing the obvious
- Keeping it clean
- Looking beyond the network

You might be inclined to think that all the fun has ended when you finally get your network installed and working. In truth, the fun is really just beginning, and it will continue to grow for quite some time as more and more users become familiar with the network and as your users begin to appreciate what the network can do for them.

Getting a network up and running is a significant accomplishment and a noticeable milestone. Keeping it running is no less of a challenge, but it doesn't seem to have the glamour — or to deliver the recognition — that making something out of nothing can confer.

Be that as it may, keeping your network running will probably become one of the most important jobs you ever do. The trick is to plan on regularly spending time on that task, and to anticipate your users' needs rather than react to them. It's always better to be proactive than reactive, and, in this chapter, you get some useful tips and advice about how to get into a proactive mode with your network. More important, you get the information you need in order to stay proactive, even as things change.

Maintenance: Paying Now versus Praying Later

Looking at your network from a new perspective — one of keeping up with its pieces and keeping things working — what do you see? We can't be 100 percent sure about what you do see, but we can be confident about what you should see:

- ✔ A collection of user machines that belong to the folks who use the network
- ✔ A collection of servers and related paraphernalia that provide the services to those users
- ✔ An agglomeration of cables and possibly some hubs, routers, or other gear that helps to glue together the users and the services

Each one of these collections is one that somebody uses some of the time. When it comes to the servers and the glue, however, they're collections that everybody uses all the time but that nobody — except the person or group responsible for the network — wants to acknowledge, let alone manage.

The sad truth is that, when networks are working properly, no one really notices them. The only time they get the attention they deserve is when they're not working; when that happens, the attention is seldom appreciated by the people who receive it. Your job, as you might have already guessed, is to maintain that state of cheerful oblivion which is the hallmark of any well-run network.

What does it take to get them to leave you alone?

Given that you would rather get no attention than have to face the ire of your collective user base, what does it take to achieve such ignorant bliss? The one-word answer to your question is maintenance.

If you keep things running smoothly and shield your users from changes and other sources of discomfort, you can achieve the sought-after status of being left alone. If you don't, you will be the scourge of your peers and the envy of no one. It's not really much of a choice, but it's clear which is the lesser of the two evils.

Contented users are quiet users

Keeping your network running smoothly and efficiently keeps those pesky users out of your hair and lets you concentrate on doing your real job without lots of testy interruptions. What's the secret, you might ask, to keeping them quiet?

Keep the network running at all costs

Because interruptions of network service get users riled, the safest course is to make sure that the network stays up during prime working hours, no matter what contortions that requires you to make. Believe us — even if you have to jump through some amazing hoops to make this happen, it's worth it.

Schedule downtime and spread the word

Every network has to go down occasionally, even if it's only for a few minutes. Backing up the server can slow things down to the point where the network might as well be turned off, and most equipment or cabling changes take the network out of service altogether.

Schedule these events at least a week in advance, preferably outside the main workday hours, and let your users know so that the folks who have to be there outside normal working hours aren't unpleasantly surprised to find themselves at work without a system to use. You would be amazed at how vociferous some people can get when they find that their plans to catch up on some last-minute changes or to meet an impossible deadline have been eighty-sixed by an unavailable system.

Keep an eye out for trouble

Half the problems on networks come as no surprise to anybody — or at least, anybody who's been paying attention. If you keep yourself on the right side of that equation, you can stay ahead of the users who otherwise would be breathing down your neck. If you think that the dragons are bad, wait till the users come after you.

Educated users are better than ignoramuses

Although time to hold hands with your users is always in short supply, it's always easier to answer a question once than to have to keep answering it over and over. Whenever upgrades or additions force changes on your network, let your users know ahead of time that things are going to change and what impact these changes might have. When things do change, tell 'em again, and give them more details about exactly what has changed and how they will have to deal with the brave new world the changes have wrought.

When changes involve upgrading software or changing applications completely, a little anticipatory training can do wonders to alleviate anxiety and prepare your users to handle what's new in a more cheerful frame of mind.

Keep an eagle eye on growth needs

It's been said that nothing succeeds like success, and networks are particularly prone to this phenomenon. After your users get a taste for networks, they may begin to bang on them beyond your wildest dreams.

Get your report card on a regular basis

Take the time, or make the time, to check with your users regularly. Don't just ask them how you're doing, or what they think of the network. Ask them what they want to be able to do, or what they want to be able to do more easily. The whole idea is to provide value to your users and to make them better able to do their jobs. Sometimes, giving them what they want isn't enough. Sometimes you also have to prod them to want more than they think they need.

If you can stay in touch with your users and keep them informed, you build a loyal base of advocates. If you can empower them to do their jobs better, you build a reputation for getting things done. Staying ahead is hard work, but it does have its rewards.

Upping the Ante: Upgrades, Uprevs, and One-Upmanship

Part of living with networks means dealing with a continually changing landscape. The technology keeps changing as it gets cheaper and faster. The software keeps changing as it gets more powerful and feature-laden. And users keep changing as they discover new and more innovative ways to use the services a network can bring them.

Maintaining a network means anticipating regular changes and planning to deal with them. In addition to scheduling changes, we strongly recommend scheduling regular network maintenance. Because change is inevitable, why not plan for it and allocate specific times to deal with it? The worst thing that can happen is to get to your maintenance period and not have to do anything special to fill the time. If our experience is any indicator, that normally isn't a problem.

So, what if the XYZ MegaSpreadsheet comes in on Tuesday and your next scheduled maintenance isn't until the following Monday? This occurrence not only lets you free up some time to do maintenance but also provides a way to build in a cushion for change — for informing your users, figuring out whether training will be needed, and getting ready to make whatever changes are necessary.

When it comes to software upgrades or new releases, you might want to consider adding to that cushion and take extra time to test new releases before inflicting them on your users. At the very least, you should keep old versions around and available on the network so that, if the new stuff doesn't work out, you can easily roll your users back to the previous version.

Generally, it's up to you to control the pace of change and take advantage of new releases and new software in a way that best fits your schedule and your users' needs. Random change is the most difficult to tolerate. After you get your users trained, the rest should be easy.

Getting Help When You Need It

Networks are like most other systems — most of the time they just chug along in a steady state of equilibrium, shifting only with user demand. But, when things change, the system gets stressed, and that's when networks are most likely to break down. If you're planning to make changes, you should also plan for the possibility that those changes may cause some unforeseen side effects. That way, if things break, you are ready with Plan B.

Before you move on to Plan B, here's what you can do to avoid having to use it:

- ✔ Schedule major changes over three-day weekends. This practice can give you an extra day to get things working if you need it.

- ✔ Find out how to contact technical support before you roll up your sleeves and start changing things. If you are planning to work over a three-day weekend, make sure that tech support also is planning to work.

- ✔ See whether your reseller (the folks who took your money for the original product) or your vendor (the folks who built the system or software or whatever and who probably took your money for the upgrade) can arrange to have someone on tap to help in case things get weird. As Hunter S. Thompson says, "When the going gets weird, the weird turn pro." Find out who the pros are at your reseller or vendor and figure out a way to get to them when you need them. Bribery is OK, as long as you can get help when you need it.

Plan B should be needed only if things get so messed up that you cannot get back to where you started (with no changes) by the time your users show up at work on Monday morning. For Plan B, you should arrange to beg, borrow, or steal (just kidding!) a replacement unit for your server or whatever unit is being mucked around so that, if worse comes to worst, you can use it to replace your hopelessly screwed-up system with a reasonable facsimile. If your users never figure it out, you can heave a big sigh of relief.

The moral of the story is, plan for disaster, but hope for a miracle. If the former happens, you will be ready to deal with it. If the latter occurs, you can revel in having a free weekend, just like everybody else.

Building a Routine

The key to successful network maintenance is to build a routine that everybody gets used to. You probably will wind up being on first-name terms with the janitorial staff and the rent-a-cop in the lobby, but notoriety isn't what it's cracked up to be.

By scheduling regular maintenance, you train your users and your management to expect and accommodate change. You also make it possible to control how and when things change, and you can plan to deal with problems if they occur.

The best thing about a routine is that you will know when things will change and what has to be done to make that happen. The worst thing that can happen is that you get stuck in the middle, unable to go forward or backward. If you're ready for this contingency, you can fire up Plan B and keep right on going.

Maybe consistency really *is* the last refuge of the unimaginative. But because imagination is a dicey quality for a network, that's probably not such a bad thing....

Noticing the Obvious

As we have already said, paying attention is a key ingredient in dealing with users. It's also a crucial element in maintenance of any kind. When the painters, or the A/C guys, or the plumbers come calling, you should keep an eye on them, especially if they're going spelunking in the ceiling where your network cables are located. When the electricians come around, you should make sure that they know which conduit is for electricity and which one is for network cables. You would hate it if they got it wrong. Another worry — and the bane of many campus networks — is to watch out for the guys with the backhoe. More innocent networks have died from an errant backhoe than anyone would ever want to pay for.

Keep your eyes peeled for what's going on around you, and your ears tuned in to what users are saying. If you can keep up with the latest gossip, you can often stay ahead of the well-intentioned but often maligned influences that otherwise could put a hex on your network.

Keeping It Clean

When it comes to dealing with resources that everybody shares, keeping things clean is an important chore. If this concept doesn't make sense, think of the company refrigerator down in the lunch room. If someone didn't post a sign that says "Anything left in here over the weekend will get tossed on Monday morning," what kinds of science experiments would you find growing in there after a few months?

Guess what? Your network server is the electronic equivalent of the company refrigerator. Everybody uses it, but nobody wants to keep it clean. And everybody, sooner or later, forgets that they left the electronic equivalent of a tuna casserole sitting in there since last Christmas.

If you want to keep your network running smoothly, you're going to have to sweep away the unsanitary buildup that always develops. Fortunately, NetWare helps you: You can set up the file system on a server so that it limits the amount of disk space users get. By keeping this number on the low side, you can make your users clean up after themselves. For the truly lackadaisical, you can purge files that haven't been accessed for a number of days (you get to pick the number). Or, on NetWare 4.0, you can use storage migration to copy unused files from the disk drive and to a magneto-optical disk, or even to tape.

From a system perspective, you should keep old versions of software around for a while after adding new ones. But, when the new stuff becomes old hat — typically, after one or two months — you have to remember to ditch the old stuff. If you're truly conservative, you can let the arrival of the next new version seal the fate of the version that's one generation back from the one you're using. That way, you have only two copies of stuff around all the time.

Even though disk space keeps getting cheaper, and the "disk farms" attached to servers keep getting bigger, it's still worth your while to keep the files pruned. Besides, you have to make room for all those Windows applications....

Looking Beyond the Network

Our last maintenance tip is to consider the world beyond the network from time to time. Hey — look — we know that it's the most absorbing thing there is, but get a life! Actually, what we really mean is that the network is usually just a piece of your business and that you should consider the impact of losing other parts of your company's systems.

What happens if the mainframe goes south permanently? What about the phone system? Or, even worse, what happens if the whole place goes up in flames and nothing remains but a charred skeleton?

Generally, this stuff falls under the heading of disaster recovery. If your company entrusts just a part of its business to the network, somebody should have a plan for recovering from its complete and utter destruction. If the network is all that your company uses, that plan becomes essential.

Many consultants can help you devise a disaster recovery plan for your network (and other key ingredients of your business environment), but they all boil down to a few essentials:

- ✔ Always have multiple system backups (for a more thorough discussion of backups, please see Chapter 18).
- ✔ Store at least one backup set off-site (preferably in a fireproof vault).
- ✔ Make arrangements to gain emergency access to systems similar to yours for fallback use. These arrangements are expensive, but at least you can get back to work without losing everything.

To take advantage of these services, of course, you have to build a detailed plan and you have to go through the motions needed to put it into action.

Don't worry — this kind of thing always seems like total overkill until the unthinkable happens. When it does, you will thank your lucky stars that you planned ahead. If you decide not to build a disaster recovery plan after what you have learned here, at least it will be an informed decision.

Part II
Gimme a Light — a NetWare Lite

In this part...

*N*ot since learning how to blink have we encountered anything as easy to learn as NetWare Lite. Lite gives you the ability to tie together two or more PCs quickly and efficiently. With NetWare Lite, you can use other people's disks and printers as though they were attached directly to your own PC. A few simple DOS commands — or access to Microsoft Windows 3.0 or higher — and a small dose of common sense are all you need. You also should read the following chapters about NetWare Lite. **Note:** There's no pop quiz at the end of this part of the book, so relax and enjoy yourself.

Chapter 8
The Meaning of Lite

*N*ow that you know all about what networks are and how they (net)work, let's discuss the best choice for a small network: NetWare Lite. Obviously, if NetWare Lite is a "light" version of NetWare, NetWare 2.2, 3.11, and 4.0 must be "heavy" versions of NetWare. During these next few chapters on NetWare Lite, therefore, the text refers to NetWare 2.2, 3.11, and 4.0 collectively as the NetWare Heavies. By contrast, NetWare Lite is simply called Lite.

This chapter outlines the features and capabilities of NetWare Lite. Just consider NetWare Lite to be a lean and mean version of the NetWare Heavies. Please don't be fooled by the term "lite." NetWare Lite offers many features that are particularly well suited to small networks. Lite also offers several features that are not available in the NetWare Heavies. As good as Lite is, it cannot do everything well — so you need to understand when Lite is not the best choice.

Lite Is Easy and Quick — and Has No MSG

Lite is the easiest-to-use offspring of the NetWare family. Lite is small, so it doesn't require lots of PC memory or a really big hard disk. Lite is easy to set up and use, so you don't need your quantum physics textbooks. Unlike the NetWare Heavies, Lite doesn't require you to assign one PC just for serving the other PCs on the network, also known as a *dedicated server*.

The price of dedication

A dedicated server is a PC you can't use to type a letter, play a computer game, or run any programs directly on the keyboard and monitor. In other words, a dedicated server is not a PC at which you can sit down and perform useful work. Many network operating systems require their servers to be dedicated PCs. NetWare 3.11 and 4.0 require dedicated servers. Under NetWare 2.2, a dedicated server is optional but questionable — among the cognoscenti, it's definitely *not* recommended.

NetWare Lite enables you to use all your PCs as nondedicated servers. While you are running a program from your local hard drive, someone else can access a file or program on your hard drive from across the room by way of the network. Nondedicated means "ready to work whenever you are." It also means "as cheap as it gets!" Figure 8-1 shows the "recipe for success" for NetWare Lite.

Recipe for Success for …

NetWare Lite

Serves 1–30

To at least one PC with a hard drive to use as a server, add
at least one more PC, with or without a hard drive, for user(s) to do useful work.

Gently whip in one copy NetWare Lite for each PC on your network.

Insert one network interface card for each PC on your network.

Add enough cables to tie together all your network cards.

Install NetWare Lite (takes about five minutes per PC).

Set up server directories (takes about ten minutes).

Set up user accounts and passwords—passwords are optional, but recommended (takes about ten minutes).

Add monosodium glutamate (MSG) to taste—just kidding!

Figure 8-1:
The recipe for success with NetWare Lite.

David versus Goliath

Lite is really the David of the PC network world. Much smaller and more agile than the NetWare Heavies, Lite beats the network giants by using very simple tools. NetWare 2.2, 3.11, and 4.0 are more complex to set up and usually require someone fairly knowledgeable to be able to run the network on a daily basis. On the other hand, Lite is easy to install and use on a daily basis. All you need is a little networking knowledge and a basic understanding of DOS. Lite is usually appropriate when the following things happen:

✔ Ten or fewer users want to share files and printers.

✔ All users are located within a few hundred feet of each other.

✔ All users have stand-alone copies of their applications (word processors and spreadsheets, for example).

✔ Cost is a deciding factor.

✔ You want to handle your network — or at least most of it — yourself, and you're not a network guru just yet.

Exceptions to those rules of thumb always exist, of course. If your situation doesn't exactly fit our guidelines, find someone who knows networks and explain exactly what you want to do. No one enjoys talking about networks more than network gurus do.

CompuServe is a great place to contact network gurus and ask questions. Novell even has a NetWare Lite forum that deals with specific questions and problems regarding Lite. You can learn more about using CompuServe in Appendix C.

We recommend Lite to people who already have the programs they want to run — word processors, spreadsheets, and so on — installed on each machine, but who need the ability to easily share documents, worksheets, and printers.

We do not recommend Lite for those who want to buy one networkable copy of a complex program such as a word processor and have multiple users run it from one server. Running a complex program located on someone else's hard drive on the network can slow down everything.

If you want to buy "networked" copies of your programs — one centrally located copy that can be shared over the network — and have all your users run them from a server, you need at least NetWare 2.2 and a dedicated server PC. Even then, more than 20 users or so can bring a network to its knees when everyone tries to start MegaSpreadsheet at the same time. Keep that warning in mind when you are considering which network operating system is right for you.

Gimme a Lite!

Back in the old days of PCs — oh, four or five years ago — most companies that had PCs used the *sneakernet* network. Sneakernet was jokingly described as the process of taking a disk from one machine, walking across the office — in your sneakers, get it? — and giving the disk to a co-worker so that he or she could update or print a file. You can imagine how time-consuming and frustrating the sneakernet process was.

Even worse, when you had multiple copies of files on different disks that were being updated by numerous people, sneakernet was confusing at best. If Jim didn't know that Mary was figuring the net profit margin at the same time he was adjusting the cost of raw materials, both could end up with misleading results and the sneakernet blues. By providing simple, easy-to-use access, NetWare Lite is a modern solution to those blues.

A *client* is the PC at which you actually do some work. You can run Lotus or WordPerfect or Harvard Graphics from a client. A *server* is the PC that offers files (in shared directories), printers, or other services for the Heavies, to others over the network. A *client-server* is a PC at which you can work while others share your files or printers. Under NetWare Lite, a PC can be a client, a server, or a client-server.

Lite enables you to hook together as many as 25 PCs and to share hard drives, floppy drives, files, programs, and printers. A server is any PC with a hard drive that enables other PCs to share its programs and printers. With Lite, at least one of your PCs must have a hard disk and be set up as a server or client-server. The other PCs can be clients, servers, or both at the same time, which is a configuration known as client-server. A client-server PC is available for access by others while it is also available for direct, local use (by you).

A *nondedicated server* is a PC you use as both a client and a server. Though all 25 PCs on a Lite network *can* be servers, you must configure at least one PC — with a hard disk — as a server. You cannot have a network without at least one server. The rest of the PCs can be diskless clients — a PC without a hard drive — or simply clients with hard drives you do not share on the network.

Less Is More (More or Less)

By this time, you're probably asking yourself, if NetWare 2.2, 3.11, and 4.0 are so great, why would anyone want to use NetWare Lite? One important reason is cost. The average price for the least expensive of the big three, NetWare 2.2, is approximately between $50 to $80 per PC (more users means less cost per user, but more dollars overall), with a minimum expense of around $500 just for the network software. Compare that price to the $69 average cost per PC of NetWare Lite and you can see a big reason to choose Lite, especially for a small number of workstations (four or fewer).

You must also consider the complexity factor. NetWare 2.2 probably requires a dedicated server. This statement means that you would need one additional PC to be dedicated to serving your users. The NetWare Heavies don't permit users to share their local drives and printers with other users, either. Only files and printers located on a server are accessible by other users on the network. NetWare Lite has these features built in at no extra cost. In some offices, in fact, users run both NetWare Lite and one of the Heavies at each workstation to let everybody get the best of both worlds.

Meet NetWare Simplicity Lite

That's right! Simplicity is Lite's middle name. Lite comes on one disk. One more disk of utilities also is supplied for those of you who plan to run Lite with Microsoft Windows. The Lite installation program takes about five minutes and requires you to answer X questions and pick X choices from a multiple-choice list. Defining the directories and printers you want to share on the network takes approximately ten minutes. Assigning user names and passwords might take five minutes. The hardest part of setting up NetWare Lite probably is installing the network interface cards in each PC and their cable connections.

From Peer to Shining Peer

Lite uses the *peer-to-peer* networking method to share local resources across the network. A server-based network requires all shared resources to reside on a centralized server. A peer-to-peer network gives everyone on the network the opportunity to share her local stuff with others on the network.

Wait! You say that you don't want other people to have access to all your top-secret stuff? You probably don't want your boss to see that new golf game and the recently updated copy of your résumé. No problem. Lite gives you control over which network users can see your locally stored stuff.

Printer Queues: Revenge of the British

Queue is the British word for "line." When you share a printer, Lite creates a queue to store print jobs waiting for that printer. Each printer has its own print queue.

As the server sends print jobs to the printer, Lite lines them up like a queue forming outside a British privy. Jobs are printed in the order in which the queue receives them. This system of print queues means that the printer doesn't have to be available at the time you ask to print something. The print queue accepts any and all print requests as they occur and then lines up all print jobs for printing as the printer becomes available.

Administering Your New Lite Network

Everyone on your network can be a Lite network administrator because every PC on the network is a potential server. We suggest that one person — perhaps you — should serve as the primary network coordinator. Your job is to educate and assist your users in such areas as backups, e-mail, rights, and security.

Over time, you and your users will become a practiced team of network administrators. As you all gain experience with NetWare Lite, you can distribute some of the coordination responsibilities to users who show an interest. This distribution of responsibilities also takes pressure off the coordinator to always be available to solve network problems. They say that the best managers always train their own replacements. "One for all, and all for one" should be the battle cry for your Lite networks.

Lite Requirements: Here's What It Takes

One of the most appealing facets of Lite is the small amount of memory and disk space it requires. Lite takes up approximately 600K of hard disk space when it is installed. The PCs on which you run NetWare Lite require no additional memory — although we recommend at least 640K of RAM. That's for DOS and Lite to use, not just Lite. If you're using Windows, you probably will need at least 4MB of RAM. All your PCs must use DOS 3.x, 4.x, or 5.x, although you can use any flavor of DOS you want (Microsoft, Novell, IBM, or Compaq, for example).

You will see many product version numbers that take the form N.x, where N is a number such as 1, 2, or 3, and x means any subversion of that software version. This statement means that we just told you that any version of DOS that is numbered 3, 4, 5, or 6 with any subversion suffix, works with NetWare Lite,

Where can NetWare Lite play?

NetWare Lite runs on almost any IBM or compatible personal computer. Everything from the old Intel 8088 — the processor in the original IBM PC — to the most modern 80486, zillion-gigahertz PC microprocessor with internal cache, built-in numeric coprocessor, and plush carpeting. If your PC runs DOS 3.0 or higher, you can also run NetWare Lite.

whether it's from Microsoft or another vendor. And even though Novell isn't shipping its DOS 7.0 version as we write this book, it's a safe bet that it will run with NetWare Lite too.

P.S. Be on the lookout for NetWare versions numbered 2.x, 3.x, and even 4.x, later in this book.

You *must* purchase one complete NetWare Lite package — software and manuals — for each PC on your network. If anyone tells you that you can buy just one copy of the software and copy it to multiple PCs, *ignore them!* Each copy of NetWare Lite contains a unique hidden code that is broadcast across the network to all the other PCs.

If Lite detects duplicate codes — which indicates duplicate installations of the same copy of NetWare Lite — everyone on the network gets a copyright violation message on his or her screen every few seconds. Have you ever tried to type a letter with interruptions every few seconds? The copyright violation messages can drive you crazy. (For some of us, that's a fairly short drive.) The only way to stop the constant license violation warnings is to replace the illegal copy or copies of Lite with a *separate, licensed copy* for each PC.

Don't NIC Yourself When You're Shaving Costs

When you buy *network interface cards* — better known as *NICs* — for your network, be sure that you also receive an installation manual and a drivers disk. The installation manual shows you how to set the switches for that particular NIC so that it can coexist peacefully with everything else inside your PC.

Drivers are small software programs that let Lite talk to the NIC and across the network cable to other PCs. Usually, each model of an NIC requires a unique driver. Make sure that the network interface cards you buy include drivers for NetWare Lite. Drivers designed for use with the NetWare Heavies don't yet work for Lite. Novell plans to change this situation by the end of 1993, but that's not the case as this chapter is being written.

The perils of compatibility

Some brands of NICs include what's known as *compatibility mode.* This term doesn't mean that the card will make someone a good spouse. Compatibility mode means that the card operates properly with a driver from another manufacturer.

Novell's NE2000, for example, is a popular Ethernet NIC. Some small network manufacturers might include an NE2000 compatibility mode on their NIC so that they don't have to spend time and money writing customized drivers for their NIC. You can use the ubiquitous NE2000 driver, included with each copy of NetWare Lite, just by setting a few switches on the card. The really cheap NICs you see in the back pages of personal computer magazines usually include a compatibility mode.

The package containing the NIC should include a list of network drivers it supports. If the list does not include NetWare Lite, you should reconsider the purchase of that brand of card. Otherwise, you will spend a great deal of time trying to track down the correct driver, if it even exists. This problem is particularly common with those very cheap NICs you often see advertised in the back of many PC periodicals and on matchbook covers everywhere.

NIC, or network interface card, is a generic term used to describe any type of network card. If you have chosen ARCNET adapters for your network, think about your ARCNET cards when we mention NICs. Your NICs might be token ring or Ethernet or baseband or jazz band, but we refer to them collectively as NICs.

Drivers...Start Your NICs

Without a driver, your average car is not very useful. A car cannot go anywhere without a driver — the same is true for your network interface cards. But it's also necessary to have the right driver for your NIC; not just any driver will do.

The reason is that your PC's processor doesn't talk directly to the NIC. If PCs were to communicate directly with the NIC, each NIC would have to be the exact same design. Instead, the PC talks to the driver, and the driver talks to the NIC. The software — the driver — must meet certain standards in order to communicate with each PC processor. The NIC manufacturers have the freedom to design unique features into their product. Little things such as network software changes or new versions of DOS also require drivers to change, so it's important to make sure that you have the right driver for your unique configuration!

How Lite Looks at the World

NetWare Lite enables users to share drives and printers by fooling your PC. Lite makes your PC think that there are more drives and printers physically attached than actually are attached. Lite performs this magic by using a type of software called a *shell*.

The Lite shell automatically loads when you turn on your PC. The shell looks at every DOS command you type to see whether it can successfully execute the command on the local PC or whether it is a network command. If it is a local command, the shell passes the command to your PC. Your PC runs the command and displays the results on your monitor screen. If the shell recognizes the command as a network command, the command executes across the network and the results are also displayed on your PC. Here's a crude example:

You type a local command to DOS:

```
C:\>dir
```

and here's what you get back (or something very much like it):

```
C:\>
DOS          <DIR>      03-07-93    8:57p
COMMAND  COM      47987 05-09-91   12:00p
CONFIG   SYS        194 03-22-93    9:42p
NWLITE       <DIR>      03-13-93   12:05p
AUTOEXEC BAT        139 03-14-93   10:53a
         5 file(s)       48320 bytes
                      61726720 bytes free
C:\>_
```

You type a network command:

```
C:\>net login supervisor
```

and here's what you get back:

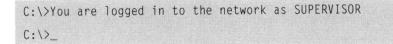

```
C:\>You are logged in to the network as SUPERVISOR
C:\>_
```

The Lite shell looks at the first command (DIR), recognizes it as a local DOS command, and passes the command to the PC's processor for execution. The shell also looks at the second command (NET LOGIN SUPERVISOR), recognizes it as a network command (that first word, NET, is a dead giveaway, eh?), and executes the command through the driver to the NIC and across the network. The result of the network command is then displayed on the local PC.

How Lite Coexists with the NetWare Heavies

Any NetWare Lite client or client-server can also be a client on a NetWare 2.2, 3.11, or 4.0 network server. Your department at work can use NetWare Lite for all of its internal networking while accessing other NetWare 2.2, 3.11, and 4.0 network servers for company-wide programs such as electronic mail.

Follow these steps to alter your PC setup if you want to attach to a NetWare server from a Lite client:

1. Change the directory to the NetWare Lite subdirectory:

   ```
   C:\>cd \nwlite
   ```

2. Use a text editor, such as the DOS EDIT program, to make changes to STARTNET.BAT:

   ```
   C:\NWLITE>edit startnet.bat
   ```

3. Delete these lines:

   ```
   LSL
   DRIVER.COM
   IPXODI A
   ```

   (The exact name of the program in the second line depends on the type of NIC you use.)

4. Insert this line:

   ```
   IPX
   ```

   You will have to get a copy of this file from your company's network guru and put it in the NWLITE subdirectory.

5. Press Ctrl-Alt-Del to reboot your PC.

It's all a matter of protocol!

IPX is the protocol that NetWare 2.2, 3.11, and 4.0 servers use to communicate with network nodes. A *protocol* is the format of the information as it travels across the wire. The sending and receiving PCs must have a prior agreement about how communications will proceed and how to handle errors. Examples of other protocols include TCP/IP, DECNet, and SNA.

Multiple protocols can coexist peacefully on the same network because NetWare Lite uses a variation of the normal IPX protocol called *IPXODI*. In order for a NetWare Lite client to attach to a NetWare Heavy server, you must delete the IPXODI programs — as described earlier in this chapter, in the section "How Lite Coexists with the NetWare Heavies" — and replace them with the regular IPX program. Fortunately, Lite servers can still talk to a PC that has IPX loaded in place of IPXODI. If you require access to NetWare Lite servers and NetWare Heavy servers, substituting IPX for IPXODI is a simple solution.

You now can share files and printers on your Lite network as usual. You also can log in to your company's other NetWare servers and, better still, use the resources available there. Though this process is relatively easy to complete successfully, we suggest that you contact your company's NetWare guru for help. That way, you are sure to do everything just right and get the latest and greatest software.

For Lite, Small Is Beautiful

Throughout these chapters, you have learned how small yet powerful NetWare Lite can be. Its economy of design enables Lite to be almost invisible on your PC. No extra memory and very little hard disk space are needed in order to run Lite. Lite doesn't require you to be a networking expert, but it's effective for most uses. Lite gives you the ability to access files and printers on your co-workers' PCs. And Lite gives you the most networking for your investments in time and money.

If you don't back up, you get run over

After you get your network up and running, we have one suggestion that we want to chisel in stone (or on your forehead): *back up, back up, back up.* Most people are too lax when it comes to developing a backup procedure for their own PC. A backup procedure becomes even more important when other people begin to store and update files on your hard drive. (That may be one of the duties your users decide is the network coordinator's responsibility!)

A Lite network is easy to back up because each PC can be a server. You can write a batch file that attaches to each user's hard drive and back up those files to a single machine. You can also install a tape backup unit on one of your PCs and make periodic — *no less often than weekly* — backups of the network files.

Note that you don't have to back up every file on the network. Because you have the original copies of DOS, MegaSpreadsheet, and Goofie Golf, you only have to back up the data files that change over time: documents, databases, and spreadsheets. The more irreplaceable the data, the more often you should back up. We strongly advise you to establish an effective backup plan before installing your network. Go ahead and ignore our sage advice — you will be sorry! Nyah, nyah, nyah!

Chapter 9
The Charge of the Lite Brigade: Installing and Using NetWare Lite

● ●

In This Chapter

▶ Installation schminstallation: A Lite breeze

▶ Defining user accounts and passwords

▶ Defining shared resources: Directories and printers

▶ Mapping isn't a city in China

▶ Capturing that port before it gets away!

▶ A scintillating overview of Lite commands

▶ Getting Lite to shine through Windows

▶ Ready, aim, fire — troubleshooting your Lite network

● ●

*T*he NetWare Lite installation procedure is short and sweet. You insert the disk labeled NetWare Lite Program and Driver. In this discussion, we assume that drive A is the appropriate floppy drive. If you use drive B instead, simply substitute B for A in the instructions.

At the DOS prompt, type the following line:

A:INSTALL

The installation program fires up and you see the NetWare Install main menu, shown in Figure 9-1. You see this same vertical list menu format throughout the NetWare product line.

The up- and down-arrow keys enable you to scroll through the list. When you press Enter, execution of the highlighted selection begins. When you finish each selection on the menu, you return to the main menu screen. To exit from the main menu screen, press Esc and then Enter.

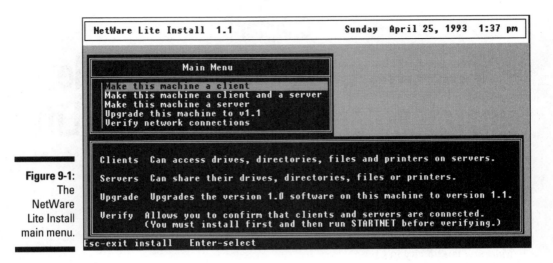

Figure 9-1:
The
NetWare
Lite Install
main menu.

You first must decide whether the machine on which you are installing will be a client, a server, or a client-server. Remember that clients can access resources — files and printers — located on server PCs. Servers can share their files and printers with clients. Client-servers can access network files and printers and share local files and printers with other clients. We suggest that you define all your PCs as client-servers. This choice gives users the most flexibility when it comes to sharing and using network resources.

1. Choose the option "Make this machine a client and a server" from the Install main menu.

2. Type a server name when you are prompted. A descriptive name your users can recognize easily is best (HOWARD or HOWARD386, for example, if Howard has multiple PCs on the network).

3. Press Enter to answer No for question 2 regarding a preview of DOS file changes. Lite adds the commands to your CONFIG.SYS and AUTOEXEC.BAT files that must load automatically. You can always edit these files later if you don't want Lite to load every time you turn on your PC.

4. Press Enter to see the list of available network interface card drivers. If the driver for your card isn't on the list, follow the directions the NIC manufacturer supplies to add the driver to the list. If you set your card to a compatibility mode, select from the list the correct compatible mode driver, probably NE1000 or NE2000.

5. Be patient while Lite copies the files to your hard drive.

6. After the installation process is complete, reboot your PC by pressing Ctrl-Alt-Del.

As your PC loads, some new messages indicate that Lite is loading successfully. After you get to a DOS prompt, type **NET** and then press Enter. Lite asks you for your user name. Type **SUPERVISOR** and then press Enter. Your login to your NetWare Lite network is now complete.

Defining Users and Passwords

The next step to successful networking is defining users and passwords. Type **NET** at the DOS prompt and then press Enter to start the Lite menu interface, shown in Figure 9-2. This menu system is the key to setting up and maintaining your network. Notice the similarities to the NetWare Lite Install main menu screen. The vertical list and screen colors will become familiar to you in no time.

Though NetWare Lite includes 15 different commands for execution from the DOS prompt, you can accomplish the same results by using the NET menu interface.

The NET interface makes defining users a snap, as shown in these steps:

1. Press the down-arrow key to highlight the "Supervise the network" option and press Enter.

2. Press the down-arrow key to highlight the User List option and press Enter.

3. You then see the entire list of network users: SUPERVISOR is the only one that's predefined.

Figure 9-2: The NetWare Lite NET menu interface is your network control center.

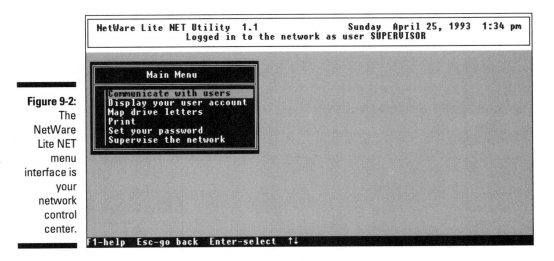

4. Press Ins to define a new user. A dialog box pops up that asks for the new user name in 15 characters or less.

5. Type the new user name and press Enter. We suggest that you use meaningful, unique names all your users will recognize. This is no time for cryptography or cuteness.

6. Press Enter again — the new user name is highlighted — and you see the user options. If you want to assign a password to this user, highlight Change Password and press Enter. Enter the new password, press Enter, reenter the new password for verification, and then press Enter.

7. Press Esc to return to the User List. Press Ins to define another user. When you're finished defining users, press Esc to return to the main menu. If you don't like pushing buttons, feel free to use the mouse.

Security on a network is a provocative topic. Many novice users don't understand the need to protect data with a password. Other users don't even consider the slightest possibility that others can see their data. Networks on which everyone knows everyone else's passwords are fooling themselves into believing that they have a secure network.

We suggest that all networks require unique passwords at least five characters long with a 90-day expiration on all user accounts. This technique keeps things changing enough to foil casual interlopers, but not enough to confuse your users. If the software doesn't remember when to change passwords, somebody else — you! — will have to take on the responsibility.

NetWare Lite gives all users supervisor-level privileges by default. You must take away privileges to restrict user access to network resources. Remember that user passwords only protect against unauthorized users logging in to the network. The setup of the network's shared directories keeps prying eyes away from sensitive files.

Sharing Directories and Printers

While you're in the NET menu interface, let's also define a network directory:

1. Highlight "Supervise the network" and press Enter.

2. Highlight "Network directories" and press Enter.

3. Press Ins to see a list of servers on which you can define a network directory.

4. Highlight the server on which you want to define the network directory and then press Enter.

5. Type a name, as long as 15 characters, for the new network directory. Again, it's a good idea to pick self-explanatory names and avoid names that are overly cryptic or cute.

6. A dialog box pops up that asks for the directory path. Enter the complete physical path (C:\LOTUS\DATA, for example) to the directory you want to share. **Note:** Users on the network can see all the files in this directory, and they can also see any files in its subdirectories.

7. After you have filled in the dialog box to your satisfaction, press Esc and then Enter to save and exit.

8. Your first network directory definition is now complete.

Defining network printers is just as easy from the NET main menu, as shown in these steps:

1. Highlight "Supervise the network" and press Enter.

2. Highlight "Network printers" and press Enter.

3. You now see a list of all network printers. Press Ins to define a new printer.

4. Highlight the server to which the network printer is attached and press Enter.

5. Type a name, as much as 15 characters long, for the new network printer. Remember what we said about names: short, descriptive, and neither cryptic nor cute.

6. Choose the port name where the printer is connected. For most parallel printers, the port name usually is LPT1:. Get some help from a PC guru if you don't know which port the printer is on or get hold of a PC diagnostic utility, such as Microsoft Diagnostics (MSD.EXE comes free with every copy of Windows 3.1), System Sleuth, or Check-It. Most of these programs can identify your current port assignments, plus much more.

7. The next dialog box is full of technical junk you never need to see, so press Esc two times to save your new printer and return to the NET main menu.

8. You now have users, network directories, and a network printer defined on your Lite network. That wasn't so hard, was it?

You Can't Take a Drive Without a Map

Now that you have a network directory defined, you can see how the users on the network get access to that directory. Lite refers to this process as *mapping a drive*.

Your PC probably has an A drive and a C drive and maybe even a B drive. DOS uses alphabetic drive letters to identify hard and floppy disk drives. The average PC uses only two or three of the available drive letters for locally installed drives. NetWare Lite can *map* any unused letters to a network directory. After that little bit of magic is complete, your PC can have many more drive letters than are physically attached. The following steps show the method to map drive letters to network directories from the NET main menu:

1. Press the up- or down-arrow key to highlight "Map drive letters" and then press Enter.

2. Highlight a drive letter that is different from any of the physical drives already installed in your PC. If you don't already have an E drive, for example, highlight the E drive letter and press Enter.

3. You now see a list of all available network directories. Highlight the directory you want to map to the E drive and press Enter.

4. Press Esc to return to the NET main menu. That's all there is to drive mapping.

Now you can go to a DOS prompt by pressing Esc and then Enter. Make the E drive the current drive by typing **E:** and then pressing Enter. You can run almost any command you run on your local drives, except CHKDSK, and your PC thinks that E is a local drive. Way cool! You can also accomplish the same mapping by using the MAP command at the DOS prompt. See the command summary after the following section for the correct command syntax.

The Capture Rapture

Lite also has a command called CAPTURE for attaching to network printers in much the same way as you map drive letters. Lite calls this process *capturing a port*. The following steps show the method to capture a port and send your print output to a network printer from the NET main menu:

1. Press the up- or down-arrow key to highlight Print and then press Enter.

2. Highlight a port other than the physical ports you are using on your PC. Highlight the LPT2 port, for example, and then press Enter if you have a local printer attached to LPT1.

3. You see a list of all available network printers. Highlight the printer you want to send your print output to and press Enter.

4. Press Esc twice to return to the NET main menu. That's all there is to capturing to a Lite printer.

All print output you send to LPT2 now is *redirected* to the network printer you have specified. Redirection is the process of mapping a drive to a network directory or capturing a port to a network printer.

A Syntax Isn't a Levy on Cigarettes

We have referred several times to the Lite commands you can run at a DOS prompt rather than use the NET main menu to accomplish network tasks. You can execute several commands only at a DOS prompt because they have no equivalent action on the NET menus. Get to a DOS prompt and try some of these commands just for practice. This section provides a quick overview of the Lite commands and shows their syntax.

AUDIT: Available only at a DOS prompt. Auditing must be turned on in the NET menus for the AUDIT command to work. This command sends the characters following the command to a special file, called an *audit file,* that keeps track of network activity. The AUDIT command is used primarily in batch files to make note of network operations.

Syntax: **NET AUDIT** *"string"*

CAPTURE: As noted, redirects local printer ports to network printers.

Syntax: **NET CAPTURE LPT1 ROGERSLASER**

HELP: Displays the built-in text that explains the syntax of each of the Lite commands.

Syntax: **NET HELP** *command*

INFO: Displays information servers, clients, and your username.

Syntax: **NET INFO**

LOGIN: Well, it logs you in.

Syntax: **NET LOGIN** *username*

LOGOUT: Orders your breakfast and a newspaper from room service. Oops! Sorry, that's the CHECKOUT command. Actually, it just logs you out of the network.

Syntax: **NET LOGOUT**

MAP: Redirects a local drive letter to a network directory.

Syntax: **NET MAP N: DEBBIES_GAMES**

NDLIST: Displays a list of available network directories.

Syntax: **NET NDLIST**

NPLIST: Displays a list of available network printers.

Syntax: **NET NPLIST**

PRINT: Enables you to print a file directly to a network printer without a capture of a local port.

Syntax: **NET PRINT C:\CONFIG.SYS KAYS_LASER**

RECEIVE: Enables your client to receive messages from other network users.

Syntax: **NET RECEIVE ON/OFF**

SEND:	Sends the included text to a user or to everyone on your network. Use the ALL option with discretion because it does what it says — sends it to everyone!
Syntax:	**NET SEND** *"text" user1 user2* or **ALL**
SETPASS:	Enables you to set a new password.
Syntax:	**NET SETPASS**
TIME:	Synchronizes the internal clock in your PC with the clock in the network server.
Syntax:	**NET TIME** *servername*
ULIST:	Displays a list of all users currently logged in.
Syntax:	**NET ULIST**

If you are ever stuck at a DOS prompt trying to remember the syntax of a particular command, type **NET HELP** and then press Enter. You will see a list of all Lite commands. Type **NET HELP** *commandname* to get specific syntax help for a particular command.

Doing Windows "Lite"ly

Those of you who use Windows already know that you are different from your average PC person. NetWare Lite requires a few special things if you run Lite as a client, server, or client-server while also running Windows on your PC. New copies of NetWare Lite now include a disk and installation manual called NetWare Lite v1.1 Utility for Windows.

You must install NetWare Lite v1.1 before installing the Lite Windows utilities. This utility is not compatible with NetWare Lite v1.0 or any Windows version before v3.0. Be sure to remove the SMARTDRV statement that Windows put in either your CONFIG.SYS or AUTOEXEC.BAT file.

Because NetWare Lite is incompatible with Microsoft's SMARTDRV disk-caching program, you cannot use both of them together. If you want to use Lite (why else are you reading this book?), get rid of SMARTDRV now!

Be sure not to choose Novell NetWare in the Windows setup program unless you are connecting to a server running NetWare 2.2, 3.11, or 4.0. Lite isn't compatible with the Novell NetWare option under Windows. Although Lite can run on a PC that doesn't have a hard drive, the Lite Windows utility is too big to fit on a single disk (the utility is uncompressed when you run the install program).

A hard drive is absolutely necessary before you can load or run the NetWare Lite Windows utility. Like we said, it's too big to fit on a floppy, uncompressed (unless you have one of those newfangled 2.88MB floppies).

To install the NetWare Lite Utility for Windows, insert the utility disk in the appropriate floppy drive and then start Windows. From the File menu, select Run. In the Run dialog box, type **A:SETUP** and then choose OK. The Install program copies all necessary files to your hard drive and the required setup changes are automatic. After you have started Lite and Windows, choose the NetWare group and then choose the NetWare icon. The NetWare Lite window that appears indicates that now you can get to the NetWare Lite resources on your network.

The NetWare Lite v1.1 Utility for Windows manual contains numerous caveats for users who run Lite under Windows. Be sure to review the information on pages 7 and 8 of the NetWare Lite v1.1 Utility for Windows manual before running Lite under Windows. If you don't, you may be sorry.

Troubleshooting Your Lite Network

Into all networks a little trouble must intrude. Now that you have a nifty new network, more sources exist for every potential problem. Suppose that you start getting a message that the printer is not responding. Is it your printer that isn't responding, or is it the network printer you recently captured to? A network can increase the likelihood of problems while also making those problems much harder to pinpoint.

The key to troubleshooting networks is to keep a complete set of records from the beginning. You should have a floor plan overview that shows the cable layout. Cable connections cause the bulk of network problems: The most common culprits behind network difficulties are loose cables, or "human error" — when users unhook their network cables.

Much of this trouble happens because users mangle their networks without realizing the effects they can cause. Ethernet networks, for example, are real picky about having each cable properly terminated and attached to a PC. When Joe in accounting unhooks his Ethernet network cable to rearrange his office, he can bring down the entire network. You must know where to look for cabling anomalies. A cable layout is essential equipment for network troubleshooting.

Specific error reports accompany many of the errors you see. Keep records of these error messages, and the time, date, and machine where the error shows up. Train your network users to write down any errors they see, whenever they see them. Most of these errors identify the offending component, and some errors even offer possible remedies.

Compare all recorded errors to the errors listed in the Lite manual, the messages in your application manuals, and the errors covered in the network interface card manuals. Determining the origin of an error can be the trick to solving problems in a network environment. As you gain experience, you learn to recognize, pinpoint, and cure common errors.

After you have determined the cause of an error, study all the relevant manuals and on-line help for possible solutions. If you're still stumped, contact the vendors who make the offending components and ask for their technical support department. Most hardware and software manufacturers keep databases of known problems and possible solutions. Talk to any PC or network gurus to whom you have access for their suggestions. Ask questions on CompuServe in the forum dedicated to the products you believe might be causing your error. A wealth of troubleshooting experience is available on CompuServe, and it's fast and relatively inexpensive to use. For information about using CompuServe, check out Appendix C.

If you suspect a network problem, start the Lite Install program. Insert the Lite Install disk in drive A, type **A:INSTALL**, and then press Enter at a DOS prompt. Highlight "Verify network connection" and press Enter. Enter a name — any name will do — and press Enter. Go to all other network PCs that you suspect are not communicating properly and repeat this procedure. Each PC name should appear on all the other PC screens. If you don't see any PCs on the list, check the card settings and cable connections according to the NIC manufacturer's guide.

Troubleshooting PC network problems is more of an art than a science, but things improve as you become familiar with the system. These procedures are your paints and canvas; try not to make a mess. We can only point you in the right direction. The skillful detective work is up to you.

When it comes to troubleshooting, these are the best three things to remember:

1. **Don't panic!** Don't let the adrenaline rush of things going wrong stop you from using your head and working from what you already know. Many simple problems seem worse than they are at first because it's so unsettling when things get weird.

2. **Be patient.** Even though your first priority is to get back to work, don't try to hurry your way through the problem-solving that troubleshooting always requires. Be thorough and methodical, and take your time. There's never enough time to do things right, but there's always time to do them over!

3. **Write things down as you go along.** That way, you won't try to apply the same fixes more than once, and you can keep track of what you have done and rejected. When you have solved the problem, you also can refer to the successful fix later on.

Chapter 10
Running a Lite (Network)

*E*ach person in charge of a server — even ol' Alice in accounting — is a network administrator. NetWare Lite's peer-to-peer network structure means that every PC can be a server, so every user can be an administrator. This structure raises the possibility, hideous to some, that users with absolutely no network experience can perform network supervisory tasks on your network. Zounds!

Peer-to-Peer Is not a Stroll Through a Harbor!

Organization is the key to successful network administration. One user — perhaps you? — should serve as the network organizer. Your job is to coordinate the actions of the various network administrators. The coordinator should plan the location of shared network files. Try to share the load so that no single PC stores more than 25 percent of network files. This number limits the potential for damage if you lose access to a single machine. It also should leave enough room on your users' desktops for their own stuff!

All users whose PCs are configured as servers should be put in charge of maintaining their own network resources. This responsibility includes making sure that their printer has paper and toner and that they back up all shared files at least weekly, if not more often. It is important that no more than three users be made responsible for the network as a whole — appoint a coordinator and two backup coordinators. Too many people making networkwide changes can lead to network anarchy. Teamwork is the name of the game in successful peer-to-peer networks.

Who's in charge here?

We suggest that only three people on the network have supervisory privileges: the coordinator and two backups. NetWare Lite defaults to all users having SUPERVISOR privileges. To change the privilege level, follow these steps:

1. Start the NET menu interface by typing NET at the DOS prompt.

2. Highlight the last selection, "Supervise the network," and then press Enter.

3. Highlight User List and press Enter.

4. Highlight the username you want to change and press Enter.

5. Press the down-arrow key to highlight SUPERVISOR privileges and press Enter.

6. Press N, to set the option to no, and then press Enter.

7. Press Esc, press Enter, and then press Esc twice to return to the NET main menu.

Generally, the network coordinator should be in charge of defining new users and passwords, defining new network directories and printers, and troubleshooting the network. If you have the luxury of owning a high-capacity tape-backup system, the coordinator should take responsibility for performing regular network backups.

When you are running a NetWare menu utility, such as the NET menu interface, press the first letter of any selection in a list box to immediately highlight that selection. If multiple selections begin with the same letter, the first selection beginning with that letter is highlighted. This feature still makes it faster to get where you need to go, especially for mouse-o-phobes!

There's more to backing up a network than just backing up a network. At least once a month, you should try to restore some of your backed-up data files. Be sure to restore to an empty subdirectory; otherwise, you might overwrite current files with older versions of the same files that were backed up earlier.

Just because the backup software says that a backup was successful doesn't mean that you can successfully restore your files. Test a sample collection of restored files at least once a month. It ain't working until you can prove it — so prove it!

Be sure to make a backup of the network system files every week as well. You can find a selection called "Server system files" under the "Supervise the network" selection on the NET main menu. Backing up these files gives you a copy of your setup for shared directories and printers, and all your user definitions — good stuff to have in an emergency. It's absolutely essential to have to get your Lite servers back in action if problems ever come up.

Dealing with Users

The main task for most network administrators is public relations. You must educate your users on network etiquette, dealing with error messages, and getting them used to the idea of other users accessing their hard drives. Some users have to be coaxed, prodded, or forced into using the network. Others complain that it took so long to get a network installed.

As a network coordinator, you also have to help your users build reasonable expectations about what networks can and cannot do for them. A new network neither fixes every communication problem in your office (though electronic mail, known as e-mail, can help), nor does the introduction of a network signal the end of civilization as we know it. Networks just make things different, and hopefully better, than they were before.

Dealing with Access Rights

The NetWare Lite default installation gives all new users supervisory privileges, and each new shared directory that gets created grants all access to users. Only the network coordinator and two backups should be permitted to retain these supervisory privileges. You should also carefully control access to directories by way of rights and user lists (see Chapter 16 for more information about NetWare security and rights).

Don't ever share the root (C:\, for example) of one of your hard drives because that access "trickles down" to all subdirectories. In other words, granting users access to your root directory also grants them access to *everything* else on your hard drive. Are you really sure that you mean to do that?

A good rule of thumb is to define each shared directory with READ default access rights. You can then grant the ALL access rights to users on a case-by-case basis through the "Users with nondefault rights" selection. As users discover that they need access to a particular network directory, they can skim the directory contents under the default READ access. If more rights are needed (WRITE, DELETE, or MODIFY rights, for example), you can simply add their usernames to the "Users with nondefault rights" for that directory.

You should try to control access to shared printers in exactly the same way. However, because printing to another user's printer doesn't imply quite the same degree of imposition as browsing through someone's hard drive, we suggest that all shared printers be left with ALL rights. When Alice starts to complain about the many pages of network printout spouting from her (formerly) personal printer, you can easily restrict access by using the "Users with nondefault rights" selection when you are defining Default access rights for network printers.

What If the Dog Eats Your Password?

There are two kinds of network users: those who have forgotten their passwords, and those who will forget their passwords. People are people. All of us forget our network passwords at least once in a lifetime. Luckily, Lite provides an excellent alternative in these situations: The SUPERVISOR can always define a new password, which means that all you have to do is remember the password for the SUPERVISOR username.

But, wait — what happens when someone forgets the SUPERVISOR password? There is hope! If any username with supervisory privileges — other than SUPERVISOR, of course — logs on to the network, its user can reassign any password, including the SUPERVISOR password. This is one reason we so strongly suggest that at least two other users also be granted supervisory privileges. Be warned, though: Anyone with a twisted sense of humor *and* supervisory privileges can reset the passwords of everyone on the network, including the SUPERVISOR account.

OK, so you admit that you made a mistake by not granting supervisory privileges to two designated backup coordinators. Now you have forgotten your password. What the heck can you do? Well, there's good news and bad news. The good news is, if you reinstall the Lite software, the SUPERVISOR account will be reset, sans password. The bad news is, you lose all the shared directories and printers, and all the user accounts already defined. It is just like starting over. Come to think of it, it *is* starting over. How's that for a pretty good incentive to give SUPERVISOR privileges to at least two backup users? Ouch!

Common Networking Gotchas

The "gotchas" are not a guerrilla group in Central America. Gotchas are important little details learned only in the school of hard network knocks. (Most of these things come from trial and error — mostly error). You can benefit from the experience of thousands of network administrators by reading and listening, and heeding what you learn.

In this section, we go through all the gotchas we can think of and then point you in the right direction to recover and learn from your own gotchas. The first three gotchas are particularly important in a peer-to-peer network, in which availability of shared resources is in the users' hands.

Gotcha #1: If the server ain't turned on, no one can access the gazillion-dollar color laser printer the server shares with the network.

It may seem like a simple concept until you try to explain it to ol' Alice in accounting. A server must be turned on for others to be able to access shared resources. Every PC on your network must now be left turned on, therefore, whenever other users need access to it. So you have to get users out of the habit of turning off their PCs every night. All server PCs must also be left on so that network backups can be completed successfully. This gotcha brings us to a corollary gotcha.

Gotcha #2: If ol' Alice reboots her PC while you are saving a file on her shared network drive, you will be an unhappy network user.

An old network proverb says that a network is only as good as long as it is *up*. A server is up when it is available to network users. If a server is rebooted or turned off, it is considered to be *down*. Being down is not at all good. Again, educate your users about the importance of never rebooting their PCs without first warning all network users. That way, shared files in use can be saved rather than lost, which brings us to the next item on the gotcha list.

Gotcha #3: Just because ol' Alice's copy of MegaSpreadsheet is locked up tighter than a drum, it doesn't mean that the shared drive or printer on her PC is also locked up.

It's common for nondedicated servers to have DOS problems that do not crash the server. When a server goes from being up to being down, the server is said to have *crashed*. Your DOS programs can lock up, yet they may not work with the Lite programs that enable other users to access your disk and printer. For this reason, you *must* alert network users, *before rebooting*, when your PC is having problems. Those users may be able to salvage a great deal of hard work that otherwise will be lost if you blindly reboot at the first sign of trouble. Old habits die hard, but network servers can crash even harder! Tell your users that they now have responsibility for more than just their PC and programs; they're not just any ordinary fools — they're *network administrators!*

Gotcha #4: Multiple copies of the same file can wreak havoc on your co-workers.

We last discussed the problem of multiple copies of the same file when we were talking about the old sneakernet in Chapter 8. Now that everyone on the network has access to each other's hard drives, you have geometrically increased the number of places for a file to get stored. Meet with your users and agree on a central location for each workgroup's files. Perhaps a payroll directory on Sue Ellen's PC is the only place to store employee electronic timesheets. And a personnel directory on Matt's PC is the only place to store employee records.

This method is the only practical way to make sure that different users don't keep multiple copies of the same file in separate places. Even with a central storage area for each group, you still have to make sure that someone doesn't already have a file open before you make changes. When another user saves his or her work, your changes may be overwritten.

Gotcha #5: The more successful your network, the greater the number of people who will use it. The more people who use the network, the slower the network gets, and the less people want to use it. So less is more, and more is less! Huh?

This most paradoxical gotcha points out that some networks become victims of their own success. When you are planning your network, *before* buying anything, consider not just what you need today but also what you need if and when things go really well.

Outgrowing your network software and hardware can be expensive. If you suddenly need to connect 50 additional users scattered across a large campus, your copies of NetWare Lite and your el cheapo ARCNET adapters can be headed for the trash bin. Obviously, if you work in a small dentist's office with two PCs, even an explosion in root canal work doesn't test the capabilities of NetWare Lite.

Gotcha #6: Cabling is usually the problem.

No such thing as an absolute exists in the network world. In our experience, however, the network cabling *absolutely* drives us crazy more than any other network component. We have chased more gremlins across more networks than we care to remember, and it usually comes down to cabling.

A loose connector on Pete's PC can make your WordPerfect print Kanji characters upside down and backward while Pete's work is unaffected. We have battled unexplained network problems for days only to find out that the carpenter installing new cabinets in Debbie's office had drilled through the network cable inside that wall. Don't skimp on the design and installation of your network cabling system. Cheap components cost you far more in the long run than buying the good stuff to begin with. Please be sure to buy quality cable and connectors for your network installation.

Gotcha #7: Twisted-pair cabling can really be a problem for network installations.

Be very careful when you are installing twisted-pair networks. Twisted-pair is the type of wiring used by the telephone system in your home and probably at your office. Twisted-pair wire consists of two small copper wire conductors covered with an insulating coat of plastic and twisted around each other every few inches.

Much of the twisted-pair wiring in older buildings was installed 30 or 40 years ago. You can easily spend more money trying to make old twisted-pair wiring work than you would spend to install new wiring that meets modern specifications. When in doubt, hire a technician to check your cabling with diagnostic equipment. It is cheaper to spend the money once than to spend it twice — trust us.

Gotcha #8: Some network things just cannot be explained (also known as The Sweet Mystery of Life).

This gotcha is the toughest one to contend with. You see some problems you can't explain. You see them come and go for no reason. You see problems recur that you thought you had fixed last week. Get used to it. If you're seeing intermittent problems that don't affect network productivity, it's sometimes better to just shrug your shoulders and go on to the next problem.

Separating Local from Networked Resources

The process of keeping your local files separate from shared files on your hard drive can get a little tricky if you don't plan ahead. We suggest that you define a NETWORK subdirectory on your hard drive and locate all sharable files in well-labeled subdirectories of that NETWORK subdirectory. The following example directory structure illustrates how you might structure your hard drive to keep your résumé from getting mixed up with the company's end-of-quarter financial results:

```
C:\ (your root directory)
   \DOS
   \WORDPERF
      \DOCS
   \LOTUS
      \WKS
   \HARVARD
      \CHTS
   \NETWORK (your network "root" directory)
      \WPDOCS
      \LOTWKS
      \HGCHTS
```

When you set up your network, you are required only to share the C:\NETWORK directory; access to its three subdirectories automatically trickles down. If you want tighter control over who accesses which files, create three separate network directories: WPDOCS, LOTWKS, and HGCHTS. You can then grant read access to some users, no access to some users, and full access to other users.

Notice the subdirectories under each application directory (WORDPERF, LOTUS, and HARVARD). This structure lets you store all your private data files and documents in these private directories. That way, no one on the network can see your personal work. If you have a private file you want to share on the network, simply execute a DOS COPY command to copy the file to the appropriate network directory on your PC.

The 5th Wave

By Rich Tennant

"PREDICT SECURITY EMISSIONS ON YOUR NETWORK? NO PROBLEM. WHAT ARE YOU RUNNING? TWISTED PAIR CABLING ON A LAN? HOW ABOUT YOUR OPERATING SYSTEM,..."

Chapter 11
Is the Lite Way the Right Way for You?

NetWare Lite's Strengths and Weaknesses

It's no mistake that NetWare Lite is the best-selling peer-to-peer network. Lite solves the basic problems of sharing files and printers among small groups of DOS-based PCs. This statement doesn't mean that Lite is the right solution for every situation, however. The things that Lite does well, it does very well, but it has limitations, like every network product. If you're not using PCs, for example, or if your PCs aren't running DOS or Windows, Lite is completely unsuitable for your needs.

A man goes to his doctor and says, "Doctor, I keep having these splitting headaches from beating my head against a brick wall." The doctor asks, "Why in the world do you keep beating your head against a brick wall?" The man replies, "Because it feels so good when I stop!" Don't beat your head against a networking brick wall. Table 11-1 makes a comparison between the time when the use of NetWare Lite is appropriate and the time when the headaches become, shall we say, acute.

Table 11-1	The Pros and Cons of Lite	
Situation	*Headache?*	*Why or why not*
Florist shop	No	Small network with two PCs in same area; perfect fit
Large doctor's office; 12 PCs in two separate buildings; continually expanding PC environment	Yes	Expansion soon outstrips Lite's capacity; separate locations are harder to hook up and support
Accounting department in small manufacturing firm; 8 PCs; Novell 2.2 network in use in marketing area	No	Lite is a great first network; easily ties in to 2.2 server; upgrade Lite to 2.2 as necessary
State agency (75 employees) with mainframe and PCs	Ouch! Don't even think about it!	Situation far outstrips the capabilities of Lite

You can see from the table that Lite is appropriate for most small offices or workgroups in which PCs are in the same general vicinity and share data files and printers. Lite is a good choice when you don't know much about networks, you don't have much money to spend, and you don't have much time to devote to running the network.

Heavy Mettle

So, if Lite is so great, why does anybody need the NetWare Heavies? NetWare 2.2, 3.11, and 4.0 have many advantages over Lite, though the difference between a benefit and a drawback is sometimes in the eye of the beholder. The Heavies require a dedicated file server PC that does nothing more than serve the needs of the other PCs.

On this file server you would install a 32-bit preemptive multitasking network operating system that is the fastest thing since greased eels. What? It's really not as scary as "32-bit preemptive multitasking network operating system" sounds. Despite the technobabble, it's a shorthand way of getting to the main differences between a peer-to-peer networking system such as Lite and the newest of the NetWare Heavies — namely, 3.x and 4.x.

For clarity's sake, here's what's going on: A *bit* is similar to one letter in a word. DOS is an 8-bit operating system, which means that DOS talks in 8-character words. NetWare Heavy talks in 32-bit words, conveying more information with each word. *Preemptive multitasking* means that numerous programs can run simultaneously on a Heavy file server without the PC losing track of any of the

TECHNICAL STUFF

The gateway to paradise

A *gateway* is an electronic or software device that connects two or more dissimilar computer systems. A NetWare-to-IBM-mainframe gateway, for example, takes the IPX from one side of the gateway and translates it to the SNA protocol required for some IBM mainframe communications. Gateways are becoming more and more common as vendors figure out how to make different kinds of computers and software talk to each other.

information. While you're sorting a database, someone else can be loading Word and a third person can be updating Lotus worksheets, all without the server missing a beat or getting confused. In fact, *hundreds* of users (as many as a thousand, in fact) all can be doing different things on a NetWare server and you will think that you're the only one who's logged in.

The NetWare Heavies shine in the area of communications with other systems. You can purchase gateways to mainframes, minicomputers, and other networks. You can also install modem gateways that enable every user on the network to share access to a "pool" of modems. Networks with more than 15 or 20 users *require* a more substantial investment in the network operating system and file server hardware — and most important — in someone knowledgeable to make it all work.

Knowing When to Say "Uncle"

OK, so you have your Lite network up and running. Things are going pretty well and more and more users are asking for access to your newly installed network.

How do you know when it's time to make the jump from Lite to Heavy? The short answer is, when you can no longer deal with the problems of an overextended Lite network. If you spend hours a day just performing backups, consider a centralized file server running NetWare 2.2. If you're trying to figure out a way to expand from 20 to 50 users, share modems and a mainframe gateway, and connect to the NetWare server in Taipei, consider NetWare 3.11. If your boss wants you to expand your little 14-PC network to the rest of your 400-person company, give NetWare 4.0 a try. Try to not become so enamored by the joys of Lite smallness that you lose sight of the big picture. Networks are just a means to an end, and if the means get too nasty, the end doesn't matter.

Mixing Lite and Heavy

One of the benefits of NetWare Lite compared to the peer-to-peer competition (LANtastic or Windows for Workgroups, for example) is the ease with which you can connect to a NetWare Heavy file server. Because Lite uses a variant of the IPX protocol that the NetWare Heavies use to communicate, it's simple to set up your Lite client as a Heavy client.

This flexibility takes some of the pressure off you for choosing Lite. You have a clear upgrade path to a more powerful network operating system, if you ever outgrow the capabilities of NetWare Lite. By using the upgrade procedure described in Chapter 8, you can set up your PC to access a Lite server and a Heavy server from the same PC — the best of both worlds, indeed!

Making the Lite Choice

Always try to keep in mind that Lite was invented in order to network PCs that have to share things without the burden of being networked. Lite eases that network burden to the point that most users will forget that their drive X maps to Fred's PC located 50 feet away. They just know that their PC does what they need it to do to get their job done. Therein lies the basic foundation for the success of Novell's entire line of network products: The products work!

Part III
Networking with NetWare

By Rich Tennant

"OH SURE! LEAVE IT TO THE FORESTRY SERVICE TO START TALKING DISTRIBUTED COMPUTING ENVIRONMENT JUST WHEN I GET THE MAINFRAME UP AND RUNNING."

In this part...

The marketplace has already selected NetWare as the champion of the commercially available network operating systems (NOSs). Because it's not a popularity contest, there must be some good reasons why.

NetWare comes in multiple flavors, with different capabilities. Despite these differences, any flavor of NetWare offers more horsepower and better network access than any of its competitors, at least according to the pundits who write for the computer trade rags.

NetWare makes it possible for PCs, Macintoshes, UNIX machines, and other computers to work together, and to share files, printers, and all kinds of other services. The big attraction is that NetWare works to bring businesspeople close together and to make them more productive.

This part of the book "opens the hood" on the various flavors of NetWare and shows what these babies can do. You are taken through the full range of NetWare's capabilities so that you can understand what NetWare offers, beginning with basic installation and configuration, through the file system, and into NetWare's security, printing, messaging, backup, and more. After you get a feel for NetWare, you are then armed with the tools and techniques you need in order to keep it performing at its absolute peak.

Because this section is liberally illustrated with examples and provides a great deal of background information, you can keep up with a tour that covers lots of ground. It's not quite as bad as "if it's Tuesday, it must be Belgium," but you will want to take the time to become familiar with each of the topics discussed. If you put in that time, you will be well on your way to understanding NetWare, and you will be better prepared to make it a part of your life.

Because we don't necessarily expect you to sit down and read this entire section from beginning to end, you can use the chapters for reference if you just want to check out a few topics. Whatever way you choose to approach NetWare, you should find it interesting and challenging. But you should also find it fun. Enjoy!

Chapter 12
A Road Map to NetWare

*O*K, now it's time for things to get heavy. If NetWare Lite lives up to its name, *real* NetWare has to be a weighty subject, right? *Not!* NetWare ain't heavy, it's where the real networking action is. The reason that NetWare Lite is called Lite is because it cannot come close to touching what NetWare can do.

NetWare celebrated its tenth birthday in February 1993. Curiously, it's also been through ten major versions in those ten years. In this chapter, you learn just enough about ancient NetWare to know where today's products are coming from. You also get a quick overview of each of today's fresh versions so that you can understand what NetWare is about and so that you can tell the differences between the three currently available flavors.

In the Beginning...

Today, Novell is a colossus of the networking world. Its 1992 annual revenues neared the $1 billion mark ($933 million). It employs more than 3,600 people worldwide, with offices in 30-plus domestic locations and another 28 locations outside the United States. During the past ten years, Novell has built an empire from networking software.

X marks the spot!

One thing you will notice in this book, and particularly in this section, is that versions of NetWare get lumped together with an *x*, like this:

- ✔ v2.*x* is used to refer to all versions of NetWare that begin with a 2 (v2.0, v2.11, v2.12, v2.15, and v2.2).

- ✔ v3.*x* is used to refer to all versions of NetWare that begin with a 3 (v3.0, v3.1, v3.11, and v3.12). New versions of 3.*x* are usually under development at Novell; by the time you read this, you should be able to find out whether there's a new v3.*x*.

✔ We sometimes refer to NetWare 4.*x*, even though there are only two versions — 4.0 and 4.01 — available now. Sooner or later, another release will appear, and 4.*x* lets us talk about it in a general way without knowing its real number.

Note: In an effort save ink, Novell has dropped the *v* in front of its NetWare version numbers, beginning with NetWare 4.0. That is why we refer to v2.*x* and v3.*x*, but use 4.*x* rather than v4.*x*. Who says that product names are arbitrary and capricious, anyway?

From the ashes rises the phoenix!

The birth of NetWare began as a part-time project for developing a disk server operating system, by a bunch of graduate students at Brigham Young University, next door to Provo, in Orem, Utah. This group called themselves Superset, and it remains one of the key technology groups within the company.

Because NetWare's origins precede those of DOS, Superset's original effort was to build server software that could service CP/M and UNIX workstations. That six-week contract was renewed several times as the project grew in size and expanded in scope. Today Superset has been fully absorbed into Novell, but the group members are still the second-largest Novell stockholder, collectively speaking. In any case, after ten years, it's obviously not a short-term relationship.

ShareNet becomes NetWare/S-Net

The original version of NetWare was called ShareNet, also known as S-Net, and was based on proprietary servers built around Motorola's 68000 processors (the same family, incidentally, around which the Macintosh is built). This version of NetWare, which became known as NetWare 68 or NetWare /S, represents the first version of the product family.

Shortly after ShareNet was born, IBM introduced the DOS operating system for PCs. Ray Noorda, Novell's president and CEO, deserves credit for realizing that DOS was an important phenomenon because he encouraged attention toward this fledgling new operating system, in addition to the focus on UNIX and CP/M. By the end of 1983, as many as 24 PCs could be attached to the ShareNet server by using serial RS-422 connections running at a whopping 232 Kbps.

In the following year, NetWare became a real network operating system, when support for ARCNET boards in the NetWare 68 server was added, connecting the server to a real network for the first time. This support also multiplied the speed by an order of magnitude, to 2.5 Mbps.

When IBM released its second-generation PC, the PC XT, ShareNet was renamed to NetWare/S-Net and Novell began to move the server software from its original 68000 server platform to run on this new PC. The first PC-based version of NetWare, known as NetWare/86, required a gargantuan 640K of RAM and a 10MB hard disk.

Counting bits and bytes in computer-ese

Speed and capacity are measured in bits and bytes in the language that computer geeks like to speak (it has only a superficial resemblance to English). For the record, here's how this stuff works.

A *bit* is the most basic unit of information for a computer. It's a location in memory, on disk, or anywhere else computers can get to that's set to either 1 or 0 in value. Because 1 and 0 comprise two distinct states, this is called a *binary system*. Everything else that computers do comes from ones and zeroes (which is pretty amazing, we think!).

A *byte* is eight bits of information treated as a single chunk. Most alphabetic characters can be represented by a single byte, which is why bytes are used to state the size of most computer-storage stuff, from memory to disk storage to tape cartridges, and so on.

Computer sizes, capacities, and speeds are often stated in terms of either bits or bytes. We cover others as they come along, but the speed stuff covered in the section "ShareNet becomes NetWare/S-Net" works like this:

- *Kbps,* which stands for *kilo bits per second,* is a rating of volume over time, otherwise known as speed. A kilobit equals 210 or 1024 bits, which is pretty close to 1,000 in base 10 (humans count in base 10, and computers count in binary, or base 2), which is why they call it a kilobit. For the record, 232 Kbps is pretty slow for network stuff.

- *Mbps* stands for *mega bits per second.* One megabit is 220, or 1,048,580 bits. Because this number is pretty close to a million in base 10, it gets the prefix *mega.* When we say ARCNET runs at 2.5 Mbps, this number is significantly faster than S-Net, but it's still pretty slow by network standards.

Even then, Novell supported multiple kinds of workstations. It kept up support for CP/M machines, even after adding support for DOS, and also offered S-Net NICs for some other microcomputers that today sound like sideshow attractions: the Victor 9000 and the ill-fated TI Professional.

At the time, it wasn't yet clear that the PC would become the dominant desktop machine, and Novell embarked on the strategy of supporting all desktops with a sufficiently large market share to command attention, if not respect. Support for CP/M continued until 1986, at which point DOS emerged victorious in the battle for PC operating system supremacy. While in its NetWare/86 phase, NetWare went through three revisions — a 1.0 version, and 2.0 and 2.1 versions.

Say hello to Advanced NetWare

When IBM introduced its 80286-based PC AT in 1985, Novell followed suit with a new version of NetWare to exploit that powerful new platform's capabilities. This version, which became known as Advanced NetWare, was released as v1.0 in 1985, which quickly was followed by v2.0 in 1986. Advanced NetWare ran on both PC XTs and PC ATs, but it was designed to take advantage of the AT and performed much better on that more capable platform.

Keeping up with Intel

By now, a NetWare trend was emerging, one in which Novell would push to develop NetWare for the most powerful Intel platform available and exploit that platform's advanced hardware and instruction set capabilities. This support also has continued to this day, with versions of NetWare available that require a minimum of an 80386-equipped PC and that can take advantage of 80486-specific capabilities, if it is present.

Advanced NetWare supported as many as 100 simultaneous users, a capability that was unmatched at the time it was introduced. The server could be configured to act solely as a server, called a *dedicated server,* or it could act as a workstation and a server, called a *nondedicated server,* to help purchasers get double-duty from one of their machines. Advanced NetWare also witnessed the introduction of read-after-write media checks, called *hotfix,* and included built-in router support for as many as four NICs in a single

server. This capability was required because of Advanced NetWare's support for 100 simultaneous users. Most networking technologies don't allow 100 devices to be attached to a single cable (and, therefore, to a single NIC). Advanced NetWare also added support for as much as 16MB of RAM (the maximum allowable amount on an 80286 processor) and for as much as 2 gigabytes (GB) of disk storage.

Today, it's not unthinkable to use a much more powerful machine on your desktop, but at the time this amount made for a raging monster of a PC. This level of capability began to command respect from the business community and represented Novell's first widely accepted network operating system. At the same time, Novell began to get a reputation for building reliable, high-performance software, reflecting its broader use in the marketplace.

SFT NetWare

SFT NetWare was released in 1987, as the first in a series of software fault-tolerant (SFT) NetWare products. The idea was to stress the software's reliability and capability, helping Novell continue to expand its increasing business market share. NetWare was beginning to step into the big time, and MIS managers accustomed to built-in integrity mechanisms and reliable software systems were making it clear that NetWare had better be capable of playing.

At this point, Novell began touting its hot fix media checks at its first level of SFT capability and started talking about its second and third levels of SFT. SFT Level II includes the hot fix feature from SFT I and provides support for duplicating data on a hard disk, either by duplicating drives through a single disk controller (called *disk mirroring*) or by duplicating drives and controllers (called *disk duplexing*) for even more reliability. These two approaches, depicted in Figure 12-1, illustrate that doubling hardware expense for disk drives can greatly improve reliability.

SFT Level II also includes transaction tracking capabilities, referred to as the Transaction Tracking System (TTS). TTS lets database and file system operations be logged as they occur and can then re-create them if the server crashes. This capability virtually guarantees that only transactions in process (and not yet complete) would be lost in the event of a system failure. In plain English, TTS makes a NetWare server very reliable.

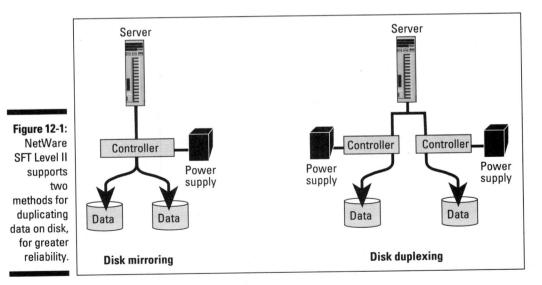

Figure 12-1: NetWare SFT Level II supports two methods for duplicating data on disk, for greater reliability.

At the same time as it introduced SFT Level II, Novell introduced the concept of SFT Level III, in which entire servers were duplexed and appeared to the network as a single server, for the ultimate in server reliability. Unfortunately, building the technology to support this level of system fault-tolerance proved more difficult than originally thought. Though Level III initially was promised for delivery in 1989, a "limited release" version did not make its way into customers' hands until late 1992, and a commercial version of NetWare SFT Level III based on NetWare 4.0 is not expected to ship until late 1993 or early 1994. Figure 12-2 shows how SFT III turns two servers into one and illustrates its use of a special link between the two machines to keep them tightly synchronized.

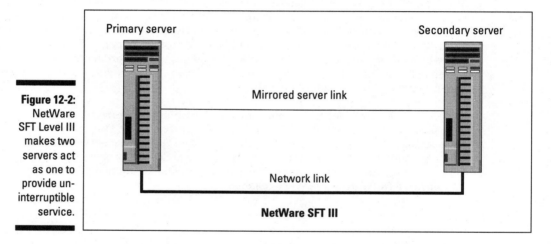

Figure 12-2:
NetWare
SFT Level III
makes two
servers act
as one to
provide un-
interruptible
service.

Collapsing the family: Getting to NetWare 2.2

By 1989, Novell offered four separate and distinct versions of NetWare written for the Intel 80286 processor. These products were based on various versions of NetWare v2, ranging from v2.11 to v2.15, depending on which flavor was purchased. Keeping track of these multiple versions was not only confusing for customers but also was a support headache for Novell: The company had to handle questions about four different versions, each of which required its own testing and support team.

Realizing that these versions were superfluous, especially with the introduction of a new generation of NetWare in 1990 (v3.0), Novell decided to consolidate all four versions into a single 286-based NetWare, called NetWare v2.2. Before this consolidation could happen, though, NetWare went through five versions of software, beginning with Advanced NetWare v1.0, to multiple Advanced and SFT versions (v2.0, v2.11, v2.12, and v2.15).

In addition, Novell created special entry-level versions of NetWare: Entry-Level System I (ELS I), which supported four users; and Entry-Level System II (ELS II), which more or less stayed frozen at a v2.12 revision until v2.2 came along and supplied five- and ten-user versions. Sound confusing? You bet! Be thankful that ELS is just a fading memory....

Introducing NetWare v2.2

Today, NetWare v2.2 is the bottom rung of the NetWare network operating system family (not counting NetWare Lite). As far as logical progressions go, v2.2 should be considered next in line after SFT NetWare 286. It offers all the features of that product and ships with a large collection of hardware drivers — for NICs, disk drives, tape drives, and the like — right in the box. Best of all, it's much easier to install than its immediate predecessor.

This list shows some of NetWare v2.2's distinguishing features:

- Sixteen-bit operating system
- Supports DOS, OS/2, Macintosh, and Windows workstations
- Aimed at small businesses, professional offices, and departmental workgroups
- Offers support for resource sharing, workgroup productivity applications, and simple administration
- Permits addition of a limited number of add-on software modules, called *value-added processes* (*VAPs*) per server (most commonly used for record management and printing)

Who's using v2.2?

Until 1992, more copies of NetWare v2.x were in use than any other kind of NetWare. Most of NetWare's users belong to its original constituency — smaller networks, of 15 or fewer users, who tend to control their own environments and who typically do not have access to centralized support from MIS. Somebody therefore gets elected to take care of most of these networks instead of managing networks as a full-time job.

Should I consider building a new network around v2.2?

Even though a fair number of first-time network buyers are still purchasing NetWare v2.2, we cannot, in good conscience, recommend it. The main reason is that NetWare v2.2 is on the trailing edge of Novell's development cycle. Because it is a "mature product," which means that v2.2 is being maintained and kept going, it no longer receives the benefits of much attention or the incorporation of much new technology. Put a different way, it's not getting much time anymore from the Superset gang.

The only valid reasons, as far as we're concerned, for considering a purchase of v2.2 today are the following iron-clad, inflexible, nonnegotiable requirements:

- ✔ The absolute lowest possible cost

- ✔ A special-purpose application that doesn't run on anything other than v2.2

- ✔ The need for a nondedicated server (you *must* be able to use the server as a workstation)

Welcoming NetWare 3.x

Because NetWare v3.0 was introduced slightly ahead of the consolidation of the v2.x family, it's possible to argue that the introduction of a next generation of NetWare is what made the consolidation of the 16-bit versions a reality. When it shipped in the fall of 1989, NetWare v3.0 represented a major step forward from v2.x capability, but not until Novell shipped v3.11 almost 18 months later were all the capabilities promised for v3.x delivered.

So what makes NetWare v3.11 special? Why is it such a significant advancement over the v2.x NetWare family? There are many reasons, but the following ones are some of the most significant:

- ✔ A full 32-bit operating system.

- ✔ Supports add-in software modules, called NetWare Loadable Modules (NLMs), to extend NetWare's basic functionality (see Chapter 14 for details). Third parties offer add-in products for NetWare 3.11 that span everything from automatic uninterruptible power supply (UPS) support, to high-performance database management systems, such as Oracle, Sybase, and Informix.

- ✔ Built-in routing and support for IPX, TCP/IP, and a subset of SNA; add-in support available for AppleTalk, OSI, and others.

- Support for DOS and OS/2 file systems; built-in, add-in support available for AFP, NFS, and OSI FTAM (File Transfer, Access, and Manipulation), with a single underlying file system, enabling users on all platforms to share common files.

- Server-based backup architecture, with built-in SBACKUP.NLM and numerous third-party enhancements available.

- Enhanced server and network management, using SNMP, IBM NetView, and third-party NLMs, and support for remote management over the network.

Whereas NetWare 2.*x* garnered accolades and recognition for Novell's file and print services, NetWare 3.*x* opened the door for an entire market of network-based services and capabilities. In addition, NetWare 3.*x*'s support for multiple protocols, multiple desktops, and built-in routing made it the integration platform of choice in businesses in which order had to be created from chaotic, scattered communities of some or all of the following: DOS and Windows PCs, Macintoshes, UNIX machines, and IBM mainframes and look-alikes.

With NetWare 3.11, Novell delivered a networking platform that could meet the needs of most business networks and did not require its purchasers to swear allegiance to one particular platform or operating system. Because this platform fostered the mentality of continued use for existing systems, instead of throwing them away or trading them in for new ones, this open-minded attitude has earned Novell its customers' appreciation and respect.

Who's using NetWare v3.12?

Today, more than half of Novell's installed base is using v3.11 or v3.12, including most of the Fortune 1000 companies. It is Novell's workhorse platform, and with nearly four years of testing and development under its belt, it also offers the broadest range of add-on options, custom services, and the like. The short answer to the question, "Who's using NetWare v3.12?" is, "Nearly everybody."

Should I consider building a new network around v3.12?

Even though NetWare 4.0 is commercially available as this book is being written, v3.12 still rules the roost in terms of all the additional features and capabilities that third parties provide to add value to a NetWare platform. Because these kinds of add-ons are a large part of why users buy and use NetWare, basing a selection on available functionality seems to argue that v3.12 is the right place to begin building networks for today.

In the next section, on NetWare 4.0, we outline some reasons you might want to consider going to NetWare 4.0 anyway, despite the broader range of options and support available for v3.12 today. Unless you need some of these special, new capabilities or are working with large NetWare networks, v3.12 is the best NetWare platform to build networks around today. As NetWare 4.0 ages and third parties catch up to its new capabilities, this will change. For now, v3.12 is a very good choice to network a business around.

Climbing to NetWare 4.x

In March 1993, Novell introduced NetWare 4.0 at the InterOp trade show in Washington, D.C. The accompanying fanfare and a whiz-bang, high-tech demonstration showed a live network of 1,000 workstations being handled by a single server, which was automatically reconfigured to 1,000 servers being managed by a single workstation. This display was intended to prove to the skeptics that 4.0 indeed could handle 1,000 users on a single server, and that large-scale integrated networks could be built on the 4.0 platform, which is where the reconfiguration to 1,000 servers came in. The demonstration was a raging success, and the skeptics were wowed. In early fall 1993, Novell shipped a multilingual version of 4.0, number 4.01, that was code-named FIGS, for its capability to support French, Italian, German, and Spanish, in addition to the English the base 4.0 version already had covered.

But there's much more to NetWare 4.x than just increased capacity and the capability to accommodate large collections of servers. In addition to doing everything that v3.12 can do, 4.x also offers a whole slew of enhancements and new capabilities. Read on for a list of what's new and interesting about NetWare 4.x:

- Shipping versions can support 5, 10, 25, 50, 100, 250, 500, and 1,000 users per server; this capability really covers systems from the smallest to the largest.

- Built-in directory services. Users can ask for things by name rather than by address, and the network appears as a logical whole rather than as a collection of individual, isolated servers.

- Optional, built-in disk compression that typically can almost double the storage capacity of most hard disks

- Foreign language support; users can run NetWare in English, French, German, Italian, Spanish, Japanese, and other languages (languages not named are supplied by third parties, not by Novell)

- Enhanced network security and audit capabilities, including single login to the network and background security checks

- Improved network monitoring and management

- Storage migration facility; seldom used files can be aged onto secondary or tertiary storage systems (typically read-write optical media, and tape)

- Improved wide-area network capabilities

- Improved system performance, memory allocation, and memory protection

- Automatic update/migration tools to help automate the process of upgrading from 2.*x* or 3.*x* to 4.*x*

- CD-ROM based installation (one disk means that no floppy shuffling is required in order to install 4.*x*)

- Built-in support for CD-ROM and other optical disk formats

- Support for application developers to build imaging, multimedia, and telephony-based applications; over time, the most interesting applications and capabilities will appear on NetWare 4.x, but they probably won't be obvious until late 1993 or early 1994

- On-line, electronic documentation; a powerful search engine makes technical data much easier to find than scanning the foot-high pile of manuals that has characterized previous versions of NetWare

This is a great deal of information to absorb, so let's try an abridged version. NetWare 4.*x*'s most significant new capability is a directory service that makes interacting with the network much easier and more intuitive. NetWare 4.0 also does a great deal to enhance performance and extend storage capabilities. NetWare 4.*x* also comes in multiple languages and is easier to install and maintain than are previous versions.

NetWare 4.*x* has much more to offer than just improved large-scale behavior and better wide-area networking support. We think that it's worth the upgrade price just for the performance improvements, doubling of disk space, and improved installation and on-line documentation. But only you can decide whether these new bells and whistles are enough to get you to make the switch in the near future.

Moving up to 32-bit software

From a CPU power standpoint, v3.12 takes full advantage of the Intel 80386 platform (NetWare v3.0 was originally known, in fact, as NetWare 386 v3.0). It's a 32-bit operating system, with the capability to address much more memory than its predecessor did. More important, it takes advantage of the multiprocessing capabilities of the 80386 to offer fast, elegant support for a multitasking environment.

In plain English, v3.*x* NetWare can keep multiple tasks around and switch among them very quickly,

providing the illusion that it can do several things at a time. This capability makes NLMs possible and gives v3.12 its extensible, flexible capabilities. Because the 80386 and the 80486 are more alike than different, Novell didn't find it necessary to build for the 80486 a new version of NetWare that was distinct from the v3.*x* versions. Instead, v3.12 can sense whether it's running on an 80486 and, if it is, take advantage of the more advanced features it offers.

Who's using NetWare 4.x?

As this book is being written, Novell is shipping more than 40,000 upgrades from v3.12 to 4.x to satisfy users who purchased advanced upgrades. It's a reasonably safe bet that these folks will use 4.x. This group of Novell customers has multiple servers (often hundreds or thousands of them), multiple locations with wide-area links, or special application needs that cry out for NetWare 4.x. Not surprisingly, this audience is the same one for which Novell is positioning the product: the larger companies who use more sophisticated technology and who have already adopted networking and are trying to expand and capitalize on its use.

Because NetWare 4.0 comes in small-user flavors (5, 10, 25, and 50), it clearly is intended to become Novell's networking flagship. Ultimately, it should make a good replacement for all v3.x and v2.x implementations.

Should I consider building a new network around NetWare 4.x?

If you're trying to put in place a large-scale, full-featured network, 4.x is not completely outfitted with all the options that make v3.12 so attractive. If you have time, you can wait for 4.x to catch up; if you don't have time, we recommend that you begin building your environment around v3.12 today and plan to migrate to 4.x as the features and functions you need become available on that platform. If you take that approach, be sure to get some 4.x training at the first opportunity, and be sure to plan ahead for your ultimate migration. That way, you can make the change smooth and painless for both you and your users.

Figuring Out What You Have

Now that you know what kinds of NetWare are available, how can you tell which kind you have (assuming that you already have some)? The answer's easy — all you have to do is look.

Let the server tell you

If you can get to your server and watch it boot up, it will tell you which version of NetWare it's running. It shows you a message that looks something like this (the details vary depending on which version you're running):

```
Novell NetWare v3.11 (250 user) 2/20/91
```

What could be easier?

Let your workstation tell you

If you're running a DOS or Windows PC, NetWare can tell you about itself, if you know how to ask. By typing **WHOAMI** at the DOS command prompt, after you log in, the middle line of the reply shows you the details you want about which version of NetWare you're connected to:

```
You are connected to Server AUS-NIX running NetWare v3.12 (250 user)
```

What does it mean?

If you're already running one of the current versions — NetWare v2.2, NetWare v3.12, or NetWare 4.01 — it means that now you know that you're OK. If you're running something else, the first thing you should consider is whether you can get an upgrade to bring yourself into synch with Novell.

You may be wondering, if what you have is working, why should you bother? There are two primary reasons you want to stay caught up:

✔ If anything breaks, it's much easier to get technical support for a shipping version of software than it is for an outmoded version. This statement is as true for Borland's SideKick as it is for NetWare.

✔ Eventually, you have to add a new user, or some additional elements, to your server. Finding drivers, shells, redirectors, or whatever for outmoded versions of software can be a form of torture so horrible that it can't even be conceived of, let alone described here.

Picking What You Really Need

Let your budget and your needs dictate which version of NetWare you use. Because the newer versions typically do more and cost more, wanting more means paying more for what you get. If you can live with a less capable version, you may elect to do so, but please consider our earlier argument about what's getting the attention and where the technology is going.

What works today may not work as your needs expand and change. Planning far enough ahead to be able to anticipate changes means not getting surprised by them. This planning requires frequent reassessments of the tradeoffs between capability and cost, and between your time spent changing things versus your time spent explaining why your users cannot do the things they want. Try to build a system you and your users can live with for a while. Then everyone can concentrate on doing their real job.

Covering the Waterfront

This book is not the be-all and end-all of NetWare information. We have deliberately tried, in fact, to keep it simple and lighthearted, and stress concepts and overview over details. If you get in a situation in which you need details, we want to recommend some places to find them:

- Novell ships a boatload of documentation with its products. Its manuals can be hard to navigate and difficult to follow, but they are an excellent source of hard-boiled technical information. When you get stuck, have problems, or need more information, always try the manuals first.

- NetWare is a popular computer-book category. You can find several yards of books about NetWare that range from introductory texts to detailed discussions of system management, troubleshooting, electronic mail, and much more. If you need more information, spend an afternoon plowing through these resources with some specific questions in mind. If a book gives you good answers, think about buying it. Then you can use your selections to augment the manuals.

- The people who sold you NetWare generally have some expertise with the product. Some resellers charge you for their time, and others help for free; don't overlook this resource, because it can save you time, aggravation, and money.

- Novell offers a yearly subscription to a CD-ROM database of technical support and other NetWare-related information, called the NetWare Support Encyclopedia (NSE). It comes in standard and professional flavors and costs between $600 and $1,200 for a year's subscription. Because it contains regular updates of all current technical-support issues and copies of all current drivers, patches, fixes, and so on, it's an invaluable source of NetWare information. For small operations, the cost may be high. If that's the case, see whether your reseller can help you get information from this valuable resource (nearly every reseller has at least one copy of the NSE).

- CompuServe's NetWire forums are a great place to go for help. Because Novell people and other experts support users there equally, you can get the benefit of both the party line and outside opinions in the same place. NetWire is one of the best places to go with questions or problems, and it is often the best source of answers. For more information about using NetWire, check out Appendix C.

- Novell doesn't do much direct customer support, and none of it is free. You can call in if you have already paid for service, or you can charge support calls to a credit card through 1-800-NETWARE. When you have exhausted other means of support, it's time to try this one.

Because there's so much NetWare out there, there are also many sources of information about NetWare. When you need details, or just need help, you can get what you need if you know where to go and what to ask.

Chapter 13
Concrete Ideas for Laying the Foundation

● ●

In This Chapter

▶ The proper way to boot a server

▶ The importance of logging in and out

▶ The importance of a well-designed login script

▶ The importance of shutting down a server properly

▶ How to recover from some common network emergencies

▶ How to maintain your network

▶ The supreme importance of backing up your files

● ●

Some of your questions about NetWare have to be "Why did Novell design NetWare the way it did — what difference does it make whether NetWare is a 32-bit preemptive multitasking operating system or not? Who cares?" The short answer to these questions is that Novell built NetWare that way because it works!

It's true that NetWare has lots of ugly details under the covers. It's also true that Novell and thousands of NetWare users have discovered and fixed hundreds of bugs in the past ten years. This adds up to numerous patches and fixes, and to many warts and blemishes if you look at NetWare up close and personal. Doesn't sound very appealing, does it?

Given all of these shortcomings, why does NetWare make up 60 percent of the network operating system market? Because NetWare demonstrates that, if you build a network around it, it will work. And it works with many different networking topologies, networking technologies, and other kinds of software, networked or otherwise:

✔ NetWare servers do their jobs by using any of thousands of combinations of different manufacturers' PCs, network interface cards, printers, hard drives, coprocessors, and food processors. Oops! Ignore that last one — we slipped!

✔ NetWare client PCs can be any of thousands of PC models built since 1982.

▌ ✔ NetWare can connect you to a multitude of other systems over its network, such as DEC VAXes, IBM mainframes, and UNIX workstations.

And it *all* works. What does NetWare's 32-bit preemptive multitasking operating
system do? *It works!*

Will Bootups Walk All over You?

You cannot have a network until you have a server that's operating, and you
cannot have a server that's operating until you are able to boot it up. The exact
procedure for booting your NetWare server varies according to which version
you install. The end result of the bootup process is that you have a server that
is up and running, until you decide to take it down (hopefully until then,
anyway). The difference between booting a server and bringing a server down
is that you can always choose when to bring it up, but you cannot always
choose when the server comes down. Occasionally, despite your best efforts, it
comes down on its own, in what is accurately called a "crash."

Getting the boot

The first step toward getting your server ready to boot up is installing and
configuring the operating system software.

The 2.2 two-step

Although Novell has vastly improved the NetWare 2.2 installation procedures,
NetWare 2.2 is still the most difficult of the entire NetWare line to configure and
install. The NetWare 2.2 installation program, called INSTALL, compiles the
server code from numerous object files spread over several disks. Object files
are the raw source files from which PC programs are built. The NetWare 2.2
installation lets you choose between a basic installation (in which most configuration decisions are made for you) and an advanced installation (which permits
you to make every single nitty-gritty decision for yourself). Most people select
the basic installation option, and we suggest that you do the same.

The NetWare 2.2 INSTALL program asks you about your particular server
hardware — the type of PC, hard drive, network interface card, and so on —
and then generates the server with the code required for your setup. This
server generation process — some people call it "genning" or "to gen" — can
take an hour or two to complete. One drawback of the genning process is that
even minor changes to the hardware, such as installing a new network interface
card, usually requires you to regen the server. Consequently, everyone who has
ever installed NetWare 2.2 has muttered, "There *must* be a better way!"

The 3.11 waltz

Meet NetWare 3.11. Novell listened to all its customers' complaints about server installation and decided to fix this awkward process with NetWare 3.0 (which was quickly upgraded to 3.1, and even more quickly to the current version, 3.11). NetWare 3.11 includes a program on one of the distribution disks called SERVER.EXE. NetWare 2.2 took dozens of steps and hours of work to get the server up. In contrast, the following list shows all the steps required to get the server up using NetWare 3.11:

1. Insert the disk labeled SYSTEM-1.

2. Type **A:** and press Enter.

3. Type **SERVER** and press Enter.

Your server is now up and running. It's that easy. Granted, you cannot do much with it yet, but this method is much quicker and simpler than 2.2 ever dreamed of.

NetWare 3.11 employs the concept of dynamic loading and unloading of server drivers and programs called *NetWare Loadable Modules*, or *NLMs*. The server install program is an NLM. The server console monitor program is an NLM. The network interface card driver is a type of NLM. The hard drive driver is also a kind of NLM. You get the idea.

To get your server *configured* — the process of installing all the drivers and definitions you need in order for NetWare to work with your other hardware and software — follow these steps:

1. Type **SERVER**.

2. Load the disk driver for the type of hard drive installed in the server PC.

3. Load the driver for the type of NIC you have installed.

Your server is now up and running. If you add a new NIC, you just have to change the driver you load rather than regenerate a whole new operating system program.

The 4.0 non-Shuffle

Installing NetWare 4.0 is even easier than installing its predecessors. Although it works in pretty much the same way as 3.11 (except for a detour to set up NetWare directory services), it all comes loaded on one CD-ROM disk. The biggest advantage of 4.0 is that there's no disk shuffling involved in the installation — mostly because there are no disks to shuffle!

You are presented with numerous options during the installation process to perform comprehensive analysis and testing of the server hard drive. These disk analyses aren't quite as critical as they used to be, because Novell-certified hard drives now ship with any bad sectors already marked. "Novell-certified" means that the hard drive manufacturer has submitted to and passed an extensive suite of Novell tests to ensure complete compatibility with all versions of NetWare.

Prepping your hard disks for NetWare

A *bad sector* is an area on a hard disk that, for some reason or another, doesn't play back what's recorded. It might be the result of a manufacturing defect, damage to the drive's platters during shipment, or the wrong phase of the moon. The fact is, that area cannot be used. By marking bad sectors in the drive's manufacturing process, manufacturers now save you the time of having to find them and mark them for yourself. It may not sound like much, but Novell's disk analysis program, called COMPSURF, has been known to take three or four *days* to do its analysis job. So it's better for somebody else to take care of this process for you, unless you have way too much time on your hands!

The comings and goings of NLMs

Note that these device drivers and NLMs are dynamically loadable. If you want to unload a database NLM to conserve memory, you can unload the NLM without bringing the server down. If you have a server utilization NLM you use to monitor server performance, you can run your test and then unload the NLM from memory. This single achievement from Novell did more to ease the administration of network servers than any other event in the ten-year history of PCs.

T-I-I-M-M-B-B-E-E-R-R: Graceful Logins and Logouts

Logins and logouts are very similar to booting up and bringing a server down. Logging in, like booting up a server, is an action required in order to gain access to the shared network resources. Logging out, like shutting down a server, is strongly recommended although not absolutely required. This section provides more information about each kind of network action.

Logins

The login process occurs when NetWare verifies that you are who you say you are — by asking for a *password* — and when NetWare grants you access to the shared programs and printers on your server. The server checks your login name and password against the database of network definitions. If you are in the database and you have typed the correct password, the server knows which files and printers you can access.

During the login process, a NetWare server can run a list of commands called *login scripts*. A login script is just like the AUTOEXEC.BAT file that your computer executes every time you boot up your PC, except that the login script executes only when you successfully log in to a NetWare server. Your AUTOEXEC.BAT batch file executes DOS and batch commands when it runs. The network login scripts can also execute DOS commands, NetWare commands, and a wide selection of batch-type commands that are available only to login scripts.

Your network probably has a system login script that runs for all users and a personal login script specific to each user. The system login script runs commands that are common to every user and executes first. Typically, the system login script maps users to directories needed by all network users, like PUBLIC and DOS. The user login script executes immediately following the system login script, but only if that user has a personal script defined. The user login script contains commands specific to that particular user, such as capturing to the nearest network printer and mapping to an application directory. Users can add commands to their own scripts or the administrator can place commands there for them.

The login script-definition process is identical for each version of NetWare, although a few minor variations exist between versions in the kind of login script commands available. Listing 13-1 shows the system login script for the 3.11 network at our company. Listing 13-2 shows the user login script for user MARY_JO. These listings have been created to help you get an idea of how flexible and useful these types of scripts scripts can be.

Listing 13-1   A sample system login script.

```
REM - System login script created on 1-10-93 by ETF
REM - Script last updated on 4-22-93 by MMC

REM - Don't show login script commands during execution
MAP DISPLAY OFF

REM - Say hello to each user by name
WRITE "GOOD %GREETING_TIME, %FULL_NAME!"

REM - MAP to public directories used by all users
MAP INS S1=SYS:PUBLIC
MAP INS S2=SYS:DOS_V60
MAP INS S3=SYS:UTILS

REM - MAP to each user's "home" directory
MAP ROOT H:=SYS:USERS\HOME\%LOGIN_NAME

REM - CAPTURE a default printer for all users
CAPTURE L=2 Q=5TH_FLOOR_LASER

REM - IF statements choose mappings and captures
REM - for members of groups
IF MEMBER OF "FINANCE" THEN
        MAP INS S4=SYS:APPS\FINANCE
        CAPTURE L=3 Q=FINANCE_LASER
END

REM - COMSPEC tells your PC where to find the DOS
REM - command interpreter
COMSPEC = C:\DOS\COMMAND.COM

REM - Use the DOS SET command to set DOS environment
REM - variables
DOS SET=PROMPT $P$G

REM - The # sign runs a DOS command or .EXE file
REM - This one runs a virus-scanning program
#VIR_SCAN.EXE

REM - Use EXIT to leave the login script
EXIT
```

Listing 13-2	A sample user login script.

```
REM - Login script for user MARY_JO created on 3-15-93 by ETF
REM - This Login script was last updated on 4-1-93 by MKC

REM - PHASERS let the user know his login script is
running
FIRE PHASERS 10

REM - MAP to a shared directory used by MARY_JO
MAP ROOT I:=SYS:APPS\PAYROLL

REM - CAPTURE to a network printer in MARY_JO's area
CAPTURE L=3 Q=PAYROLL_LASER

REM - MAP shows the user all defined drive mappings
MAP

REM - EXIT quits the login script and runs a batch file
EXIT "WIN31.BAT"
```

You probably will notice in these login scripts some commands that don't look familiar, such as FIRE PHASERS 10 and WRITE "Good %GREETING_TIME, %FULL_NAME. These commands are part of the NetWare login script language. This script language gives you extensive control over tasks NetWare performs when users log in. You can learn more than you ever want to know about the login script language by studying the supervisor guides for each version of NetWare.

Logouts

As mentioned, logging out is not an absolute requirement for NetWare users. NetWare automatically logs you out if you just turn off your PC. If you don't log out, however, you can make your local network administrator mad at you in a hurry.

The most obvious reason to log out is to prevent anyone else from accessing the network on your account. While you're out to lunch, your workplace rivals can send prank e-mail messages to the boss and sign your name to them. This situation may seem like a minor joke, but it can become a serious breach of network security if you have access to sensitive information on the server.

We cannot tell you how secure you want your network to be. We can point out, however, that the majority of unauthorized uses of corporate networks are from people who leave themselves logged in while they are away from their

desks or from users who set their password to an obvious word or number —
such as their spouse's name or their own birthday.

Although we suggest that you *always* require passwords on all your servers, we
know of many networks that don't use passwords. A network that has no
required passwords is safer than a network that requires passwords but has no
password policing. A network without passwords has no illusion of security,
and a network with poorly protected passwords may lull users into a false
sense of security.

Logging out is also *very* important for each user because of limitations in some
network tape-backup programs. A user who remains logged in overnight has
files open on the server. Open files prevent some tape-backup programs from
backing up properly. One file that is sure to be open when users are logged in is
the network database of user and resource definitions. This file is one that is
crucial to network operation and critical for inclusion in system backups.

Without a current backup copy of the server database file, you might have to
totally redefine your network in the event of a server crash. That's no big deal if
you have three users. It might take you days, however, to reenter each user and
resource definition in a complex 150-user network. Please be aware of the open-
files problem when you buy tape-backup software (some programs can circum-
vent open files) and when you are training your users in proper network
etiquette.

Do you have several users with various kinds of
local DOS-based menuing programs, such as
AUTOMENU or MENUWORKS? If so, here's a
convenient way to restart a local menu from your
network menu for all those users, regardless of
which particular local menu system they use:

1. Define a RETURN TO LOCAL MENU selection on your network menu. That selection
   can EXIT your network menu and then
   execute a command called LMENU, for
   local menu.

2. Create a batch file on each PC called
   LMENU.BAT and place it in a directory in
   each user's local path. LMENU.BAT just

needs to start the local menu system to
work, like this:

```
C:
LOGOUT (optional)
CD\AUTOMENU
AUTOMENU
```

Now, no matter what changes you make to the
network menu, and no matter what changes users make to their local menu, users will always
return to their local menu after exiting from the
network menu. You can also define the network
menu on each user's local menu so that they all
can go back and forth with ease between network and local resources.

Lower Than a Snake's Belly: Bringing the Server Down

Shutting down (with the DOWN command) a NetWare server is important because it provides for an orderly shutdown of all server files and resources. File corruption is a real possibility if you simply turn off a server PC. You can end up with the PC equivalent of scrambled eggs when someone turns your server off rather than shuts it down.

In fact, you usually see some error messages during the next bootup following an improper shutdown. Also, NetWare may take a few minutes to resynchronize those system files that it keeps duplicated in memory following an improper shutdown. (Improper shutdowns are one of the reasons it keeps those duplicates!) Although the NetWare operating system is pretty good at recovering from such unexpected interruptions, the best way to ensure a smooth bootup of a NetWare server is to always bring it down correctly.

Always try to notify your users before shutting down your server. It can be quite a shock to someone who is about to save a ten-page document when he or she gets an error saying that the server is not responding. All three versions of NetWare include the capability to broadcast a message to all users from the server console. Use this broadcast capability to warn your users that the server will shut down in a certain number of minutes. They will thank you.

To shut down a NetWare 2.2, 3.11, or 4.0 server, go to the server console and type **DOWN** at the : (colon) prompt.

We say that computers are either *booting, up,* or *down.* When a computer starts up, it begins by reading a small program that tells it where to go to find the information it needs in order to get itself started. It then uses that short program to read the programs it really needs, and starts itself up by beginning with a small, dumb program and winding up ready to rock 'n' roll. Because it's similar to the phrase "pulling yourself up by your own bootstraps," this program became known as a bootstrap loader. What does a bootstrap loader do? It boots up the computer. End of story.

As long as a computer is running properly, it is said to be "up." A server that stops working abruptly because of software or hardware failure is said to "crash." A server that has just crashed or is turned off is said to be "down." A server in an airplane performing a loop that hits a tree is said to be in an "upside-down crash." A server wearing a pair of boots would just look plain silly.

Lightning Can Be a Real Charge!

You cannot keep emergencies from striking your network, but a contingency plan for each of several common problems is absolutely essential. The collective experience of a generation of computer-keepers says that it's not a matter of *whether* emergencies hit, but rather *when and how often*. Boy Scouts make great network administrators because their motto is "Be prepared."

Frequent server backups are de rigueur for the successful network administrator. Find a good, automated, tape-backup unit with twice the capacity you can ever imagine needing in your wildest server dreams (or nightmares). This item on your contingency plan is so versatile that it can be used in almost every imaginable emergency recovery situation. As Karl Malden says: "Don't leave home without it!"

A philosophical question: If a server crashes in the middle of a forest, is there any sound? Of course! It's the sound of a forest of network users feverishly dialing the phone number of their network administrator (who is at home, sleeping — it's the middle of the night on a weekend). Then there's the sound of users calling the network administrator's boss to complain that the server still isn't up. Then there's the sound of the network administrator's boss calling the network administrator demanding to know why the server isn't back up already. You think we're kidding, don't you? *Not!*

Double your hardware to double your life expectancy

The NetWare operating system has the capability to perform disk mirroring and disk duplexing on server-attached hard drives. *Disk mirroring* means that you can install duplicate hard drives, one active and one backup, that NetWare then writes to simultaneously. If a crash or other problem occurs with the active drive, NetWare automatically begins to use the backup drive and notifies you of the switch.

Disk duplexing not only mirrors the drives but also provides the capability to use totally backed up and redundant disk controllers. *Disk controllers* are the adapter cards that make the drive go round. With disk duplexing, you have redundancy of most of the critical moving parts inside your server. We always use disk duplexing and strongly suggest that you do too, whenever your budget permits. Duplexing beats just having spare controllers and hard drives in stock because it doesn't require you to bring the server down immediately to make repairs. You have the luxury of postponing repairs until a more convenient time for both you and your users.

Novell's latest development in server redundancy, what Novell calls *fault tolerance,* is a product called SFT III. SFT III is a copy of version 3.11 that mirrors the entire server PC to another PC. Server fault tolerance gives you the ultimate backup plan if any hardware component in the active server fails. A dedicated network connects the two servers, usually over fiber optics, and keeps both servers in synch. Granted, this solution can be expensive, but it is well worth it in truly mission-critical environments.

Look, Ma — It Eats Out of My Hand!

The proper care and feeding of a new network guarantees that you don't grow any new gray hairs as your network matures. It also means that any balding you experience as a network administrator is the result of your genes, not the result of tearing clumps out as you recover from your own mistakes. Neglect or mistreat a network, though, and it's not your hand that it bites. The rest of this section covers the list of some of the most important things you should remember when it comes to maintaining your network.

Backups, Backups, and More Backups

You absolutely *must* develop an effective server backup strategy *now* or pay dearly for the lack of one later.

Your first line of defense for any network problem, emergency, or anomaly is a current set of server backups. One of your first decisions as a network administrator is to decide how important the server data is to your organization. You might talk to your boss and other managers to get a good feel for this issue. We suggest full server backups — that means every single file on your server — at least once a month, and incremental file backups — a backup of all files that have changed since the last backup — at least once a week, if not every day. This rule of thumb is for noncritical server data. You should back up mission-critical data every night, if possible. If only we can find a way to back up data before we even know what it is....

Chapter 18 is completely devoted to backing up — and restoring — your network. If you're responsible for a network — any network — you should read this chapter, hopefully before you have had cause to weep!

Documentation, Documentation, Documentation

The one thing every administrator despises is documenting the network. There is no substitute for a paper backup of your server directory structure and user accounts. Many network performance-monitoring programs include sophisticated options for documenting your server hardware and software. The goal of this paper trail is to retain the ability to accurately rebuild the server if your tape backups fail to restore properly following a catastrophic server failure.

Get a big binder and print every login script and server configuration file you can get your hands on. Find a good network configuration report utility and run it weekly. You save hours or days of downtime later with good server documentation because you don't have to scramble to find the information you need. Who needs to poke around a scrambled hard disk with a sector editor in the middle of the night, anyway? You shouldn't have to if you compile this information.

You also need good documentation of the network cable installation for troubleshooting purposes. We have seen one loose network connection in an office blow another user down the hall completely off the network, while the user directly hooked to the bad connection remained unaffected. This kind of troubleshooting is impossible without at least an idea of which cable connects to which PC and how it gets there. If you have a cable-installation company install your cabling, be sure to get several copies of their cabling diagram before you pay them. Again, a little work now can save hours of agony later, not to mention the recriminations.

Did We Mention ... Backups, Backups, and More Backups?

Don't forget that the long-term success of your network is tied directly to the quality of your server backups.

We cannot emphasize this point enough: *Back up your server often!*

Uninterruptible Power Supplies

The savior of many a server is the *uninterruptible power supply*, or *UPS*. UPSs contain a rechargeable battery that provides your server with a backup power source if its A/C power fails. The UPS senses that A/C power has gone away and automatically kicks in to supply power to your server on a few milliseconds' notice. If your server contains critical data, you shouldn't go without one; even if it doesn't, a UPS is still a good idea.

Spare Parts

Purchasing spare replacement parts for critical server components is not only great insurance, it's now cheaper than ever. PC prices have dropped dramatically in the past few years and your spare parts inventory plan is a primary beneficiary. Critical items such as hard drives and network cards can be purchased for less now than at any time in recent memory.

Clean power is good power

Modern UPSs frequently also have line conditioning and filtering built in. Although a power outage can certainly be a critical occurrence for a server, your server is more likely to suffer hardware damage from normal fluctuations in line voltage, called *sags* and *spikes*. A good UPS smooths out the drops and surges in the power going to your server. We consider a line conditioning UPS to be a no-brainer requirement for all servers.

Recent advances in technology have endowed UPSs with brains: UPS manufacturers are including a microprocessor in the electronics of the

UPS. This feature lets the UPS talk intelligently to the server. A UPS can tell the server about the quality of the incoming electrical power, notify you when the battery backup is supplying power, and even perform an orderly shutdown of the server when the battery nears exhaustion. Many UPSs also have a NetWare NLM included to give you sophisticated control of the system. Some UPSs can even dial your pager or home phone number, through a modem hooked to the server, to let you know when the power is out.

Now, if we could just teach our UPS how to make us fresh coffee in the morning....

Having these common parts on hand can mean the difference between one hour of server downtime and one or two days of server downtime. The price reductions should also benefit your users' efforts to upgrade their local PCs. You can purchase a 486 PC for much less than what a 386 cost in 1990. Take advantage of the buyer's PC market to purchase spare server components and upgrade equipment for user PCs.

We recommend a 25 MHz (megahertz) 486SX PC with a super VGA monitor, 8MB of RAM, and a 200MB hard drive as the minimum PC purchase for new network users. It's not that existing users can't get by on much less, but a PC configured as recommended should be ready for any new networking developments in the next few years. For your new server purchases, we recommend a 486 50 MHz or 66 MHz PC with as much RAM and hard drive space as you can afford (at least 16MB of RAM and 1GB (gigabyte) of disk space, at a minimum).

Last but not Least — Backups, Backups, and More Backups

Did we mention the importance of server backups yet? Just in case — don't forget a good backup-and-restore strategy!

Chapter 14
The File System:
Center of the NetWare Universe

· ·

In This Chapter

▶ The NetWare File System (simplified)

▶ Common server file-system layouts

▶ Finding your way around the file system

▶ Setting up utilities, applications, and more

▶ File system access

▶ 2.x, 3.x, 4.x file system specifics

▶ Inoculate your server from nasty viruses

▶ Taking care of business

· ·

*W*e talked earlier about the key to Novell NetWare's success: that it simply works as advertised. This chapter shows you the nitty gritty of exactly how NetWare's file system works and why it works the way it does.

We discuss the general principles behind the NetWare network operating system philosophy and how Novell's design decisions affect your fledgling network. We also talk about the specific differences between the version 2.x, 3.x, and 4.x file systems.

No matter how hard we try to make this material light and entertaining, things still get pretty technical. So hold on to your thinking cap and dive right in. Just don't file it under F, for forget.

Just What Exactly Is a File System?

A file system is the way the network operating system handles and stores files. NetWare "fools" your PC's DOS operating system into thinking that the server hard drives are local hard drives. This sleight of hand is called *redirection.* On the server side, NetWare's file system is a total replacement for the functions of DOS. In fact, you cannot even run DOS commands directly on a server after the server is "up." Only special NetWare commands, called *console commands,* are run from the server keyboard. Of course, users can use most DOS commands on the server network drives they access.

DOS stands for *disk operating system.* It was originally written for mainframe computer systems many years ago. The NetWare file system completely replaces DOS on the server with an optimized, 32-bit, preemptive, multitasking, multiuser, file server network operating system. The phrase *32-bit* means that NetWare can handle data in bigger chunks than 16-bit DOS can. *Multitasking* means that the file server processor doesn't have to wait for the completion of one task to begin another task. If the processor has to wait for a hard drive to retrieve data, the server can process the next request in line until the hard drive finishes fetching the original request. Each of these steps takes less than 1 millisecond to occur. That's pretty fast!

NetWare divides the file server disks into areas called volumes. A *volume* is a logical, or nonphysical, division of hard disk space. You can define multiple volumes, though we don't recommend multiple volumes unless you are using NetWare 2.*x.* Version 2.*x* restricts volume size to no more than 255MB. Obviously, if you have a server hard drive that is bigger than 255MB, you have to define multiple volumes.

Version 2.*x* also has the restriction that each volume must reside entirely on one disk (that is, volumes may not *span* multiple physical hard drives). Versions 3.*x* and 4.0 support a total disk space of 32 terabytes, and volumes can span or be spread across multiple hard drives.

The NetWare Prairie: Navigating the Server Plains

Think of the NetWare volume as analogous to the root directory on a DOS-based PC. In other words, the volume is the top of the NetWare directory structure. Underneath the volume, you can have lots of directories and subdirectories and even sub-sub-sub-subdirectories.

When you install NetWare on a file server, the INSTALL program creates the default volume named SYS and four default directories on volume SYS called LOGIN, PUBLIC, MAIL, and SYSTEM. Here's the deal:

- ✔ LOGIN is where the server stores programs necessary for users to log in.

- ✔ PUBLIC is the directory in which the server stores general server utilities for use by all users.

- ✔ MAIL contains unique directories for each user in which the server stores all their individual login script and printer configurations. (Go figure!)

- ✔ SYSTEM is the directory in which the server stores files necessary for server upkeep and administration, as well as some utilities intended for use by only the network supervisor and supervisor equivalents.

You should plan carefully how you organize your file server directories before you install the NetWare software. We suggest that you keep all individual files out of the server "root" directory. Create directories in the root called DOSAPPS, for your DOS applications, and WINAPPS, for your Windows applications. Each application should have its own subdirectory under the appropriate directory, as shown in these examples where the application files are located:

```
SYS:DOSAPPS\WORDPERF
```

and

```
SYS:WINAPPS\WINWORD
```

With this kind of organization, it is easy to control access to each application because these directories can be *flagged* as *read only* so that none of the users can accidentally erase your applications files. You can also give each user a *home directory* in which he can store anything he wants (anything you have the server disk capacity to store).

You can limit a user's storage capacity on each server volume by using SYSCON for versions 2.2*x* and 3.*x,* and by using NetAdmin for version 4.0. Define a directory in the root called HOME, as shown in this example:

```
SYS:HOME
```

and then create home subdirectories using each user's login name:

```
SYS:HOME\ED_BURNS
```

Generally, you should give each user full rights to only her own home directory. Users should not be allowed to browse through another user's home directory. What if your users want to share files with each other? Create a directory in the server root called SHARED with subdirectories for each department or group of users that wants to share files, as shown in these examples:

```
SYS:SHARED
```

and

```
SYS:SHARED\MARKETNG
SYS:SHARED\ACCNTING
SYS:SHARED\ADVRTSNG
```

This system makes it easy for you to grant rights to shared directories by using the NetWare group feature. Create a group called MARKETNG, made up of all the members of the marketing department, and give the group all rights to the SYS:SHARED\MARKETNG subdirectory. Other departments cannot see the group's shared data, but users can copy files to the server and notify other group members to retrieve the file from the shared directory.

If you want a common area in which the entire company can share files, grant all users full rights to the SYS:SHARED directory but restrict each department's subdirectory access to group members only.

Navigating the Server

Now that your directory definition is complete, how do you get around in this monstrosity of a file server? Finding your way around does get tricky when your server directory tree has more branches than an anthill has ants. This is one reason that the server directory structure is so important.

Name every directory with a meaningful name so that even a stranger can understand which programs are located where on your server. Organize similar programs under a general directory, such as DOSAPPS, and then let each succeeding subdirectory get more specific. Remember that many programs require subdirectories under the application directory for system files and accessories.

You should handle server security with NetWare's trustee rights and directory flag capabilities. Trying to hide programs and data on your server eventually grows frustrating and tiresome for both you and your users. Even a medium-size server can have so many different directories that you can get lost in your own network. Our server directory motto is, "A subdirectory for everything and everything in its (well-labeled) subdirectory."

The good ol' DOS CD, or Change Directory, command is one way to get around in your file server. Be careful, however, when you are changing the directory if you have mapped a search drive to a particular directory (you can find more information about MAPping drives later in this chapter). Some of your applications may not run if you change a mapped directory to another directory.

Suppose that you have set up MegaWord to run from the G drive. If you go to the G drive and change the directory to another directory, when you type **MW** to start MegaWord, the program will not load. We suggest that you map an unused drive letter to the subdirectory you want to explore and leave any predefined or application drives alone.

Another way to navigate around your file server's directory tree is to use a directory tool such as PC-Shell or the File Manager application from Microsoft Windows. These types of utilities give you a graphical overview of the entire server disk so that you can point and click to determine which directories and files you can see and manipulate. These graphical directory interfaces typically make it simple to move, copy, and even delete files with the click of a mouse or keyboard key. Of course, you can only delete files you have the NetWare rights to delete; if you are logged in as supervisor or an equivalent, however, you can accidentally do lots of damage.

Set Up for a Smash: Utilities, Applications, and More

Most network-aware applications you install have sophisticated installation programs that do all the dirty work for you. You usually only have to pick a suitable spot in the server directory structure, press OK, and insert the disks on demand in order to install a modern network application.

The tricky part is making those applications and utilities available to your users. Many good DOS menuing programs are designed specifically to run on a NetWare file server. The network administrator must set up each application only once on the menu, including any required MAP commands or printer CAPTURE statements, and all network users can highlight the program they want from a menu list.

Some DOS menu programs include sophisticated filtering, application metering, and security features. *Application metering* keeps track of the number of users concurrently running a particular application. If you have purchased only five licenses for MegaWord, your DOS menu can ensure that you stay legal by limiting access to five users at a time.

Some DOS menuing programs also enable you to control which users can execute or even see specified selections on the network menu. If you have sensitive data in a particular application, you can easily limit access to a NetWare group, called MANAGERS, for example. Users who try to execute sensitive applications and are not a member of group MANAGERS receive a message that unauthorized access is not allowed. This feature gives you an easy way to dynamically control who can and cannot execute certain programs on your menuing system.

You can allow your users to run network applications in several other ways. One simple way is to create batch files that execute any required MAPpings or CAPTURE commands and then start an application.

Create a subdirectory on the server just for network batch files. We call the batch directory on our server SYS:NETBATS. Every user maps a search drive to the NETBATS subdirectory in the system login script. (Read more about system login scripts later in this chapter and about the relevant commands for login scripts in Chapter 19.) All a user has to know to run a network application is the name of the appropriate batch file. The rest of the commands are issued automatically.

One other option for allowing access to network directories is through Windows. A distinct drawback to this approach is that each application must be defined for each user's Windows Program Manager. If a change is required in the properties or working directory of an application, you have to go around to every single user's PC and make the required changes.

You can avoid a little of this misery by defining program icons that point to the network batch file on the server for each program. Most setup changes are made once in the batch file itself without disturbing each user's Windows setup.

Unfortunately, more bad news comes when you are using Windows to run network programs. Because Windows gives you the "opportunity" to start multiple programs at the same time, you must be sure that your batch files don't map to the same drive letters. If your MegaWord batch file performs the following map statement:

```
MAP G:=SYS:DOSAPPS\MEGAWORD
```

and your MegaDraw batch file performs the following mapping:

```
MAP G:=SYS:DOSAPPS\MEGADRAW
```

Windows gets *very* confused. Windows accesses the MegaWord directory OK, until you execute the MegaDraw batch file with MegaWord still running. Windows then changes to the MegaDraw subdirectory on the G drive to run MegaDraw.

The next time MegaWord scans the G drive for a file it needs in order to operate correctly, the file will not be found because Windows is still sitting in the MegaDraw directory. Strange, but true. If you decide to give your users access to network programs in Windows, be very careful that none of your batch files maps different directories to the same drive letter. You can also look into third-party Windows utilities, such as SabreMenu, that remove this restriction from Windows use on a network.

How to Use the File System

Users gain access to the file system primarily through the MAP command. MAPping a drive letter to a directory on the file server lets your users directly access that directory like any other DOS drive. The following line shows the syntax of the MAP command:

MAP [option] [drive letter:=volume name:path]

where *option* is one of the following (for each of these options, the characters in bold are the acceptable abbreviations; if you don't want to key in the entire word, you can get by with just the bold parts):

INSert: Inserts the search drive mapping without deleting other mappings

ROOT: Maps a drive to a fake root

DELete: Deletes a currently assigned drive mapping

REMove: Same as DELete

Next: Assigns the next available drive letter to the drive mapping

Note that the options shown here are optional components of the MAP command.

Drive mappings can be a regular mapping or a search mapping. A *regular mapping* gives the user access to a specific volume, directory, and path on the server only when the drive letter is the current directory. The user can access the directory and path by referencing only the assigned drive letter rather than the entire server path.

You add a *search mapping* to your PC's path for locating commands not in the current directory. You do not have to be at the drive letter prompt of a search mapping in order to find and execute the program. You can create search mappings by using the combination of S and a number, as shown in this example:

```
MAP S1:=SYS:DOSAPPS\MEGAWORD
```

You can issue drive mappings in the system login script, in individual user login scripts, in batch files, or manually at the DOS prompt. The operating system executes MAP commands in the system and user login scripts every time the user logs in to the file server. The process of logging out of the server deletes all drive mappings automatically. NetWare allows a total of 16 drive mappings to a server or a total of 26 drives, including local DOS drive letters.

NetWare 4.0 also introduces the concept of *directory map objects*. A directory map object enables the network administrator to define map commands that point to an object rather than to a specific directory on the server. If the path to that object ever changes, you have to update only the object definition, not all of your user's MAP commands. This new feature gives the administrator the flexibility to change object features and locations and not worry about breaking previous commands set up for each user.

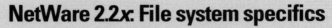

NetWare 2.2x: File system specifics

NetWare 2.2 offers a wrinkle that the other versions don't: You can configure NetWare version 2.2x servers as either dedicated or nondedicated file servers. Dedicated servers perform only NetWare file and print services. Nondedicated servers can also be used as a DOS workstation while the server is running. We strongly discourage anyone from using a NetWare server in non-dedicated mode. The slightest problem on the DOS session can lock up the file server processes. A forgetful user can accidentally reboot the DOS session and, therefore, reboot the server too.

You can boot a dedicated server either from a floppy boot disk or directly from the server disk. You must boot a nondedicated server from a floppy boot disk.

NetWare 2.2x supports 32 volumes of as much as 255MB apiece. Each volume must be located entirely on one hard drive, and a volume cannot span drives, although multiple volumes can be on one drive. You enter volume definitions with the INSTALL utility, and, after they are defined, you cannot change the size or location details of that volume without destroying all information currently stored on it.

NetWare 2.2x supports add-in programs called *value-added processes*, or *VAPs*. These processes run on top of the NetWare operating system, much like the NLMs that run on version 3.x (see the sidebar "NetWare 3.x: File system specifics"). VAPs can be any application developed to take advantage of the special privileges NetWare gives to VAPs. VAPs for tape-backup applications, server monitoring software, UPS monitoring, and so on are available today.

NetWare 2.2x supports a maximum of 100 users and can address a total of 12MB of file server RAM. Because of a definite lack of sophisticated memory-management capabilities, a 2.2x administrator must always monitor cache buffers, dynamic memory pools, file service processes, and communications buffers. Because NetWare 2.2x doesn't allow dynamic reallocation of these memory resources, you may have to shut down the server and run INSTALL (with the -M option) to change the memory configuration of the file server. See the NetWare 2.2 *Using the Network* manual for more guidance in making this decision.

NetWare 3.x: File system specifics

As mentioned, NetWare 3.x supports as many as 250 users and massive amounts of RAM and disk space. As much as 4GB of memory and as much as 32 terabytes of disk space is pretty impressive stuff. Version 3.x also supports as many as 64 volumes with as many as 8 volumes or volume segments supported on each hard drive, and each volume can consist of as many as 32 segments. Clearly, NetWare 3.x is a huge step up in complexity and performance from the days of NetWare 2.x. Version 3.x enables you to configure and tune the server while the server is up and running. Much of the memory management required for version 2.x is now dynamically allocated by the file server operating system in version 3.x.

NetWare 3.x uses the concept of NetWare Loadable Modules, or NLMs, rather than the VAPs found with 2.x. NLMs provide low-level operating system access for programs designed to run directly on the server. Novell-certified NLMs meet design guidelines for memory usage and are tested extensively by Novell. Obviously, a privileged program running on the server has the potential for crashing the server if everything is not running properly, and we have certainly seen it happen. So far, third-party companies have released everything from database engines to virus scanning programs in NLM form. The NLM concept is a great way to encourage developers to write extensions to the operating system without sacrificing NetWare's famous compatibility.

Turn Your Head and Cough: Your Server versus Computer Viruses

You spend a great deal of time and effort in the modern network environment fighting the infection and spread of computer viruses. Computer viruses are malicious or prank programs that can do everything from displaying a humorous message on your monitor to deleting every file from your hard drive.

The server file system is an ideal breeding ground and point of infection for computer viruses. Users can unknowingly store rogue programs on the server, and every other PC on the network can be infected. We strongly recommend that you purchase a virus scanning program for both local PCs and the server itself.

To a network user, virus scanning resembles backing up vital files: Even if it's available and convenient, some users simply don't see the importance of it. On our network, the DOS menuing program our users employ to access network resources includes a selection to scan the user's local hard drive for viruses.

NetWare 4.0: Now for something completely different

All bets are off with the introduction of NetWare version 4.0. The radically new design of almost every aspect of the file server operating system throws even the most experienced LAN administrator for a loop. Gone is the old bindery (although 4.0 includes bindery emulation to retain some compatibility with 2.*x* and 3.*x* servers). Gone is the administrator's familiar menu interface, SYSCON. You must now come to grips with a redefinition of the way networks are structured and maintained. Version 4.0 introduces the concept of NetWare Directory Services and network *objects.*

An object can represent real-world objects such as users, printers, countries, and groups. Basically, we stop defining application directories and server paths and instead define objects with certain characteristics. After an object is defined, you can refer to anywhere else you want in the directory by defining an alias. If the original object changes, you don't have to go back and change the setup of every alias of that object in the file system. By changing the object itself, the other references to it are not affected, but the changes are made through the directory structure. For example, if you define a printer object as an HP LaserJet Series II, you then can copy references to that object wherever a printer object is needed in your organization. If you upgrade that printer to an HP IIIsi, you have to update only the original object definition. All other references to the printer remain unchanged. Make sense?

NetWare 4.0 also includes new features to help network administrators deal with enterprise-wide computing needs. Automatic file compression is one such feature. The new 4.0 built-in file-compression capabilities enable you to set a threshold number of days before a file is automatically compressed. When a user accesses the compressed file, NetWare 4.0 automatically uncompresses the file on the fly. The compression and decompression process is totally transparent to the user.

NetWare 4.0 also introduces the concept of the High-Capacity Storage System (HCSS). HCSS uses rewritable optical disks, similar to audio CDs, to "migrate" less frequently accessed data from the server hard drive to the optical disk jukebox subsystem, called near-line file storage. The server hard drives contain on-line files that are available almost instantly. If files have migrated to the jukebox, the server must copy them back to the hard disk before they can be used. Just like file compression, where "stale" files get compressed in the background, the least active server files are migrated automatically to optical disk according to a predetermined threshold. By using both file compression and HCSS in NetWare 4.0, your server can store and access larger file capacities than a similar server can with NetWare 3.*x.*

Although many of the technical specifications for NetWare 4.0 are identical to those for version 3.*x,* a fundamental change will occur in the way we administer our NetWare networks. We are no longer concerned with paths and programs; instead, we are concerned with objects, aliases, and organizations. This shift will cause many people a great deal of confusion. One day soon, however, the NetWare 3.*x* server operating system will be looked at in much the same way as we currently look at the 2.*x* server operating system, as an anachronism.

We recommend that users perform the virus scan at least once a week. We also have a dedicated virus-scanning NLM we run on the server to watch for virus infections. Your best defense, however, against a virus wiping out large amounts of data is to have regular and up-to-date backups. That way, if a virus does infect a disk, either network or local, you can restore your most recent virus-free backup and get back to business.

With this technique in mind, think about the importance of timely backups. If you have to go back a month or even several weeks to get a clean backup to recover from a virus attack, you will have lost *a great deal* of work. In case you still haven't gotten the message ... BACK UP, BACK UP, BACK UP!

No Rest for the Weary: Taking Care of Business

A network administrator's job is never done, or so it seems to network administrators. Even when things are running smoothly, you have your hands full doing all matter of upkeep and housecleaning. We consider everything from network backups to sweeping the server room floor to be part of your job description, no matter what your job description says.

By now, you should be acutely aware that server backups are an integral part of any LAN administrator's daily routine. Prompting your users to back up their local hard drives is also time very well spent. Pick one of the many tape-rotation schemes and stick to the schedule.

Be sure to store regularly at least one full, current copy of your backups off-site, to protect yourself from fire, theft, or other catastrophe. One company we know of simply mails a complete set of backup tapes to a division in another city once a week. The contact in the other division mails back the "old" tapes every time she receives a new backup. The tapes then can be reused in the normal backup scheme. This company is comfortable that at least two complete copies of the server backups are off-site (either stored or in transit) at all times.

Other companies spend much more time and money having tape backups professionally stored by disaster-recovery specialists in climate-controlled caves deep underground. Some administrators we know simply keep a set of backups at home as a form of off-site storage. Other companies do nothing at all. Determine what kind of backup strategy you can afford and are comfortable with and stick to a regular schedule.

Another regular duty of a NetWare 3.*x* or 4.0 LAN administrator is to monitor server disk usage and deleted files. Particularly if you choose not to limit each user's storage space on the server, you have to monitor how much disk space is being used by each user.

There is no faster way to crash a server than to allow the server hard drives to become full. Users neither know nor understand that server disk storage is a finite resource. We have had users back up their entire 500MB local hard drive to the network server so that they can reformat. It doesn't take many users to store that much data at one time before your server runs out of disk space.

Again, users consider the files they store in their home directory on the server to be personal property. The average user typically stores lots of games, résumés, and recipes in her home directory. Though your company may have a clearly stated policy that such personal use of network resources is forbidden, don't just begin erasing files at will. Explain to the user that these types of items are against company rules; then give her a reasonable amount of time to copy the files to disk and let *her* erase the server copies.

Only when users repeatedly refuse to delete personal material from their home directory do we advocate that the administrator delete those files. Many users keep complete copies of applications stored in their home directory. This practice can be a massive waste of space because you might have 10 or 20 copies of the same program being stored in different places on the server.

A gentle reminder that the application is either already available elsewhere on the network or is known to be an illegal copy usually prods the user into deleting the files.

One final bit of housekeeping with versions 3.*x* and 4.0 is to keep track of the number of deleted files retained on the server. The server erases all visible signs of a deleted file yet retains the file for salvaging as long as disk space remains. When the server runs out of disk space, deleted files are purged on a first deleted, first purged basis.

As a conscientious network administrator, you should occasionally browse through the list of deleted files, using the SALVAGE utility in version 3.*x* or the FILER utility in version 4.0, for any files deemed important enough to be salvaged right away or trivial enough to be purged right away.

Chapter 15
Network Security: It's Not Just for Cops and Robbers

*N*etWare's security isn't a laughing matter unless you're the butt of the joke. You should expect to be vulnerable if you haven't done everything you can to secure your LAN rights. Security means keeping the good guys in and the bad guys out (the ones who want to destroy your data — or just steal it) so that they cannot wreak havoc on an otherwise stable LAN. The way NetWare creates security, by limiting access to directories and the precious files within them, makes sense — if you know how to deal with it. It helps, of course, to have a twisted mind. You don't have to be the type of paranoid person who reads the obituaries in the newspaper to see whether you're in them, but it can help. Security can be completely under your control. It's your turn to play cops against the robbers trying to get in.

Without giving NetWare security some passing thought, the security on your LAN is about as effective as having a toy poodle guard your home. Users who aren't allowed on the LAN can get on; users who are allowed on the LAN may sneak into areas they shouldn't. At best, chaos can ensue; at worst, your company's competitors may be better informed about your secrets than are most of your own insiders.

With some thought to how security will run on your LAN, you can make it as impenetrable as Alcatraz, without having to buy a private island for your network.

Keeping Watch: Setting Up the Right Controls

After you let users on your LAN, to keep them from running amok and destroying files and data in their wake, you can set access controls on the network. The controls make security as tight or as loose as you want. If you know that Joe cannot be trusted with Sally's files, you can keep his prying little fingers out and limit him to playing with his own stuff. Or you can give groups of users access to common files so that those who work together, stay together. These rights and attributes tell you what you can do with a file or directory; they can also control who has access to the network, which files and directories they can access, and how they can use these resources. Pretty heady stuff.

You have to ask these types of questions: What's the right level of security for my network? Do I need to act like the warden at Alcatraz, or can I be entirely trusting of my LAN users? If you don't know the answers, it's better to begin by locking things up tight and shutting all gates to intruders. Then you can relax your security procedures as you find that you can trust the people working on your LAN. You don't want to let everyone in on the company's salary records and then find the lone gossip in the crowd who tells everyone else. Think about it.

This chapter covers the Byzantine, confusing, and thoroughly abstruse topic of NetWare security, with a heavy dose of general-purpose LAN security thrown in. The danger is that the level of detail, stupefying as it is, might put you to sleep. Don't be lulled. This stuff, as tricky and odd as it is, is really important. Stay awake! Pay attention! It's your LAN, your company — and, ultimately, your job — that are at stake here.

It Ain't Easy Being a NetWare Supervisor

Security starts before you begin to think about configuring the network you have just installed. During installation, NetWare automatically creates two accounts: the one called SUPERVISOR has unlimited privileges, and the one called GUEST — you guessed it — doesn't get any privileges. More about that later.

The user of the SUPERVISOR account controls the network. The supervisor can create and delete users and change those users' access to files and directories. The supervisor creates the initial directory structure for the specific file server and has access to the entire system — quite a formidable responsibility. The responsibility for a badly built file system or for loosely administered security can be pinned directly on the supervisor. That's who everyone looks for when something goes wrong.

Because the supervisor has access to the soft underbelly of the network, he or she is one of the only people who can control whether NetWare security works.

If a LAN is big enough, supervisors can grow their empires and create other managers, called *workgroup managers,* who have limited capability to grant access to files or directories for workgroups under their control; and *operators,* who can perform certain operations from the file server console or print server.

The supervisor's rights don't end with the creation of users and the administration of the NetWare file system. The supervisor can modify the system login script, which is the part of NetWare that controls the drives a user automatically maps to and that defines the printers users print to. The supervisor also can decide whether users see those cute "Time to get to work" messages when they log in.

Finally, the supervisor gets to be head inquisitor and prosecutor. The supervisor can run programs that detect intruders trying to break into the LAN. Because the supervisor is so powerful, no one, including the supervisor, can delete the SUPERVISOR account.

Visiting Hours

The other account automatically created in NetWare v2.x and v3.x is GUEST. Network administrators usually have two views of GUEST. One is that guests shouldn't be allowed on the LAN. Because GUEST is automatically a member of group EVERYONE (the group that contains everyone else on the LAN), visitors using the GUEST account can get into anything a member of EVERYONE can see. And because guests are simply that — guests on the LAN — you cannot expect them to know what they are doing.

Many supervisors delete GUEST immediately with the SYSCON utility in NetWare v2.x or v3.x, or the NetWare Administrator (NWADMIN) or NETADMIN in NetWare 4.0. This capability brings out the downside of security, which, as everyone knows, is called *paranoia!* (As they say, though, if they're really out to get you — and they might be — it isn't being paranoid, it's being realistic.)

The other view of GUEST is more magnanimous and much less paranoid. Many administrators keep the GUEST account to help their regular users with printing. If you create GUEST as a queue user with PCONSOLE on each file server, when users choose CAPTURE or NPRINT to print to that file server, the print job logs in as GUEST. If you do this, users can CAPTURE to file servers they wouldn't otherwise be able to use, and because you can use this technique to make all your printers generally available, your users also won't complain that they can't get to the 17-page-per-minute printer in the marketing department. If you decide to keep the GUEST account, you should grant GUEST exclusive rights to PUBLIC only for printing and limit that account's access to other parts of the file server.

For more information about printing, see Chapter 17.

If You Don't Want Help, Don't Do This

Supervisors can also create superusers just like themselves. Called *supervisor-equivalents,* these users have the same rights and privileges as the supervisor. If you're the system administrator, you don't want to create superusers often because it can get out of control, just like too many cooks in the kitchen. You might want to create a back door to the system for yourself because the SUPERVISOR account can be susceptible to virus attacks and other devious measures. This account can be a secret supervisor-equivalent that nobody else knows about, for instance.

If you're the supervisor, the best approach to working on your network is to create an account without supervisor equivalence (like everyone else), where you do your day-to-day work, and reserve SUPERVISOR logins for strictly supervisory duties. Believe it or not, this technique can prevent problems that might otherwise spoil your day. It also keeps you from forgetting that you can trash the whole file system and then do just that accidentally.

Supervisors and users can also set user accounts to be security-equivalent to each other or to group accounts. You can set security equivalence through SYSCON in v2.*x* and v3.*x,* and by way of NWADMIN or NETADMIN in 4.0.

Using Other Empowered Entities

Supervisors aren't the only ones who have power over the LAN, but control starts with them and trickles down to others on the LAN. If day-to-day responsibilities get to be too much to handle, you can create workgroup managers in v2.2 and v3.*x* who manage subsets of users to help you. In NetWare 4.0, partition managers take care of their own fiefdoms, which are the individual partitions of the NetWare Directory Services (NDS) database.

Suppose that Jenny in the accounting department can create users when new people are hired. She can delete those users when they are fired. Jenny has a fiefdom in accounting — she controls the disk directories and files her users can access, when they can work on the LAN, and when their passwords change. She

Technical stuff you want to read if you use NetWare 4.0

Doesn't it bug you when everything is going along fine and then someone changes the rules? That's just what Novell did. NetWare 4.0 gets rid of the SUPERVISOR account in favor of specialized users who have supervisory rights for different parts of the LAN and tasks. Because NetWare 4.0 views the network not as a single file server or even as a collection of file servers but as a single entity (the network taken as a whole), no sole person has, or needs to have, control over the entire network. Individuals exist who may be responsible, for example, for the directory partition that marketing uses or for the sales partition.

Or a specialized user may exist who has the ability to audit the network.

ADMIN itself has access to the "root" of the directory tree. ADMIN therefore can create the network's initial directory structure, and it can create administrators to manage segments of the directory tree, called *partitions*. Or ADMIN can create a portion of the initial structure and let partition managers create the rest. The result is a more flexible and capable administrative environment, but one that must be thought through and matched to your organization's structure and needs.

can assign to the network any access that she herself possesses. If Jenny decides to be generous, she can create an account manager to help her out. The account manager can do everything Jenny can do, except create and delete users.

The primary determinant of who manages a network, or a portion of a network, is who's knowledgeable, available, and nearby — in that order. This approach doesn't always produce the best results, but it's better than nothing. If you want to take security (or other convoluted networking topics) seriously, ask for some training.

Ack! A Bad Hair Day: NetWare Attributes Need Managing Too

Just like hair, NetWare files and directories have attributes that determine what you can or cannot do with them. Mismanaged attributes are similar to out-of-control, flyaway hair; when they are managed correctly, however, they permit you to style your LAN any way you want. NetWare's file and disk directory attributes differ, based on the version of NetWare you are using, but certain attributes are common to all versions to date.

Table 15-1 shows the attributes that apply equally to NetWare v2.15, v2.2, v3.x, and 4.0. These attributes are the ones you use most commonly — the tools you need in order to manage your file system and control access to your server. Don't memorize them unless you're a compulsive control freak, but do learn how to use them. Over time, they will become your best friends. For now, though, they probably will seem a little confusing.

In NetWare v3.0, Novell added other attributes that are specific only to that version. Because file and directory attributes didn't change for 4.0, these attributes work with NetWare version 4.0 too.

Table 15-1	Common NetWare Attributes
Name	**Description**
ARCHIVE NEEDED (files only)	If you back up your system, you use this attribute. The operating system changes it when the file is modified — you don't have to worry about setting it yourself.
EXECUTE ONLY (files only)	.COM and .EXE files are the only files that have this attribute, which keeps these files from being copied or changed. Use this attribute with caution: After you have assigned it, you cannot remove it. The only thing you can do to override this setting is to copy the files again from their original disks.
HIDDEN (files and directories)	This attribute lets you hide files and directories so that they cannot be found with the DIR command. If you know how to use NetWare, you still can see files and directories with NDIR, NetWare's command-line utility, but only if your rights include FILE SCAN. If you don't know how to see hidden files, you're probably not a real NetWare aficionado!
SHARABLE (files only)	In NetWare, this attribute lets two or more users access the same file simultaneously. When files are created or copied to a file server, they are nonsharable. Before making files sharable, it's wise to be sure that the application which uses these types of files can handle multiple simultaneous users (sharable rights are required for programs such as database managers, whose files must be shared in order to do what they're supposed to).
SYSTEM (files only)	This attribute hides the file from the DIR command. This attribute is another one that lets you see files with NDIR. (The same rules apply: You must have the FILE SCAN right.) This attribute is intended to keep NetWare's own system files from being snooped — or worse.

(continued)

Table 15-1   Common NetWare Attributes *(continued)*

Name	Description
TRANSACTIONAL (files only)	NetWare's transaction tracking system uses this attribute, which keeps database files from being deleted.
READ ONLY (files only)	The look-but-don't-touch attribute lets a user read or execute a file but not write to, erase, or rename it. RENAME INHIBIT and DELETE INHIBIT are assigned as part of READ ONLY.
READ/WRITE (files only)	This attribute is similar to having free rein in a candy store — it lets users read and write to files and overrides the READ ONLY attribute. All files are set to READ/WRITE as a default.
COPY INHIBIT	This attribute sounds like what it means. It doesn't allow copying of files having this attribute, and it applies only to Macintosh files.
DELETE INHIBIT	This attribute is the same as COPY INHIBIT. You cannot delete or erase these files or directories. It applies to both DOS and Macintosh files, however.
PURGE	The bulimic security option is an irreversible attribute. After you have assigned PURGE to a file and it is deleted, you cannot do anything to salvage it. Don't mess with PURGE, unless you're feeling suicidal. If you do, you had better have a backup handy just in case.
RENAME INHIBIT	This attribute doesn't let you rename files or directories, so don't change your mind. If your current rights include MODIFY, though, this attribute has no effect. It's as obscure as it sounds and is seldom used.

Audit: The day of reckoning

NetWare v3.0 also shares attributes with v2.2 that v2.15 doesn't have: the READ AUDIT and WRITE AUDIT attributes. READ AUDIT didn't have any use until 4.0; it just shows that Novell was thinking ahead — or not thinking at all — when it created these attributes. Finally, in 4.0, READ AUDIT and WRITE AUDIT are used to provide audit trails of users' access attempts. If you're using any other version, forget about these attributes unless you use Novell's special audit NLMs for version 3.11 or higher.

NetWare v2.15 and v2.2 have an attribute in common, the INDEX attribute. INDEX is rather useless as far as security is concerned, so we don't talk about it in this book. If you think that you have to learn about it, check your NetWare manuals.

The Easy Way Out: Tips for Setting Attributes

Now that you know which attributes files and directories can have, you're curious about how you can change them. Aren't you? *Not!*

You can set file attributes in several ways. You can use the FILER utility, the FLAG or FLAGDIR commands in NetWare v2.*x* and v3.*x,* or NWADMIN or NETADMIN in 4.0. If this concept sounds confusing — it is. If you're not sure about what to use, try these utilities one at a time. If one of them works, use it and stick with it.

The following list gives some tips for learning what you need to know about attributes:

- ✔ Flag EXEs and COMs as SHARABLE, READ ONLY, and EXECUTE ONLY. If a file modifies itself, don't set it to READ ONLY (or it will not work properly).

- ✔ Flag OVL and DAT as SHARABLE and READ ONLY.

- ✔ Set files such as database files that use the Transaction Tracking System (TTS) to TRANSACTIONAL. This action helps to ensure proper handling from NetWare for transaction-oriented files.

Stand Up for Your Rights: Directory, File, and Trustee Rights

Before users log in to the LAN, the only disk directory they're permitted to access is SYS:LOGIN. From that directory, they can log in to the LAN or run SLIST to see which servers exist on the LAN. As users log in, their usernames (also called login names) are verified by the system. If the users are known to the system, they may be asked to enter a password. If they aren't known, their login attempt is rejected. After the correct password is entered, they are admitted to the system. Incorrect passwords lead to rejection, just like invalid usernames do.

Users' access to the system depends on the rights they have to files and directories on the file server and the attributes assigned to those files and directories. These rights are stored in a database called the *bindery* in v2.*x* and v3.*x.* The NetWare directory replaces the bindery in 4.0, but the schemes remain pretty similar. When you assign to a user access rights to a particular directory or file, the user becomes a *trustee* of that directory or file. The rights the user possesses are called *trustee rights.*

All versions of NetWare share common rights to disk directories, files, and trustees (remember, that's what they call a user who possesses these rights). Table 15-2 presents a comprehensive list of NetWare rights that apply to security concerns (it doesn't cover storage-specific rights added with NetWare 4.0, however). These rights are worth getting to know because you use them to determine who gets to do what to your file system. It's just like the law: With security rights, ignorance is no excuse!

Table 15-2	NetWare Security Rights
Name	*Definition*
ACCESS CONTROL	Gives the user who possesses it ultimate control. It lets you control all other users' rights. You can change the inherited rights mask and trustee assignments for directories or files.
CREATE	Lets you make directories and create files.
ERASE	Lets you erase files if their attributes are not set to READ ONLY or some other attribute that prohibits deletion.
FILE SCAN	When you use DIR, you do not see files unless you have the FILE SCAN right.
MODIFY	You should treat this right carefully and give it only to users who need it. MODIFY lets you change or rename files or directories and their names and attributes.
READ	Lets you open files that another person isn't using or as long as they have not been set with the EXECUTE ONLY attribute. READ also lets you run executable programs.
SUPERVISORY	The ultimate right; it grants access to everything. The inherited rights mask cannot touch this right.
WRITE	Like READ, WRITE lets you open files. It also lets you write to them as long as they aren't in use by another person or set to READ ONLY.

NetWare v2.15 and v3.0 have some quirks that differ from NetWare's other versions. In v2.15, the PARENTAL right replaces the ACCESS CONTROL right, and DELETE replaces the ERASE right. The OPEN right, which lets you open a file even before you can read it, exists in v2.15 but isn't used very often. Also, SEARCH replaces FILE SCAN.

NetWare v3.0 adds the SUPERVISORY right. NetWare 4.0 complicates an already complicated set of access rules. Because NetWare 4.0 introduces NetWare Directory Services (NDS), it adds a whole new set of rights related to who gets to do what to the directory database.

Two Approaches to Network Security

In NetWare 3.0, you log in to a single server with LOGIN and use ATTACH to attach to the other servers you want to access. Novell calls this approach *server-centric*. NDS uses a network-centric approach instead, which makes life much easier. With NetWare 4.0, when users log in to the network; their rights may include access to other servers without those users knowing anything about it.

NetWare 4.0 uses the same file and directory rights as v3.0. It adds to the list two directory-specific rights, object and property. Object rights give users permission to access and use certain NDS objects, such as printers or file servers, on the LAN. Property rights let a user view information or modify information about NDS objects.

The Right Way to Assign Rights

Just as with most things in life, there's a recommended way to assign rights to users and groups for NetWare. Rather than have to learn from the school of hard knocks, follow these steps to avoid the bumps and bruises that this type of a diploma can cause:

1. Assign users to groups and assign rights to the group. It's easier than assigning the same rights to a bunch of people who use the same applications.

2. Don't give users rights to the SYS:SYSTEM directory. This directory contains the bindery. Access to the bindery invites trouble on your LAN.

3. The SUPERVISOR should not have a home directory or mailbox. Both are encouragements to do day-to-day work in the SUPERVISOR account, which is exactly what you should avoid.

4. Never give users SUPERVISOR or ACCESS CONTROL rights to their own directories.

5. Users should have CREATE, MODIFY, FILE SCAN, and WRITE rights to the files to which they need to write.

6. Some applications use temporary files, which they store in a data directory. If you are using one of these directories, give users WRITE, ERASE, MODIFY, FILE SCAN, CREATE, and READ rights to those directories.

7. Don't assign CREATE and MODIFY rights to executable files.

8. Don't give users READ or FILE SCAN rights to other users' personal directories.

9. Give users all rights except ACCESS CONTROL in their mail directories.

10. Don't give users WRITE rights in the SYS:\PUBLIC directory.

11. Don't give users access to the root directory of the volume. Rights flow down the directory structure. If you do this, you have a system in which anyone can go anywhere and do anything.

12. Set the four main NetWare system directories (SYSTEM, PUBLIC, MAIL, and LOGIN) off the root to DELETE INHIBIT and RENAME INHIBIT.

Protecting Your Inheritance

In this section, you learn how rights pass down through directory structures in the NetWare file system, whether you assign them explicitly or not. Understanding how inheritance works can keep you from inheriting unnecessary headaches.

Trickling down the directory tree: Trustee or inherited rights

Sharing work on a network means sharing files with colleagues and coworkers. Whenever you're using files that belong to someone else, some of your rights to those files or directories will be those that their owner has explicitly assigned to you (as a trustee); the remainder of those rights, however, are inherited from those of their real owners. Knowing the difference between trustee rights and inherited rights can sometimes be important, so it's important to understand the distinction.

Sound confusing? For a better understanding, suppose that you use these directory paths:

```
SYS:\APPS\DOSAPPS\WP\DATA
SYS:\APPS\DOSAPPS\WP\DATA
SYS:\APPS\WINAPPS\WORD
SYS:\APPS\WINAPPS\SPREAD\EXCEL
SYS:\APPS\WINAPPS\SPREAD\PARADOX
```

If a user on a DOS-based machine has rights to the directory DOSAPPS, he has the same rights to the subdirectories WP and DATA unless other rights have been imposed for those subdirectories that limit rights. The user is called a *trustee* of the subdirectory DOSAPPS. A Windows-based user may have rights beginning at the directory APPS because he needs access to both DOS and Windows applications. A Paradox user who doesn't do any word processing may need to be granted rights only to the PARADOX subdirectory and not have rights any higher on the directory tree.

Using the maximum rights mask to set effective rights

The notion of a maximum rights mask (a mask is a quick way of blocking things off, or limiting options in computer-speak) in NetWare v2.x limits the rights a user has in any given directory. Suppose that Bob has rights to CREATE, MODIFY, READ, WRITE, and FILE SCAN for a particular directory, but his *maximum rights mask* allows him only to READ, ERASE, and FILE SCAN. You could then say that Bob has *effective rights* only to READ and FILE SCAN. You could change the maximum rights mask with the FILER utility and extend or curtail Bob's capabilities. Think of using the mask as a way of reducing the fullest possible set of rights — the maximum rights — to the set of rights that can be used — the effective rights.

NetWare v3.x and 4.x have their own version of the maximum rights mask, called the *inherited rights mask*. It shows which rights a user has inherited from the parent directory. This mask can further limit the rights a user has. By default, a user inherits from the parent directory all rights to the system. You can revoke these rights and limit them by using FILER, SYSCON, GRANT, REMOVE, ALLOW, and REVOKE. As in v2.x, the resulting rights are called the effective rights.

Examining and Changing Your Rights and Attributes

A number of utilities exist to let NetWare users look at or change their rights and attributes. These utilities work for both supervisors and regular users (but of course, supervisors inevitably get to see more than normal users do). These utilities are covered in this list:

- **RIGHTS (v2.x, v3.x):** Lets you view trustee and effective rights.

- **ALLOW (v3.x only):** Lets you view and modify the inherited rights mask for files or directories.

- **REMOVE (v2.x, v3.x):** Lets you control and remove effective rights for users or groups.

- **REVOKE (v2.x, v3.x):** Lets you control and remove trustee rights.

- **FILER (v2.x, v3.x):** Lets you view and set file and directory attributes and control rights. Shows the maximum rights mask for v2.x and the inherited rights mask for v3.0. Shows trustees to users with PARENTAL rights.

- **FLAGDIR (v2.x, v3.x):** Lets you view and set directory attributes.

- **SYSCON (v2.x, v3.x):** Lets you view and control trustee rights.

- **GRANT (v2.x, v3.x):** Lets users or groups assign rights, remove rights, and control rights.

- **TLIST (v2.x, v3.x):** Lets you view trustees of a directory.

NetWare 4.0 consolidates all the preceding utilities into three new utilities:

- The NetWare Administrator — NWADMIN (4.0)

- NETADMIN (4.0)

- NETUSER (4.0)

The 5th Wave By Rich Tennant

"AND JUST WHAT THE HECK PART OF THE NETWORK _DID_ YOU SAY YOU'RE FROM?"

Chapter 16
Keeper of the Keys: Managing LAN Security

. . . .

In This Chapter
▶ Creating and changing passwords
▶ Controlling disk space on your LAN
▶ Restricting a login to certain workstations
▶ Logging in and out of the LAN, and why it's a good idea
▶ Keeping vital information assets under lock and key

. . . .

*N*ow that you have the rights and attributes you can use to control your LAN under lock and key, so to speak, you need some really important information about keeping your LAN secure. This is the fun stuff — you get to show your true colors and keep tabs on what's going on out there on the desktops of America.

By way of SYSCON, NWADMIN, or NETADMIN, you can put additional limits on a user's access to the system. You can limit the number of workstations a user can work from at a time (typically one) and control which particular workstation a user can work from (her own).

If you have users who are always greedy about getting more disk space, NetWare's management utilities let you limit the amount of space they can use. For all users, you can require that users enter passwords to log in to the file server and that the password have a certain minimum length, be changed periodically, and remain unique. Doing these things keeps users on their toes, and it keeps any would-be intruders guessing.

Eighty-Sixed from Working on the LAN

If you really want to get strict about security and don't think that keys to the building do the job, you can restrict the period when a user can log in to the system by time of day or day of the week, or by setting a date after which logins are no longer permitted. You can also corral your users into a defined space and define the "home" directory that they first must log in to. This directory typically is \USERS\\xxxx, where xxxx is the name of whatever user you want it to be.

The Ins and Outs of Logging In and Out!

Most intruders are easy to catch. They casually stroll up to a workstation when someone isn't looking and try to read the rightful owner's e-mail while he's away. Logging in to the network when you start, and logging out when you finish working or leave your desk, is one of the easiest ways to protect your data on the LAN and keep your mail about the boss private.

Every night before going home, log out. Some companies may even require you to log out every time you leave your workstation. If you don't, some companies are mean and take your login rights away. Don't tempt fate. Use this mantra whenever you are around a LAN: Log out, log out, log out! Do it. It's a cheap form of protection. Think of it as "safe computing."

There are two ways to log in to the network: You can put the commands in your workstation's AUTOEXEC.BAT file, which is a stupid method, especially if you also add your password. Or you can enter the commands manually.

To log in, you have to enter the file server name, followed by your username, like this:

```
LOGIN LAMBIE_PIE/JANE
```

Notice that the server name LAMBIE_PIE is separated from the username by a forward slash mark (/). If LAMBIE_PIE is the only server on your network, you can dispense with its name and simply enter your username, like this:

```
LOGIN JANE
```

If there's more than one server on your network, it's vital to supply the right server name when you are logging in, especially if it's the only server you're allowed to use.

Next, you are asked to supply your own unique password, as discussed in the following section.

Passwords: How to Build 'Em, Use 'Em, and Keep 'Em Fresh

As though all the other forms of security weren't enough (and they aren't), NetWare also lets you protect your files and directories from prying eyes. You can assign a unique password for yourself and for each user on the LAN.

Choosing passwords: Not the dog's name — or the cat's, either

People have all sorts of schemes for assigning their passwords — some weird and some quite ordinary. A study has shown that most women in their 20s name their passwords after sex, love, or their husband's or boyfriend's name. Men, on the other hand, like to use the names of their favorite sports teams — GOCOWBOYS.

CompuServe recommends that a password consist of two unrelated words, such as CROUTONS and SUMMER, separated by a nonalphabetic character, such as a slash mark (/). The U.S. government recommends making a password from the first letter of each word in an eight-word sentence. Personally, we would never be able to make up an eight-word sentence that we thought was witty enough to remember.

A plethora of password information

NetWare lets users have passwords that range in length from 1 to 127 alphanumeric characters. Passwords aren't mandatory, but you use them to log on to most networks you see. We don't recommend overly long passwords (more than 12 to 15 characters is too hard to remember), but excessively short ones aren't very secure, either. Follow Goldilocks' example — use a length that's just right, to balance the trade-offs between easy break-ins and forgetfulness.

When the network manager creates your user account with NetWare's SYSCON utility (v2.x and v3.11) or NETADMIN (4.0), he decides your password's minimum length and how often you have to change it.

You can change your password yourself by using SYSCON or NETADMIN. Or, if it's simpler, you can use the command-line utility SETPASS (in v2.x and v3.11) to change your password.

Simon says this about passwords

When it comes to passwords, there are several dos and don'ts worth remembering, especially when it comes to keeping your users able to use the network without opening the door to anybody who happens to cruise by. The following list specifies things you definitely should do and some things you assuredly should avoid:

Do:

✔ Change your password periodically. A network manager can set an expiration period for passwords in SYSCON; a good network manager uses this capability. Requiring changes once a month is a good interval.

✔ Require passwords to be at least five characters long. Shorter passwords are easier to guess.

✔ Use a password you will remember. It's embarrassing to have to ask for help when you forget something very important, like that guy in *Annie Hall* who couldn't remember his mantra.

Don't:

✔ Use the name of your dog, cat, wife, or husband as your password.

✔ Tape your password to your desk.

✔ Give your password to anyone else.

✔ Use a password less than five characters long.

✔ Make your password too long, either. NetWare lets you create passwords of as many as 127 characters. Only a fool would create a password that long. *Don't* be a fool.

If you forget your password, the network manager can easily change it with SYSCON, the NetWare Administrator, or NETADMIN. As a user, you can't. Nor can you save the old password. That's the penalty you pay for forgetting: a new opportunity to forget again.

Stuff only code-breakers need to know

Before the introduction of NetWare v2.15c, passwords were sent across the wire in clear text, which made them susceptible to password snooping. Now, all subsequent versions of NetWare can send encrypted passwords across the wire, and it even stores them in encrypted form in the bindery (v2.15, v2.2, and v3.x) or in the NetWare directory (4.0 and higher), whichever applies to the version you're running. The algorithm is so complicated that supposedly even Turing would have a tough time breaking it. Our advice: Don't bother trying!

Security Begins at Home — But It Doesn't End There

As you get used to dealing with NetWare security, you will notice that some situations tend to keep occurring. Some things can go wrong, or get weird, because of inadequate security planning. Table 16-1 documents some typical security problems — some of which can have extreme consequences — that are totally avoidable. If you spend some time thinking about the subjects it addresses, you can save yourself, and your users, some unnecessary heartaches.

Table 16-1	Avoidable Security Problems
Problem	*Prevention or solution*
Password problems	Password problems of all types exist. You have less-than-savvy network managers who never require users to have a password, who never change their own passwords, or who allow passwords that are short and easy to guess. Be proactive and set up password security in SYSCON, the NetWare Administrator, or NETADMIN.
Supervisor equivalence	Make as few users as possible supervisor-equivalents.
Access to root directory	The first rule of security in NetWare is "Don't let users get to the root directory." When they have access there, they have access everywhere. Enough said.
Login script (or lack thereof)	Login scripts both permit and prohibit access. Each user on the network can have her own login script that extends, or overrides, the system login script.
More than enough rights	Give users the rights to only those directories and files they need to use. Don't be lazy. If you can't trust certain members of a group, restrict their rights.
Workgroup managers	If your organization is large enough, set up workgroup managers so that they can manage the users in their departments. This process frees you to do something really important on your LAN, like your work.
Lost users	Users disappear, they get fired, they leave the company. Don't leave them on your system — you leave gaping holes in your security when you do. Whenever a user should no longer have rights on the LAN, delete the account or have the workgroup manager, account manager, or partition manager do it. Right away, don't delay — or you will pay!

And at Your Neighbors' Too!

Many network managers use diskless workstations to better control what goes on, or what comes off, their LAN. If users cannot copy stuff to or from floppies, it does have a way of severely limiting what users can do. Also, if you want your LAN to be really secure and you have users who work from home, don't let them transfer files to the office. Make them bring in any new or changed files on a disk so that you can scan them for viruses. Or install virus-scanning software in NetWare's system login — which always runs when a user logs in and precedes individual login scripts — that automatically scans any floppies before letting them be accessed.

Now for Some Audit Checks

NetWare v2.x and v3.x had rudimentary auditing features. You could run the SECURITY utility to show the holes in your file server's security. You could even view a log that listed possible intrusions as unauthorized users tried to log in to the network. But you could not do any full-scale auditing (not from a utility designed for that purpose) of the network without buying special-purpose add-on software from Novell — and that was for NetWare 3.11 only.

NetWare 4.0 includes a new utility called AUDITCON. Users defined as auditors for segments of the network can monitor specific events on the network. They can see when users log in and log out; when any rights or attributes change; and when users create, modify, or delete files. This utility offers a great deal more information and provides considerably better accountability. It also takes up space and adds overhead to your system; only you and your company can decide whether it's worth it. Because the stuff was designed for banking and securities trading audits, if what you're doing resembles those industries, you probably will find it interesting. It's also a great source of info for the insatiably curious.

Say It Loud and Clear: Intruders Aren't Welcome Here

NetWare lets you protect your LAN from unwelcome guests with the SYSCON utility. You can record invalid login attempts and even lock out users after a specified number of incorrect logins and keep them off the network for a specified period of time. If you have intruder-detection turned on, you can record the workstation address the intruder is using to try to get into the system — if you keep a list of the locations that correspond to workstation addresses. (And you wondered why we thought creating and maintaining a map of your LAN was a good idea.)

For Peace of Mind, Keep Servers Under Lock and Key

The truism that a determined miscreant can always find a way to subvert security is as true for LANs as it is for your home or office. If the bad guys want in, they will find a way. The best approach is to advertise that you're hip to security and to let them know that other places may offer easier pickings.

Where networks are concerned, this technique means that you put servers in locked rooms to which only authorized individuals have keys. Novell has always recommended that servers be stored in physically secure locations for the very good reason that anyone who knows what he is doing can bring down an accessible server and bring it up under DOS. If the bad guy *really* knows his stuff, he can use a low-level disk editor to change some key values and set himself up as the SUPERVISOR. From there, everything else falls into place, and your precious information becomes a wide-open book.

For the truly paranoid, a simple lock isn't sufficient. If your application is sensitive enough to create concern, you should consider using an entry-control system that tracks who's coming and going, or install a camera to monitor entries and exits. This method is a little extreme for most companies, but controlling who gets at your servers is the best way to keep out of harm's way. Whether they are techno-bandits, disgruntled employees, or your star salesperson's inquisitive three-year-old, the wrong hands on a server in the open can cause grief like you wouldn't believe. Lock 'em up and keep 'em safe!

Troubleshooting the Fearless 14 Security Gotchas

In administering a network, garden-variety network mistakes can be as common as fleas on a dog, and as uncomfortable when you get bitten. Fortunately, they're easier to get rid of; if they're not caught in time, however, they can be even more devastating.

Table 16-2 includes most of the common security mishaps you're likely to encounter. You will get to know them anyway, so why not check them out? It's better to learn by reading than by doing — or not doing, as the case may be.

NetWare's minimum password length defaults to five characters, and most supervisors we know stick by this rule.

Table 16-2	14 Common Security Gotchas
Gotcha	*Prevention or cure*
Front door is missing; no back door.	Not having a back-door account to the network if you are the supervisor is a common and costly mistake. It's similar to forgetting your password, a costly and all-too-common mistake. Several utilities exist that enable you to change the SUPERVISOR password; if you have forgotten it, however, you probably don't deserve to be able to use those utilities.
I forgot my password.	If you're a user on the system, you're luckier than the supervisor who forgets her password. At least you have an out — you can have the supervisor change your password (if the supervisor is there and assuming that we're not talking about the idiot referred to in the preceding gotcha).
GUEST accounts were left on the system.	Having a GUEST account with broad privileges on your system can be worse than having houseguests. Houseguests smell like dead fish within three days; GUEST users begin to stink even sooner! Networks that have GUEST accounts are more susceptible to unwanted visitors than are networks that don't encourage GUEST users for anything except printer access. If you have any temporary users on the LAN, set them up with an account and give them passwords. It's the least you can do to protect your LAN, and it may even make your GUEST users feel special.
The SUPERVISOR account was misnamed.	Dopes and dunces are a way of life. Any supervisors who name their supervisory accounts something like SUPER or leave it at SUPERVISOR are inviting trouble. Furthermore, if your supervisor's name is Homer, that's not a good name for the account either. It's too easy to figure out. Call it GUS, unless someone named Gus works for your company.
The account the supervisor works in	If you have supervisor-equivalence, don't use that account for your day-to-day work. Use it only for managing the LAN. When you use a word processor or tweak a spreadsheet, use a regular user account. If you leave your desk to get water because your wastebasket's on fire, who knows what can happen? You might just return to find charred and discarded notes. But then again, someone could take advantage of your absence to delete the entire file system or to lock everyone out of the server. Ouch!

Gotcha	Prevention or cure
You left your file server in an unlocked area.	Everyone knows that leaving your car unlocked at the mall is a stupid thing to do — your CDs may disappear or someone might trash your stereo — but you are the only one affected. Leaving your file server unlocked in a common area can have similar consequences, but it affects many more people than just you. Lock up your file server. Don't leave it unprotected, even from naive users who don't know what they are doing. And don't let just anybody mess with it. Consider Harry, who works on the weekend rather than going to his four-year-old kid's soccer game. Harry's company has a stupid system administrator. Harry's kid, on the other hand, likes gadgets and thinks that the red on-off switch is neat. You get the picture.
The supervisor's keyboard was made accessible.	If you're the network supervisor, have supervisor-equivalence, or are a console operator, lock your keyboard when you leave your workstation. See "fires" and "kids" in the preceding two gotchas.
I didn't lock the file server console.	Ditto. NetWare v2.*x*'s FCONSOLE and v3.*x*'s MONITOR let you lock the file server console. Do it. In 4.0, use NETADMIN. Whatever your excuse might be, making excuses instead of locking the console just isn't worth the potential trouble an unlocked console can cause.
Not logging off	When you leave your workstation, log off the network. This pointer goes hand in hand with unlocked cars, kids in the office, and people who want to get into places they shouldn't be in. Some third-party utilities automatically log you off after a specified period of inactivity. If you can't remember, maybe you should get some electronic help.
Someone is trying to break into your system.	Intruder detection tells you the network address, the node address, and the IPX socket that any intruder might be trying to use. If you have a list of network addresses matched to locations, you can quickly find which workstation is under attack. Or, if you have a similar list for node addresses, you can sometimes use this list to determine which workstation to look for. Don't count on the node address being helpful though. Smart hackers can change the node address for any access method that supports locally administered addresses. This statement applies to ARCNET, Ethernet, or token-ring networks. If the intruders are that smart, the IPX socket address doesn't do you any good.

(continued)

Table 16-2   14 Common Security Gotchas *(continued)*

Gotcha	*Prevention or cure*
I ran out of grace logins; now what do I do?	You have obviously run out of the luck that has kept you running until now. You cannot log in anymore, and you cannot change your password. You aren't totally out of luck, though. The supervisor can assign you more logins using SYSCON, or he can change the expiration date of your password. Take advantage of the situation — change your password whenever NetWare says that it's time to change it.
I forgot my password.	There's one good reason not to change your password too often — you will forget it. If you do, the supervisor can change it for you by way of SYSCON. But you have to create a new password. Just don't forget it again (but don't tape it to your desk, either).
Help! I can't get into the network.	Several reasons can explain your being unable to log in to the LAN. They are shown in this list: ✔ You have entered the wrong username. You are asked to enter a password or, if passwords aren't required on your LAN, you receive the error message `Invalid Login`. Try again. ✔ You have entered the wrong password. You receive the error message `Invalid password`. Try again. If you try unsuccessfully too many times, intruder detection may lock you out. ✔ The SUPERVISOR has disabled login. Sometimes, when maintenance is necessary or when a SUPERVISOR wants to keep a particularly misbehaved user off the LAN, she disables login from SYSCON or NETADMIN. Whatever you do, you cannot log in to the LAN until login is reenabled. Don't worry — be happy! ✔ The network is down. You receive the message `File Server Not Found`. Again, there's not much you can do.
The computer says that my password's too short.	NetWare lets the supervisor set a minimum length on passwords. Imagine if your password were a single character long. With the password limitation of 40 possible characters, it would take only that many attempts to break in to the system. It's not that someone doing that without getting locked out by intruder detection isn't possible, but it can happen. Same thing with two-, three, or four-character passwords.

Chapter 17

Hard Copy: Printing in the NetWare Environment

· ·

In This Chapter

▶ Looking at the printing basics: users, printers, and queues

▶ Using NetWare's user print utilities

▶ Setting up and configuring NetWare printers

▶ Managing print jobs

▶ Sharing workstation printers on the network

▶ Using special printer functions

· ·

*F*rom its inception, one of the biggest arguments for networking has been its capability to share expensive peripherals, particularly printers. Everyone appreciates the good looks, fast output, and fancy font-handling capabilities of today's generation of laser printers, but hardly anyone can afford to put one of these puppies on everyone's desk.

You get a much bigger bang for your buck if you spend a pile on a single printer and then make it available over the network. If you had to buy printers for everyone, they would have to be slower, noisier, and of lower quality just to be affordable. For better or worse, our tastes in hard copy have become too finicky for that kind of a solution to be palatable.

Networking printers also make it possible to provide better services, such as color or duplex (both sides of a page) printing. It makes it easy to situate printers conveniently for users, and it helps consolidate expenses for electricity and consumables (paper and toner cartridges or ribbons, for example).

In short, networking's capability to deliver high-speed, high-quality printing to its users is still one of the best and most powerful reasons that people and businesses use networks. Doesn't it make you wonder why the press keeps talking about "the paperless office"?

In this chapter, you get a grip on what it takes to set up, manage, and use networked printers with NetWare. You learn how users work with printing and how to manage this service for them as a network supervisor. By the time you're finished, you should be ready to deliver hard copy to everyone who needs it.

Networked Printing: Spoofing the Printer Port

When you have a single PC with its own private printer attached, printing seems like the easiest, most natural thing in the world. The trickiest part is getting Windows and your applications set up with the right printer driver so that your PC knows how to get the most from the printer it's using. So what's the big deal about printing on a network? It should just be an extension of stand-alone printing, right?

As it turns out, when something like a printer is shared on the network, a mechanism (called a *queue*) must be put in place to be capable of handling and arbitrating among competing requests for service. The job of the queue is to accept requests for service as they arrive and to hand them off to be serviced as the printer becomes available.

In other cases, the workstation's software is built with an understanding of networked printing services, like the Macintosh, and it directly initiates moving the print job over the network to a printer or print queue for service.

In the NetWare environment, print queues are usually handled by NetWare servers or dedicated PCs, either of which is acting as a print server. The print server's job is to accept incoming print jobs from workstations and to store them. In Figure 17-1, the left side is an exact illustration of how a stand-alone PC with its own private printer works. The right side is a more accurate description of how the process works on a network. It shows the print job being shipped across the network into a queue, where it waits its turn to be sent to the printer (which may or may not be across the network, too), and then it gets printed.

Figure 17-1:
Two views of printing: what users think (stand-alone printing) and how print queues work.

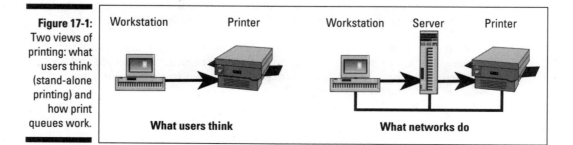

| Workstation | Printer | Workstation | Server | Printer |

What users think   **What networks do**

The printing players: users, printers, print servers, and queues

Network printing is made possible by the network access software that runs on a workstation. In most cases, network printing takes advantage of the functionality supplied by the network access software on a workstation (discussed in Chapter 1) to redirect print jobs from a local destination — typically, that machine's printer port — and ships it over the network to a print queue instead. In other cases, the workstation's software is built with an understanding of networked printing services, like the Macintosh, and it directly initiates moving the print job over the network to a printer or print queue for service.

In the NetWare environment, print queues are usually handled by NetWare servers or by dedicated PCs, either of which is acting as a print server. (The print server's job is to accept incoming print jobs).

In the spirit of good printer housekeeping, NetWare print servers also offer lots of additional functionality, including these capabilities:

- Send all status messages to a queue operator and to the print server supervisor, as well as to users (as you no doubt will want to do, in case a user fires off a long print job and leaves for lunch, only to have the printer run out of paper ten minutes later).

- Define and request printing on particular forms (legal- versus letter-size paper, envelopes, and letterhead, for example).

- Service multiple printers from a single queue, or multiple queues from a single printer.

- Control a printer's print modes (use regular, condensed, or expanded fonts, for example) or enable landscape printing (across the long dimension of a regular page) or portrait printing (across the short dimension of a regular page).

- Manage the contents of print queues (delete, redefine, or rearrange existing print jobs).

The three faces of NetWare's print servers

Three kinds of print servers are available for use in the NetWare environment. First, for server-based printing, NetWare v2.x offers a value-added process implementation of a print server, called PSERVER.VAP, and NetWare 3.x and 4.x offer a NetWare Loadable Module implementation called PSERVER.NLM. Second, both NetWare v2.2 and v3.11 also offer an implementation that runs on a dedicated PC set up as a dedicated router. Third, all three NetWare varieties include a DOS program called PSERVER.EXE that offers the same capability, except that it requires you to set up a DOS PC to act as a dedicated print server. Each of these approaches has its pros and cons, as you see later in this section.

PSERVER.EXE

The PSERVER.EXE implementation runs on a dedicated workstation that can be placed anywhere on the network. Using PSERVER.EXE reduces the load on your network servers and eliminates any need to let users close to those servers (which they might need to do if printers were attached directly to those servers). Novell recommends using a 10 MHz PC AT or better for this purpose, and we concur. (Although it works on older, slower machines, using PSERVER.EXE on anything slower than a 10 MHz PC AT may be too painful for your users.)

PSERVER.EXE can be loaded on as many machines as you might want to dedicate for print services. If you're using PSERVER.EXE, changing print server configurations requires shutting down the print server and rebooting the workstation (or workstations) running PSERVER.EXE in order for the changes to take effect.

PSERVER.NLM

If you're using NetWare 3.x or 4.x, you can install your print server as a NetWare Loadable Module running on your file server. If your printing activity is minimal or your file server is not too heavily loaded, PSERVER.NLM probably makes good sense.

Just as you can do for all NLMs, you can load and unload PSERVER.NLM at will. To make configuration changes, you must unload only the PSERVER.NLM, make the necessary changes, and reload that NLM for the changes to take effect. However, you may use only one copy of PSERVER.NLM per server on NetWare v3.11 (4.0 allows the NLM to be loaded a multiple number of times for more print connections and services).

PSERVER.VAP

The VAP version works with NetWare versions v2.15 or higher, including v2.2, or on a dedicated NetWare router (which Novell calls an *external router*). The software for the external router — including PSERVER.VAP — ships with both NetWare v2.2 and v3.x versions. If your v2.x server or your external router have additional processing power available, PSERVER.VAP can supply printing services for your network.

PSERVER.VAP must be loaded before the server or external router is started. It cannot be loaded after the server or external router is up and running, nor can you make any printing configuration changes without turning off print services beforehand and restoring them afterward. In addition, you cannot load and unload print servers on the network without also rebooting the server that is running PSERVER.VAP. Because this requirement makes PSERVER.VAP more of a pain to use than either the NLM or EXE version, we do not recommend it.

Getting It Out: NetWare's User Print Utilities

Typically, NetWare users access printers in one of three ways:

- ✔ From network-aware applications that know how to interface directly with NetWare print queues

- ✔ By redirecting output away from a local printer port across the network to a NetWare print queue

- ✔ By using an explicit NetWare network print command to interface directly with NetWare print queues

Because printing is such an important need, you should explain these options to your users and make sure that they understand the basic principles of print servers, print queues, and network printing.

And-a-one, and-a-two, and an NPRINT

NPRINT is a networked version of the DOS PRINT command. Rather than send data to a local printer port, NPRINT ships its data directly to a NetWare print queue. NPRINT also has the advantage of not remaining resident after it's used: The DOS PRINT command leaves a terminate-and-stay resident portion of itself in memory to handle any future print requests, whereas NPRINT completely vacates memory as soon as it has finished its job.

NPRINT was designed to handle printing needs from programs, such as CAD packages, that cannot print to a parallel port, which are typically designed to print to serial-attached plotters. To work around this issue, you can instruct your CAD package to print to a file instead and then use NPRINT to send the print file to a network print queue.

To use NPRINT, type the command at the DOS prompt, and specify one or more filenames separated by commas. The DOS file wildcard characters (* and ?) are also supported. NPRINT recognizes a range of options, and its syntax looks like this:

```
NPRINT path\filename...[options...]
```

For NPRINT to work properly, the files specified must be formatted to work with the target printer. NPRINT default options work only if no print job configuration has been defined for the target printer; if a print job configuration has been defined for that printer, its defaults override any of the information specific to the command-line options. When in doubt, use explicit option settings.

The CAPTURE rapture revisited

The NetWare CAPTURE command redirects output intended for a PC's printer port to a NetWare queue. The NetWare shell or redirector watches for service requests that involve network activity; if it sees any, it passes them on to the network access software. CAPTURE fully earns its name because it "captures" output headed for the PC's printer port and passes it across the network to a NetWare print queue.

CAPTURE was designed to grab output headed for the local printer and redirect it to a network print queue. It's reasonable to think of CAPTURE as something that replaces built-in printer access with network printer access.

CAPTURE is typically used in a NetWare login file, either the system login shared by all users or the user's individual login file. It establishes printer redirection for as many as three LPT ports (as many as eight for the new NetWare 4.0 VLM environment). Instead of being invoked as a specific one-shot command, like NPRINT, it becomes a part of your (net)working environment. CAPTURE recognizes a broad range of options, but the basic syntax looks like this:

```
CAPTURE [options...]
```

The print job Terminator: ENDCAP

You can use the ENDCAP command at any time to end the capture of an LPT port. You use it, for example, if you have been capturing LPT1: to a network printer and want to revert to the local printer attached to your PC's LPT1: port. The syntax for ENDCAP is terse:

```
ENDCAP [options...]
```

If no options are specified for ENDCAP, it ends the capture of the LPT1: port.

The important distinction among the ENDCAP options is whether data already in the queue gets discarded; those options that have the word *cancel* in their names discard the data in the queue, and those that don't have it let whatever has already entered the queue get printed.

Printing from applications

Most DOS applications print to an LPT port; they should be handled by CAPTURE. Those applications that need to print to serial or special ports probably will require manual intervention and judicious use of the NPRINT command. Some applications, especially in Windows, are network-aware and can print to NetWare print queues on their own.

Traditionally, the problem is to properly configure the application (like WordPerfect) or the environment (like Windows) with the right print drivers for the printers at the receiving end of the NetWare print queues. After this hurdle is overcome, though, network printing for these kinds of applications is quite straightforward.

The introduction of NetWare 4.0, with built-in directory services, promises to make it much easier for applications to find out which kinds of printers are available and to configure themselves accordingly. Because directory services serve up the menu of available printer choices for selection, end users and administrators are relieved of what can only be called a tedious chore on today's older NetWare networks. Directory access does, however, require applications vendors to write their applications to take direct advantage of NetWare Directory Services; consequently, we don't expect to see many choices on the directory services printer menu until mid-1994. In the meantime, it's business as usual: Users and administrators will have to continue making manual printer selections until directory services can give them some help.

What's in a (Utility) Name? Setting Up and Configuring NetWare Printers

Now that you have looked at NetWare printing from a user's perspective, it's time to lift the hood a little and take advantage of the insider's view. In this section, you learn how to define printers for use on the network and to set up queues to drive them. You also learn how to configure print jobs and print forms so that you can enhance the types of services your network printers can deliver.

NetWare has three primary print-management utilities: PCONSOLE, PRINTDEF, and PRINTCON. In this section, you learn how to tell them apart and, hopefully, how to avoid what is sometimes called "P-Confusion," a state that often strikes those who fail to master the differences between these utilities.

The short version of this course tells anyone who's never grappled with the NetWare print utilities that all three utilities are kind of self explanatory. If you know that a console is a control program for managing computer stuff, the name PCONSOLE might tell you that it's the right choice for managing printers, queues, and other related functions. You use this information to install printers on the network and to make them available to users.

Likewise, if you know that a printer definition is a database of functions that can be sent to a printer to make it perform special functions, the name PRINTDEF might indicate a utility that helped to establish and manipulate this type of definition databases. You use this information to make your printer do tricks.

And if you know that print configuration jobs are used to set up special collections of print settings that otherwise would require fiddling with arcane NPRINT or CAPTURE options, the name PRINTDEF might tell you that it gets used to define common print configurations as a labor-saving device for users. You use it to set up common print job definitions that users can ask for by name to make their printing requirements easier.

It's amazing how much sense things make, if you only know what they mean. It's even more amazing when your users begin to catch on.

PCONSOLE

PCONSOLE is the control center for NetWare print servers. If you're setting up queues, print servers, or print queues, its use requires that you log in as a SUPERVISOR, or supervisor-equivalent. If you're just changing existing definitions, a special class of user called the PRINT OPERATOR can do these things too. PCONSOLE covers a broad range of capabilities, as discussed in the following sections.

Defining and managing print queues

Queues are created, named, deleted, and managed from within PCONSOLE's Print Queue Information menu. The keys to creating, deleting, and renaming queues are special function keys specific to the NetWare console menus. Ins is used to insert new entries, Del is used to delete highlighted entries, and F3 is used to rename highlighted entries. Figure 17-2 shows the main menu choices for Print Queue Information.

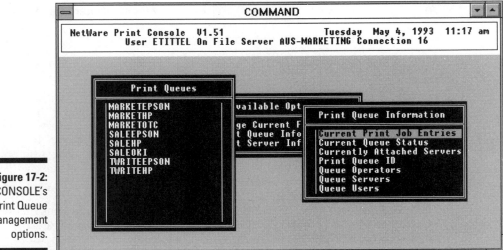

Figure 17-2:
PCONSOLE's
Print Queue
management
options.

When you are creating Print Queues, use short, self-descriptive names. A name like 2ndFQ is much better than Second_floor_queue, even though they are similar. Shorter names mean fewer keystrokes, and because queue names get used much of the time, this technique eventually wins your users' gratitude.

Print Server management

The Print Server Information menus are used for the following tasks:

- ✔ Creating and deleting Print Servers
- ✔ Managing Print Server passwords
- ✔ Assigning Print Server full names
- ✔ Defining network printer and hardware configurations
- ✔ Adding and removing Print Server users or operators
- ✔ Changing forms
- ✔ Problem notifications and notify lists
- ✔ Assigning and adding queues to printers
- ✔ Setting and changing queue priorities

Figure 17-3 shows the top-level menus for managing Print Server information; you probably will spend most of your time in the configuration and status/information submenus.

PCONSOLE offers considerably more functionality than we have discussed here. For more information about the topics we have discussed, please consult the NetWare Print Server manuals (or use the on-line help for printing-related topics if you're using NetWare 4.0).

```
┌──────────────────────── COMMAND ──────────────────── ▼ ▲ ─┐
│─│                                                          │
│ NetWare Print Console  V1.51            Tuesday  May 4, 1993   11:19 am │
│              User ETITTEL On File Server AUS-MARKETING Connection 16    │
│                                                                          │
│                                        ┌─ Print Server Information ─┐    │
│          ┌─ Print Servers ─┐           │ Change Password            │    │
│          │ AUS-MARKETING   │  vailable Opt │ Full Name              │    │
│          │                 │           │ Print Server Configuration │    │
│          │                 │  ge Current F │ Print Server ID         │    │
│          │                 │  t Queue Info │ Print Server Operators  │    │
│          │                 │  t Server Inf │ Print Server Status/Control │  │
│          │                 │           │ Print Server Users         │    │
│          │                 │           └────────────────────────────┘    │
│          │                 │                                              │
│          │                 │                                              │
│          │                 │                                              │
│          └─────────────────┘                                             │
└──────────────────────────────────────────────────────────────────────────┘
```

Figure 17-3: PCONSOLE's Print Server controls.

PRINTDEF

After PCONSOLE, PRINTDEF is a bit of a letdown. It enables you to define forms and print devices. The forms section of PRINTDEF handles definition of form names and numbers. The print devices section lets you select print devices and the device modes and functions to go along with them.

PRINTCON

The last member of this triumvirate of print managers is PRINTCON. Its job is to control print configuration information that users might otherwise have to supply in lengthy option lists for NPRINT or CAPTURE.

One of the most unfortunate aspects of PRINTCON is that print configurations are defined per individual user. PRINTCON lets the network supervisor copy printer definitions from one user to another, but it's a slow and awkward process, especially for large numbers of users. The best alternatives are to use a utility to copy the same PRINTCON.DAT to all users (XTreeNet or LAN Director can do this easily) or to share a public PRINTCON.DAT file rather than create a unique one for each individual user.

Print job configurations include the following information:

- Number of copies
- Type of file to be printed
- Tab size (spaces per tab for expansion)
- Form-feed handling (suppress or pass through)
- Notification (active or disabled)
- Printer ID
- ENDCAP handling
- Originating network server, print queue, print server, device type, and print mode
- The form to be selected
- Print-banner handling
- User name
- Time-out handling
- Time-out interval

PSC

For macho command-line users, NetWare also offers a purely command-oriented printer-control utility called Print Server Controller (PSC). PSC is cryptic and powerful — just the thing for printing nerds and other power users. It's faster than starting up PCONSOLE for quick changes to print configurations, print job setups, forms, and the like, but the consequences of even trivial typos can be, well, interesting, in the sense of the Chinese curse ("May you live in interesting times.")

We think that you should heed the curse and steer clear of PSC. If you can't avert your curiosity, though, you will have to look this one up in your NetWare manuals.

Managing Print Jobs

PCONSOLE provides the best source of printer-management information. Fortunately, though, because print servers need little management, most of your activities focus on managing print jobs and the queues and printers that service them.

Checking Print Server operation and status

PCONSOLE's main menu, Current Print Server Status, provides useful information, including the following:

- ✔ Version number of the print server software
- ✔ Print server type (VAP, EXE, NLM)
- ✔ Number of printers configured
- ✔ Available queue service modes
- ✔ Current status of print server

You probably will be most interested in the last line, which tells you whether it's running.

Checking printer status

PCONSOLE's Print Server Information menu contains an option called Printer Server, which in turn offers an option called Print Server Status/Control. Selecting Printer Status calls up a list of active printers from which you can select the printer whose status you want to know. The resulting Status menu includes information about the following:

- Printer status (Paused, Printing, Waiting, Offline, or Online)
- Service mode
- Mounted form
- Server and queue information
- Current job number
- Current job filename
- Information about number of copies, size of file, percentage completed, and completion status

Again, you will be most interested in the status field or possibly in the completion information if you're wondering why your job isn't finished yet.

Checking printer control

PCONSOLE or PSC lets you control most printer functions, including the following (and more):

- Start or stop printer
- Pause printer
- Abort print job
- Mount different form
- Send form feed (or feeds) to printer

You usually use these kinds of controls to handle print job changes, or to kill print jobs that are running too long or have formatting or other problems.

The benefits of well-trained users

Users who understand how to get the most from NetWare's print services are better able to do what they want and less likely to bother you for help. It's another case of spending a little time in advance for training — you can even get everyone together at once or at least deal with them in groups — versus fighting fires on a regular basis and doing for your users what they could otherwise do for themselves. Not much of a choice, eh?

Sharing Workstation Printers on the Network

NetWare also includes a DOS program that can act as a remote print server for printers attached to individual workstations. Basically, you must install a smallish piece of software that can catch output from a NetWare print queue at the workstation. When it is installed, it can turn individual printers into network printers.

The name of this program, RPRINTER.EXE, is short for Remote PRINTER. It's not really a print server, per se, but it provides many of the same capabilities. RPRINTER.EXE is particularly useful for small, isolated groups of users who may not be close to a print server but who have at least one printer in their midst. RPRINTER provides a method for those users to use NetWare to share that printer and provide the printing services.

RPRINTER is a terminate-and-stay-resident (TSR) DOS program. It incurs some RAM overhead and imposes some CPU consumption on the user's machine where it is installed. Its needs are modest: It consumes between 9K and 13K of RAM for the first printer and an additional 3K to 4K for each additional printer. For best results, you should install it on a workstation that isn't heavily used; a power user is likely to feel somewhat hampered by the processor overhead RPRINTER requires.

RPRINTER uses a connection slot to the print server that is servicing it, so in many ways it acts just like a remotely attached printer being run by that print server. It's still important, however, to recall that RPRINTER is running on a machine that someone else is using.

The Pros and Cons of Workstation Printing

To be most effective, the machine with RPRINTER installed should be left up and running all the time. This is RPRINTER's biggest drawback — the user on whose machine it is installed can terminate print services at any time by simply crashing or turning off his machine.

RPRINTER generally does not perform as well as a printer attached directly to a print server, particularly if the workstation running the program is also running Windows. For the most reliable performance, we recommend that it be loaded automatically in the workstation's AUTOEXEC.BAT file; then the user on that machine doesn't have to remember to load it so that others can share the printer.

Despite these cons, it's important to remember that RPRINTER offers terrific convenience for users who need network print services from its printer. The program has proved to be much more popular than Novell ever anticipated.

If you intend to use RPRINTER, check with CompuServe or your reseller to make sure that you have the most recent version. This program has gone through a remarkable number of revisions, and a newer version can make the difference between a working remote printer and an inert one.

Printing in the NetWare 4.0 Environment

All the old, familiar utilities are still available in the 4.0 environment, but a couple of new kids on the block are much easier to use than the well-worn standbys. For one thing, the Windows administration utility, NetAdmin, lets you do anything that PCONSOLE, PRINTCON, and PRINTDEF can do. The benefit is that you can manage users, queues, device definitions, job configurations, and printers from a single utility rather than have to pick the right character-mode utility for the job you need to do. This technique goes a long way toward eliminating "P-Confusion."

You have the option to move up from the level of 3.11 printing to 4.0 capabilities on existing servers that are being upgraded, or you can leave things alone. To upgrade, you have to use the PUPGRADE.NLM.

RPRINTER has been replaced by a similar but more robust cousin, NPRINTER, that comes in both NLM and EXE flavors for use on a server or remote workstation. A new character-mode utility, called PSETUP, can handle the management of print servers, printers, and queues if you want to work with a slightly friendlier adjunct to PCONSOLE.

As for the new 4.0 print utilities, our advice is to investigate NetAdmin's capabilities because of its friendly, easier-to-navigate Windows interface. Otherwise, stick with what you know. If you're starting fresh with 4.0, don't bother to learn the old stuff — focus on the current generation.

Most of the printing changes in 4.0 are cosmetic rather than deep-seated. Because some of these improvements make print management simpler — especially NetAdmin — this is not a slam! Get to know 4.0 printing — you won't be disappointed.

Chapter 18

Covering Your Assets: Backing Up and Restoring Your Data

*B*acking up your hard disk or the network is much like buying insurance. You may never need it, but it's good to have, just in case. Backing up your network servers ensures against loss of critical files and data.

As more companies use computers to store their files and data, the value of that data increases. If a company loses data because of a power surge or hardware failure, drops in revenue and customer confidence can result. If you lose data you need for a report the next day, you pay the price of not backing up your data by having to re-create it. If it's the boss's data you lose, you may wind up using a different LAN at another company, where we hope that you will put your hard-earned lessons to work.

Why Back Up Your LAN? (Why Buy Insurance?)

NetWare supports a number of backup methods and technologies. NetWare includes built-in utilities for all versions of the product that let you simply back up the data you want and restore it when necessary. Third-party vendors also supply backup software, and it is more complete than NetWare's utilities. As with everything else, with backup software, you get what you pay for.

Currently, nearly every backup package you purchase works with only specific types of backup devices. The cost of backup hardware, whether for tape- or optical-drive-based devices, typically constitutes the major portion of your backup investment. Even though the hardware is expensive, don't skimp on the work involved in choosing the software, either — ultimately, it's what you encounter most frequently, and it usually dictates hardware selection anyway.

Don't even *begin* to think that software which backs up DOS can effectively back up NetWare. Although DOS-based backups back up files, directories, and their attributes, they don't back up the NetWare bindery, trustee assignments, user rights, or extended attributes that NetWare supplies. If you want your system to look unchanged if you ever have to restore from a backup, buy software that is NetWare-compatible. Anything less leaves you twisting in the wind.

Backup Technologies

There are three kinds of backups: *on-line,* in which data is stored to the file server's hard disk; *near-line,* in which data can be retrieved for occasional use; and *off-line,* which means what it says — human intervention is typically required to retrieve it if it ever needs to be brought back into use.

Off-line: Not readily accessible, but lots of it

Off-line data storage is the most common method for backing up the file server's hard disk and the disks of workstations attached to the file server. Tape-backup devices are the most common equipment used for off-line backup. Files must be copied from off-line storage to the on-line device before they are readable.

Near-line: In the neighborhood, but not on your disk drive

Near-line storage is quickly accessible storage like that used in read-write optical disks or CD-ROM. It enables users to store large amounts of data on a secondary device when the file server drives fill up, or it provides a place to store static information, such as encyclopedias, dictionaries, or other documentation. Because CD-ROM is read-only, it's not often used for recording, but it is a handy medium for accessing large, prerecorded collections of data. For backup, you typically work with a read-write technology, such as optical or magneto-optical drives.

On-line: On tap when you need it

On-line, which consists of a local hard disk or file server disk, is the same as primary storage. On-line storage is probably the most unusual type of backup storage and is the least commonly used, probably because it's the most expensive. If a hard disk fails, the data it contains may be lost and is difficult to recover — unless you have a backup.

DIS, DAT, and QIC

Three common tape-based technologies exist: *digital audiotape (DAT)*, *quarter-inch cartridge (QIC)*, and *8mm cassette*. Each of these technologies allows storage of as much as 5GB of uncompressed data. If the tape drive supports compression, two-to-one compression is possible.

Tape

The nine-track, half-inch tape you use for backing up mainframes and minicomputers is seldom used in PC environments and is seldom worth adapting for use in a LAN. The tapes are big, yet they have a lower capacity than most of the other technologies you can choose, and the drives are typically big, loud, and ugly.

Quarter-inch cartridge (QIC)

Quarter-inch cartridge comes in two forms: DC-600 and DC-2000, which has a lower capacity. QIC cartridges hold between 40MB and 2.1GB of uncompressed, standard format data. QIC drives write data on the tape with back-and-forth movements along the length of the tape.

Digital audiotape (DAT)

Digital audiotape is 4mm wide, half the size of 8mm tape. It comes in one of two formats; either *DataDAT* or *Digital Data Storage (DDS)*. Many users prefer DDS over DataDAT because it supplies better error detection. Both formats use helical scan technology, which writes data diagonally from edge to edge of the tape. Even though DAT tape for voice-grade applications is available, don't use it. Use data-grade tapes instead — they have a capacity range of 1.3GB on a 60-meter tape to 2GB on a 90-meter tape.

8mm EXATAPE

The helical-scan technology that 8mm EXATAPE uses is similar to what 8mm videocassette players use. The similarities end there, however. Again, don't use consumer, video-grade tape for your data. You don't need to use data-grade tape to record "The Waltons" — nor do you want to pay that much for the tape. End of story — almost. EXATAPE has a capacity of between 2.5GB and 5GB.

Nearly There: Near-Line Storage

Think of near-line storage as data that can be retrieved easily by NetWare when it's needed but is not stored on the file server's disk drives. As the amount of data typically stored on a LAN grows, the use of near-line storage increases. Typically, near-line storage is used for information, such as encyclopedias, that are supplied on CD-ROM or for data that needs to be used less frequently than in primary storage. Most near-line storage used for backup falls in a class called read-write optical. This list shows some examples:

- **Optical:** Optical drives are much more expensive than traditional tape media, but they hold larger volumes of information — typically from 250MB to 1200MB. Data on optical drives is faster to access than is data on tape, and the shelf life of optical disks is long.

- **WORM:** *Write-once, read-many* devices do what their name implies — you can write data once, mainly for archiving, but you can reread that data repeatedly.

- **MO:** Magneto-optical drives, with capacities of between 128MB and 1100MB, combine laser technology with magnetics to read and write data stored on a magnetized surface. (This kind of drive is sometimes called electro-optical, or EO.)

- **CD-ROM:** You have had CD-ROM in your home and in your car for years, and you know how inexpensive they are getting. The same holds true for CD-ROM data disks. They can contain from 550MB to 600MB of data.

A variant of CD-ROM, called O-ROM (for optical read-only technology), works on magneto-optical drives. Several manufacturers are supplying software on these disks. P-ROM (for partial read-only memory) is also available for magneto-optical drives. What's next — Q-ROM (for quick read-only memory)? All those who swim in alphabet soup had better have large appetites for noodles!

Juggling Multiple Media: Changers, Stackers, and Jukeboxes

One of the best ways to automate backups is to use a *changer* or *stacker.* These devices, sometimes called *autoloaders,* look like jukeboxes. When one record (in this case, an optical disk or tape) finishes playing, the changer puts on a new one. Changers and stackers are expensive, but for users who either have a great deal of data to back up or don't find it worthwhile to baby-sit a tape unit, a changer is a good idea. For the enterprise LAN, on which performing even incremental daily backups means shuffling numerous tapes, a changer is essential. You can get stackers for QIC, DAT, and 8mm drives.

Racking Up Backup Issues

When it comes to performing backups, you must consider a number of interesting technical issues. To get the best bang for your backup buck, you should think about how much the data you're backing up can be squeezed to get the best use from your media. You should also make sure that your backup is reliable and usable and that your system runs faster than a glacier moves. Obviously, if backing up takes all your time, your users won't be able to do anything.

Compression: Putting a squeeze on

Most QIC, DAT, and 8mm drives support some form of data compression. Although compression varies based on the type of file and how much can be compressed from it, generally a two-for-one compression can be expected. Compression makes your drive *seem* as though it operates faster, but that's not really true: Because compression reduces the amount of physical data that has to be transferred to the drive by about 50 percent, as long as decompression is quick, reading a compressed file from the drive may be faster than an equivalent uncompressed version. When you combine backup compression with the disk compression that NetWare 4.0 uses, backup speeds can be pretty fast!

Reliability: Be there or be square

The reliability of backed-up data is the primary concern in a tape-backup system. Errors can occur. To prevent soft errors, which are caused by dust or other electromagnetic interference, store tapes in a clean, protected environment. To avoid hard errors, treat your tapes or CD-ROMs better than you treat your tapes and CDs at home.

Other errors, caused by writing data to tape, can be overcome by error-correction software included with most QIC, DAT, and 8mm drives, and with read-after-write verification. In read-write verification, the tape unit matches the data in its write buffer with the data it wrote to tape. An additional safety measure is tape verification, which involves determining that the data on the tape is readable.

Performance: Waiting for the paint to dry

The speed at which your system can back up data has a direct correlation with the sanity of your users. Tape drives that are slow increase stress; drives that are fast lessen stress. Three factors can increase the speed of your tape backup: the speed of the drive you're using, the speed of the network media, and the degree of achievable compression.

QIC drives, which can back up data at 30 to 800 kilobytes per second (Kbps) are almost as fast as DAT and 8mm drives.

The network access method (Ethernet, token ring, or ARCNET) also influences the speed of your backup. Data to be backed up that is flowing across the wire can easily be too slow but, alas, never too fast. A number of proprietary technologies exist, such as Thomas-Conrad's 100 Mbps TCNS and PC Office's Fast Ethernet, to speed up the process and make it palatable.

Facing Backup Head-On: Managing the Process

Network managers all approach the backup process differently. Some back up all their data every night; some never back up their data. Backing up data is a mundane, boring task; automating and regimenting it as much as possible is what makes it manageable, if not relatively painless. Take advantage of mechanical aids for backup — you might forget, but the computer won't!

Getting it all: A full system backup

The amount of data you have on your LAN determines how you should back up. If your data collection is small enough for you to back it all up overnight, do a *full system backup*. This process consists of backing up all files and directories on the file server, as well as backing up the NetWare bindery, rights, attributes, and directory structure. Make sure that the system you buy does a full restoration of the data as well as a backup.

A good backup isn't any good if it cannot be restored quickly, easily, and reliably. Testing is the only way to be sure, and it's the only way to be practiced at restoring when the real thing happens. Like getting to Carnegie Hall, the only way to manage a good backup is to practice, practice, practice.

Catching changes: Incremental backups

If your data collection on the LAN gets so big that you can no longer do a full backup overnight, consider incremental backups as the cornerstone of your backup routine. Incremental backups are normally organized as follows:

1. Once a week, back up all data on the file server.

2. Every day, back up all the data that has been modified since the previous backup (one day's worth, in other words).

Any good backup program should let you perform incremental backups. If your package doesn't support incremental backups, throw it out and get something else.

Use it, but don't abuse it: Rotation methods

Vendors offer a variety of methods for rotating the tapes you use for backup. Palindrome, for example, relies on the "Tower of Hanoi" method. Following that approach, five sets of tapes are used. When you add a new tape to the backup process, you use it once every two weeks. Tapes that were previously used every two weeks now are used every four weeks, and so on. This method ensures that new tapes are introduced into the mix every so often and that, as tapes get older, they are used less often (until they get phased out).

Another scheme, which is more common, is called the "grandfather, father, son" (GFS) method. In GFS, 20 tapes are used. Four of those tapes are used to back up daily work (Monday through Thursday). Three tapes back up work done on the first three Fridays of the month. The fourth week, you use one of the 13 "grandfather" (monthly tapes). There are 13 four-week intervals in the year. This method keeps tapes circulating regularly and ensures that none of them gets too much wear.

Desiderata: What Should a Backup Package Bring to the Party?

Like everything else, you have to be a smart shopper when you buy tape-backup software and hardware. Here are a few tips for making this venture successful:

- ✔ **File-by-file backup and restore:** A tape backup writes files by one of two methods: image or file-by-file. In backups that save file-by-file, you should be able to restore files on an individual basis. An image makes a physical copy of a drive and should be used only when a drive is nearly full. (When it is full, an image backup saves you valuable time; otherwise, go file-by-file — the only way to restore from an image backup is to restore the whole thing!)

- ✔ **Ample file-selection criteria:** You should be able to select files and directories for backing up and restoring by file or directory name by using wildcards (*.* or *.TXT), or from a pick list of files and directories.

- ✔ **Back up everything:** The system you choose should be capable of backing up the files, the directory attributes and rights, the NetWare bindery or NDS information, and all files and directories on all drives.

✔ **All file types:** The backup system should be capable of backing up the files created on different machine types. For each file type you want to use, you load a name space at the file server console. These name spaces include DOS, Macintosh, OS/2, NFS, and FTAM names and attributes (the DOS name space is loaded automatically). Tape-backup software that is SMS-compliant supports all these options and can extend itself to support new ones as Novell adds support for them.

Because SMS-compliant systems can continue to perform their backup functions no matter what changes Novell may make to the NetWare file system and its file formats, SMS-compliant backup systems for NetWare are the only way to go! Fortunately, most major backup system vendors are now SMS-compliant or will be by the end of 1993. They have many of these features:

✔ **Open files:** The software you choose should accommodate files that are open during backup. Hopefully, you will back up the system when there is no activity on the LAN, but you cannot always expect that. You may also have to back up when applications are running that may keep some files perpetually open; a good backup program should be capable of working around that limitation.

✔ **Unattended backup:** Nothing is worse than sitting and watching the paint dry. The same idea applies to backing up: Get software that enables you to start the backup and then leave. You have better things to do with your time, right?

✔ **Sufficient storage capability:** A backup rule of thumb applies here: Buy a tape-backup system that can accommodate twice as much data as is currently on your file server. You will grow into it fast enough and still be hungry for more anyway.

✔ **Comparison of files on tape to files on disk:** Some software compares data it has backed up to files on the server's hard disk to see whether it matches. Get that type of package if you can, because it saves you time — copying a file on top of itself is similar to watching paint dry. Got that? (See the discussion under the section "Reliability: Be there or be square.")

✔ **Nonfatal errors shouldn't kill your network:** The last thing you want is for errors that occur during the backup process to cause the backup to fail or, worse, to cause your network to fail. The software you buy should log these types of errors, tell you which files they occurred on, and let you decide what to do about it later. In the meantime, it should continue to back up whatever it can.

✔ **Span multiple tapes with a single volume:** Some disk volumes are larger than the capacity of a single tape. Make sure that the software you buy lets you span a volume across multiple tapes. This capability is almost as important as being able to leap tall buildings in a single bound!

To take a step further, the following list shows some features that are "nice" to have — you can live without them, even if you don't want to:

- **Backing up individual hard disks:** So you want to be a nice guy and volunteer to back up your users' hard disks too. Some software lets you do it, but if you don't have it, you can encourage your users to keep the data they want backed up on the file server instead. If you have this type of software, you can back up their workstations across the network (if, of course, the workstations are turned on).

- **Grooming, migrating, cataloging, and archiving:** Backing up resembles running a household. You have to do some spring-cleaning every so often. Some backup software offers you ways to rid your file server disk of files that haven't been used recently or to migrate them to near-line storage or even to store them away off-line (archiving). If your package is worth anything, it will also do the necessary record-keeping and archiving for you too. In NetWare 4.0, you can enable migration to high-capacity storage systems such as WORM or OM at the volume level in the INSTALL.NLM.

Do You Want Backup Standard or with Air?

NetWare has its own backup system, but it also supports backup systems from other vendors. The most common backup software included with NetWare v2.*x* and v3.11 is NBACKUP. You can rely on NBACKUP in a pinch, but if it's all you have, do yourself a favor — go out and buy something else for everyday backups.

Really basic: NBACKUP

NBACKUP is a workstation-based backup utility that backs up information on directories. System administrators who have FILE SCAN and READ rights to a directory can back up any information it contains. To restore files from a backup takes CREATE, ERASE, FILE SCAN, MODIFY, and WRITE rights.

NBACKUP must run from a workstation that does nothing else on the LAN, and it can back up data to floppies, tape drives, or optical drives. We recommend the higher-capacity media for backup, especially for some of today's mondo servers. Who wants to sit and back up data to 1,000 or more floppies? (That's not even 2GB, a modest amount of disk space by today's standards.)

From a file server, you can direct NBACKUP to back up other servers you are ATTACHed to. NBACKUP, however does not back up hidden or system directories on NetWare v2.*x* LANs, nor can you use wildcards for backing up Macintosh files. NBACKUP backs up only DOS and Macintosh files. If you have OS/2 or NFS files on your server, you have to use another utility, called SBACKUP.

Basic basic: SBACKUP

SBACKUP works with both NetWare 4.0 and v3.11. As a server-based backup system, it can handle DOS, Macintosh, OS/2, and NFS files on workstations or on the server's hard disk. SBACKUP works with a *NetWare Loadable Module (NLM)* called the TSA.NLM to see that data on a "target" is backed up. The target can be another file server or workstation on the LAN. In case you haven't guessed already, SBACKUP beats the pants off NBACKUP. To run the program, the SUPERVISOR starts SBACKUP from the file server console.

Buy some options, please: Third-party backups

Third-party backup systems are available with a variety of features. Because you have to pay real money for them, most of them are more complete than either NBACKUP or SBACKUP. Some popular vendors of tape-backup systems include Tallgrass Technologies, Cheyenne, Emeritus, Connor (formerly Maynard), and Emerald Systems.

User basics: 2.1x backup utilities

NetWare v2.1x includes four utilities to let you back up and restore data from your network drives to other network drives or to disks or a local hard disk. These utilities shouldn't, however, take the place of a whole-LAN backup, which typically is performed by a supervisor. To ensure that your personal data gets backed up daily, you might consider using one of these utilities. These utilities are command-line programs, which means that you execute them from the DOS command line:

- **LARCHIVE:** Backs up network drives to local drives or disks
- **LRESTORE:** Restores data on local drives or disks to network drives
- **NARCHIVE:** Backs up network drives to other network drives
- **NRESTORE:** Restores data from network drives to the original drive

If you want to use these utilities, refer to the NetWare documentation for details. We just want you to know that they exist, in case no one on your LAN does regular backups. If you have no other choices, they're OK; if you do have other choices, though, these utilities are pretty lame tools, as backup utilities go. Honestly, the only thing right about them is the price.

Storage for the Masses

The *Storage Management Services (SMS)* is Novell's method for standardizing backup for its third-party vendors. Before the introduction of SMS, whenever NetWare changed, vendors had to change their backup software to follow suit. When OS/2 and UNIX workstations began showing up on users' desktops, the same software that backed up DOS files couldn't be used. The backup vendors got really tired of having to rewrite their software with each major release of NetWare. Wouldn't you?

SMS separates the details needed to support the network file system from the backup method used and, incidentally, from the type of machine format used for those files (DOS, Macintosh, OS/2, NFS, and so on). SMS provides standard media formats and ensures compatibility among similar backup devices. Software from third-party vendors, therefore, can back up any kind of file. Even better, it means that vendors no longer have to rewrite their backup software to track additions or changes to the NetWare file system.

SBACKUP, which users of NetWare v2.*x* and v3.*x* might already know about, is also based on SMS.

What's Different About Storage on NetWare 4.x?

NetWare 4.0 enables you to add to your network high-capacity storage devices such as tape drives, optical erasable drives, and WORM and CD-ROM drives. These devices, which can create free disk storage space on the network, use NetWare's *High-Capacity Storage System (HCSS)*. HCSS assumes that data is stored on the primary storage device until a capacity threshold is reached. When the disk reaches that storage threshold, the files that have been least recently used are migrated. When files are needed again, HCSS enables them to be copied back to disk so that they can be used again.

In HCSS, files are migrated to and from primary storage on a file-by-file basis; files that reside on the alternate storage device can be viewed with the DOS DIR or NetWare NDIR command. Although you cannot create or delete directories on an HCSS-based device, you can assign access rights in the same way as you would for any other NetWare directory. A file on an HCSS device appears to be no different from files on a local drive, even though it may be someplace entirely different.

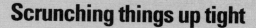

Scrunching things up tight

Another feature of NetWare 4.0 is its support for compression of files on the file server. The reason that NetWare compression is tighter and faster than Stacker or SuperStor or whatever DOS compression utility you favor is that it uses a *two-pass compression* method. In this method, it reads through a file once, just to analyze and record everything it can about the data it holds. It then uses what it has learned on a second trip through the file to squeeze things down as tightly as possible without compromising expansion time.

NetWare's disk-compression routines are built to be faster overall when they are reading compressed files from disk—where decompression is required—than when they are reading equivalent uncompressed files. This capability accounts for a 10 to 15 percent performance improvement for the file system between NetWare 3.*x* and NetWare 4.0. (We just thought that you would want to know.)

Hold Still — and Back Up Those Users Before They Get Away

Backing up users is one of those "damned if you do, damned if you don't" issues. Many third-party backup packages let you back up the users' local disk drives as well as network drives. This list shows some things to consider before you decide what to do:

- ✔ If you back up local drives, it takes additional time and it leaves any unattended workstations vulnerable to attack (because they must be logged in, in order to be backed up).

- ✔ If you don't back up local drives, you can be sure that someone will holler at you sooner or later. All you can hope is that it's not your boss who just lost a file. That could be career-threatening (we hate when that happens).

Farm Teams and the Big Leagues: Workstation- versus Server-Based Backups

Two backup approaches are common: workstation-based and server-based. Both have their pros and cons, as you would expect.

Workstation-based is strictly small-time

In *workstation-based backups,* a workstation is dedicated to the backup process. Because the backup is based on the workstation, it doesn't affect the file server processing. You can add to the backup system without affecting the file server. On the other hand, data needs to travel across the network from the file server to the workstation, which can be slow. Several high-speed access methods are available to alleviate that problem. Also, the workstation you are backing up from must be logged in to the network, which may pose a security threat, especially if the workstation is unattended during the backup.

Server-based is smart, fast, and less fattening

Server-based backups are generally faster than workstation-based backups and can be left unattended without posing threats to security. The backup process can slow down file server performance, however, which is why it's typically performed during the wee hours, when your users are fast asleep. That's also why this kind of backup is run unattended, because you probably want to get your sleep, too.

Practice Makes Perfect: Knowing What to Do Before Disaster Strikes

Most network managers test fate every day that they show up at work. They hope that the backup they began the night before has worked. They have never tested their backup system to see whether it does what it says it will — restore the data they have been backing up so regularly and reliably. They have forgotten the three cardinal rules of backup safety:

- ✔ **Document the backup process.** You won't live to regret it. Write down whether you do a full backup or an incremental backup or whether you use some other scheme. Indicate where you store the tapes so that they won't burn if the building goes up in flames. Relay everything you know about backing up the system, in case you burn up too!

- ✔ **Test your backup system.** Back up the LAN and then restore it. Try to retrieve files. See whether the restored bindery is as it should be. It doesn't work until you can prove that it really works.

- ✔ **Cross-train other users.** Find an assistant and show her everything you do. Make your assistant learn backup and restore procedures cold. Getting run over by a train is a remote possibility, but it can happen. Of course, you probably wouldn't care . . . but somebody else might.

The basic idea is to learn the mechanics so that, when the unthinkable happens, you don't have to learn or think. You can just go through the motions and reserve your cranial capacity for blind panic.

Take Care of Your Backup System, and It Will Take Care of You

Proper care and feeding of your backup system is also a terrific idea because it improves the odds that things will work when you need them to. And because a backup resembles a life preserver and should be used only in drills and when there's a man overboard, improving the odds is always a good thing. Follow these guidelines:

- ✔ Clean your tape drives often. Use a cleaning kit for tape-backup units. Cotton balls or Q-Tips don't cut it. They leave fibers on the tape and the heads.

- ✔ Rotate your tapes and introduce new ones on a regular basis.

- ✔ Watch NetWire for the latest backup patches and fixes and for new drivers.

- ✔ Keep in touch with your vendor for hardware and software upgrades.

- ✔ Store your tapes in a dust-free, fireproof environment, preferably off-site.

- ✔ Before you use your tapes, re-tension them each time. Do this in the same way as you re-tension a tape cassette: Put a pencil inside one of the gears and rotate the gear until it is tight.

Just Do It: Tips for a Safe and Secure Backup

Practice and routine are the hallmarks of preparing for a crisis. No opportunity to restore a backup is anything less than a crisis, so we recommend the following guidelines:

- ✔ To encourage regularity, schedule your backups at the same time every day.

- ✔ Use a software package to record the users and groups on your LAN, along with their rights, attributes, and trustee rights.

- ✔ View the logs your software generates after each backup to make sure that everything happened just as it should have.

- ✔ If at all possible, back up your system when nobody's on the system. If you do this, you reduce the likelihood of files being open during the backup.

✔ If you can, make sure that the capacity of your tape drive is larger than the data set you want to back up. A system manager we know has to go into the office halfway through the backup to change tapes, every day of the week. Bummer!

Tangled Tapes: Troubleshooting the Top Three Problems

Although tape is a nice, reliable medium, it doesn't mean that you will never have problems. Again, a little practice ahead of time lets you discover what real problems you might have. For the record, this section lists some of the likely candidates you will encounter:

✔ **Messing with Macintosh files:** If you have Macintosh files on your LAN, make sure that the software you buy backs them up. In a Macintosh file, you have both a data and a resource fork. The software should back up both.

✔ **The trouble with tape:** Tape can suffer from all sorts of problems. It can break or wear out. Rotate your tapes periodically. Because tape is constantly in contact with the read/write heads of the tape unit, it may become worn in places. When this happens, "dropouts" occur, and the magnetic media is not capable of retaining data in those areas. Temperature and humidity also cause tape to wear.

✔ **Shiny shoes:** When the backup software supplies data to the tape drive at a rate slower than the unit's rated speed, it's called *underrun*. If you hear the tape unit starting and stopping repeatedly, it's likely that underrun is occurring. The tape drive must back up the tape to read the last block it wrote, and then it must move forward to write the next block. It resembles the sound of a shoeshine — back and forth, back and forth. It might make your shoes look good, but it's murder on your tape drives. If you hear this, you should investigate thoroughly. In most cases, a new software driver for your backup device or more server memory should help alleviate the problem.

Chapter 19
Mysteries of the Organism: System Configuration

• •

In This Chapter

▶ Installation overview overload

▶ Why your configuration changes whether you want it to or not

▶ When to leave well enough alone

▶ The configuration utilities: SYSCON, FCONSOLE, and MONITOR

▶ The book on bindery basics

▶ Setting up groups, users, and groups of users

• •

*H*ow do you make your new network work for you? There is no substitute for rolling up your sleeves and diving right in. This chapter discusses the big picture of how and why you install the NetWare network operating system. Where it is appropriate, we discuss the specifics of the installation process for version 2.*x*, 3.*x*, and 4.0. So, off we go, into the wild blue yonder....

Installation Basics: An Overview

Before you learn to run, you learn to walk. Before you learn to run the server, you must learn first to walk through the server installation. The basic installation process for all three versions of NetWare is shown in these steps:

1. Gather the correct hardware and software for server installation.

2. Run the installation program.

3. Prepare the server hard disk for the NetWare file system: Partition and format the drive from the installation program.

4. Create volumes and load the NetWare SYSTEM and PUBLIC files on the hard drive.

5. Start the server.

This view is obviously a simplified one, but you get the idea.

The NetWare installation manuals generally do a great job of explaining the installation process step by step. You have many decisions to make along the way, so be sure to keep good records.

The installation process is also when your life as a network documenter begins. Keep a written record of the jumper settings for each adapter board you install in your server PC. Also make note of the total amount of RAM installed and the types of hard drives and storage capacity.

You want to have a clear picture of what kind of hardware resides in your server and how that hardware is configured. It's frustrating to have to stop in the middle of the installation to pry open the PC case so that you can check some bit of hardware minutiae. A little work up front saves you mountains of work later.

To Grow or Not to Grow, That Is the Question

As you proceed, keep an eye planted on the here and now and one eye looking to the future. No matter how thorough and careful you may be in the initial planning of your network, it is nearly impossible for you to anticipate what your network needs might be a year from now.

Start thinking about the future of your network and particularly the possibilities for your server. Don't buy a PC with just two drive bays because you don't think that you will ever need more than two hard drives. Likewise, don't buy a PC with room for only 16MB of RAM on the motherboard just because you think that NetWare 2.2 (with its 12MB RAM limit) is all you will ever need.

Networks and their servers tend to be wildly successful even among people who say that they don't have any use for them before installation. After people see how easy networks are to use and how much networks can improve their productivity, you will have more than enough enthusiasm for continued network expansion.

Considering the drastic price cuts in PC hardware during the past few years, we suggest that you avoid cutting corners on your server PC just to save a few bucks. Buy the biggest, fastest, most expandable, and most upgradable PC you can afford. Avoid the minority of PC manufacturers that still engineer proprietary hardware in their products in an attempt to lock you in to their architectures. You save money in the short run — and in the long run as well — if you have an industry-standard PC with interchangeable parts.

With the possibility of later network expansion in mind, you have to consider that changes in network hardware can mean changes for the network software. With NetWare 2.x, making any changes requires you to regenerate (REGEN) the server operating system because its hardware drivers and configurations get compiled into the server software as a consequence of the installation program. You must recompile or REGEN the server operating system to take advantage of hardware upgrades.

NetWare 3.x and 4.0 are easier to upgrade because their hardware drivers and configurations are "loadable." In fact, their drivers can also be unloaded at will so that you can swap out system software components on the fly. This feature gives you the ability to easily change software settings or configurations to match hardware changes or additions and not have to jump through lots of hoops. We like this capability, and you probably will learn to like it too.

If It Ain't Broke, Don't Fix It

Now that you have learned how easy it is to change your server setup, particularly with NetWare versions 3.x and 4.0, we now want to encourage you to never do so. OK, not never, but we want you to think long and hard before making even minor changes.

Of course, the amount of caution should be directly proportional to the importance of the server. In environments in which the network is considered a mission-critical resource, changes should be well researched and well planned. If your company uses its network server to store games for employees to use on their breaks, you can probably make server changes with little or no warning. The primary reason for caution is that things don't always go according to plan.

SYSCON, FCONSOLE, and MONITOR: Configuration Utilities Deluxe

NetWare's SYSCON, FCONSOLE, and MONITOR utility are the most frequently used network administrative utilities. You use these programs to manage users and view server information. SYSCON comes with all three versions of NetWare and is devoted primarily to directory, group, and user management.

FCONSOLE is the server monitoring and tuning utility for version 2.2. MONITOR serves the same function for versions 3.x and 4.0. Both FCONSOLE and MONITOR include extensive information about file server memory utilization and overall operating statistics. Let's take a closer look at each utility in its native environment.

SYSCON! Yeah...that's the ticket

SYSCON, short for *system configuration*, is your primary utility for managing groups and users on your network. SYSCON also contains a host of supervisor options for behind-the-scenes control of which, when, and where users can access your server. The top line of the SYSCON main menu tells you the day, date, and time. The second line tells you who you're logged in as and to which server you're logged in. Each selection on the main menu takes you to a submenu or information window.

Accounting for the action

The first selection on the SYSCON main menu is Accounting. The Accounting capability enables the network manager to keep track of user connection time for charge-back purposes. The server keeps a running tally of file server services used by each user. You can also assign a charge rate for the access time.

Changing focus

Option 2 on the SYSCON main menu is Change Current Server. This option enables you to select between available file servers for SYSCON activities.

File server information at your fingertips

Option 3 on the SYSCON main menu enables you to view file server information. The ensuing window shows the name of the file server, the NetWare version, the SFT version, and several other server statistics.

Groping for the Groups

The next option on the SYSCON main menu, Group Information, enables you to manage all aspects of NetWare groups. You can create, rename, and delete groups. You can also assign or delete users to a group. After a group is defined, you can assign and modify group trustee directory and file rights.

Setting your sights on supervisor superlatives

Supervisor Options, the fifth selection on the SYSCON main menu, is the heart of an administrator's user-management toolbox. You can create the system login script, view the error log, activate intruder detection, and reassign file server console operator status.

Getting closer to your users

The last option on the SYSCON main menu, the User Information selection, enables you to create and control users. You can define where and when a user is allowed to log in. You can assign and change user passwords. You can also define user login scripts that are executed every time a user logs in.

From defining groups and users to enabling the accounting features of NetWare, SYSCON is your network security blanket. It's the main utility for managing your user community, unruly or otherwise.

FCONSOLE: A LAN administrator's best friend

The NetWare 2.*x* file server configuration and monitoring utility, called FCONSOLE, enables you to keep a close eye on the operation of your file server. From the FCONSOLE main menu, you can send a broadcast message to all users logged in to the current file server. You can also change the current file server.

Connection information, anyone?

If you change servers, you are prompted for your username and your password. The Connection Information option gives you the opportunity to see all logged-in users by login name and connection number. Any users who have loaded the network workstation software but have not yet logged in are shown with a connection identification number; rather than a login name, however, you see NOT-LOGGED-IN.

Down, but not out

The Down File Server option enables you to do just that: to shut down the file server from a workstation. Be extremely careful when you use this option because you can cause users a great deal of discomfort when you shut down a file server. The good thing about this option is that you do not have to be at the file server console to shut down it down.

Get a LOCK on this

Your next FCONSOLE option displays all file-locking activity on the current file server. Files are locked when an application, usually a database but potentially any kind of application, puts a lock on a file so that no other network user can make changes to that file. This feature prevents a user from changing a file in use by somebody else. If you are updating a record in a database and someone else tries to make changes while you have the file locked, the other user gets an "access denied" error message. After you update the file and save it, then other users can access and make changes to the file.

If you are the one trying to access a file that is locked, a quick glimpse at the FCONSOLE file lock activity option shows you the login name of the person who has the file locked. Supervisor and supervisor-equivalents can even clear a file lock currently held by any users. We don't recommend that you ever do this, but, under dire circumstances, it is possible that you may need to.

Do you know what the LAN drivers know?

The sixth option on the FCONSOLE main menu, LAN Driver Information, shows you all the software and available hardware configuration settings for the network interface card or cards in the file server. You can only view this information — it cannot easily be changed. To change these settings, you must regen the server operating system.

Purging is good for the file system, if not for the soul

The next option in FCONSOLE is Purge All Salvageable Files. NetWare keeps the most recently deleted files in a salvageable form that's hidden from normal users. In case the hard drive space is needed or you have files you don't ever want anyone to be able to recover, the purge option does the trick.

FCONSOLE statistics: These numbers never lie

The Statistics selection on FCONSOLE tells you all kinds of neat stuff about memory use, disk use, LAN I/O, and volume information. These statistics tell you how healthy your server is. Watch the cache statistics for signs that you need to add more memory to the server.

Disk statistics can tell you that a disk problem or crash is imminent. LAN I/O statistics indicate whether the server network interface card is a bottleneck on network performance. We like to print all the server statistics screens weekly to track server performance and possible problems. We put these screen prints in our server documentation log for future reference. We're always sifting through the statistics history folder after a server crash or other problems to see whether the warning symptoms were there all along.

Monitoring miscellany

Many file server monitoring programs monitor the statistics and produce reports or trouble alerts automatically. Some type of monitoring is crucial to the continued success of your server. Disk use trends can alert you to potential shortages of disk space. Without enough RAM, your memory statistics will begin to show problems. When your server gets critically short of RAM, your server crashes. By that time, however, it's usually too late. Be proactive in your network management and avoid situations in which the server croaks unexpectedly.

Remaining options

The remaining options on the FCONSOLE main menu are mostly informational. Status tells you the current server data and time, whether new users are free to log in (when would you not want new users to log in?), and whether transaction tracking is enabled. FCONSOLE is really the network administrator's best friend in maintaining a NetWare 2.*x* server. The more familiar you are with the information in FCONSOLE, the better you can anticipate and react to server problems. FCONSOLE is one of your best tools in effective management.

Yo! MONITOR this!

MONITOR serves an identical yet expanded role for the NetWare 3.*x* and 4.0 network administrator. MONITOR is an NLM that is loaded at the server console. To keep track of server statistics, you must either go to the file server console and run MONITOR, or load the RCONSOLE utility (also known as remote console) and run MONITOR from your workstation.

As you browse through the options in MONITOR's main menu, you can see a great deal of similarity between MONITOR and its earlier incarnation, FCONSOLE. Almost all the functions in FCONSOLE in NetWare 2.*x* are now part of the MONITOR program. In addition, the new name better fits the purpose of the utility.

The MONITOR main menu screen, lists a boatload of server-configuration and - utilization options. At the top of the MONITOR screen, you see up-to-date statistics about the server, including the ones in this list:

✔ Server up time

✔ File server utilization or which percentage of server processing power is being used

✔ Cache buffers and other memory use statistics

✔ Disk I/O statistics

✔ Packet receive and directory cache buffers

✔ Service processes

✔ Connections in use

✔ The number of open files

Connections redux

The first selection, Connection Information, shows you the login names of all users currently logged in. Any user who has loaded the NetWare client software (IPX and NETX) into his PC but has not yet logged in is shown as NOT-LOGGED-IN. NetWare assigns a unique connection number to each individual user. You can also view which files each user has open on the server. You can also see the user status and a list of all files on which the user has a file lock.

Doing disks right

The second option on the MONITOR main menu is Disk Information. This choice shows you many statistics about the server's hard drives:

✔ The driver used to operate the disk.

✔ The total disk size.

✔ Whether the drive is mirrored. *Mirroring* is the process of having two identical copies of data on two separate disks. If the primary drive fails, the backup drive is immediately brought on-line so that there is no interruption in server operation.

✔ The Hot Fix status. The Hot Fix feature automatically relocates data whenever a bad spot on the disk is discovered.

✔ The total number of blocks on the disk.

✔ The total number of blocks used for Hot Fix.

✔ A cumulative total of the number of bad blocks found and redirected by Hot Fix.

✔ The number of blocks used by Hot Fix for administrative purposes.

Keeping an eye on these disk statistics is a must. A disk burp is a warning that your disk has problems. For example, a growing number of Hot Fix blocks can indicate that a disk crash is imminent. Print these screens once a week or purchase a monitoring utility to help you keep track of disk information.

Leading the LAN

The next selection on the MONITOR main menu is LAN Information, where you get more LAN driver and communications statistics than you can shake a stick at. Most of these statistics are informational only, although a high count in some areas can indicate LAN hardware or cabling problems. Again, monitoring this stuff is mandatory.

Making the most of your modules

The next selection on the MONITOR main menu is System Module Information. Here, you see a list of all LAN drivers, disk drivers, and other NLMs loaded on the server. The amount of detail available for each NLM depends on the developer's design. Some NLMs and drivers keep statistics for troubleshooting and monitoring purposes, and most simply show resource use and copyright information.

Holding back the great unwashed: Lock File Server Console

One of the simple but beautiful features of the MONITOR menu is the choice called Lock File Server Console. This option lets you walk away from a server situated in public — or one that nonsupervisory personnel can get to — by making this selection from the menu and then typing in any password you want in order to lock up the keyboard. Until that correct password gets reentered, the keyboard is useless to everyone. Because this situation is exactly what you want, it is an important security step to take whenever you have to leave a server unattended.

Locking up file access, strictly for safety

The File Open/Lock Activity screens show you which files are open and locked and by whom. This is the easiest way to find out which network user has a particular file open or locked. You can also clear or close a file that is in use in case of emergency, as a way to avoid open files in shutting down the server, for example.

Wrestling your resources: how they get used

The next selection from the MONITOR main menu, Resource Utilization, displays numerous memory pool and cache statistics. Because NetWare 3.x and 4.0 use dynamic reallocation of memory, these statistics are not quite as important for you to monitor as they are under NetWare 2.x. With NetWare 3.x and 4.0, if a memory pool runs out of RAM, the operating system automatically allocates more memory to that pool. You can also get more information about memory processes in the Resource Utilization option.

You can see from this overview that the MONITOR NLM is a comprehensive LAN performance- and configuration-monitoring tool. Most of the information available in MONITOR is just that — information. You have to look to other configuration tools, such as the SET console command, to change some of the options you see in MONITOR. But that's why they call it MONITOR rather than CHANGETHEFILESERVER (it's shorter, too).

Bindery Basics: The Glue That Holds the Server Together

The NetWare *bindery* is the backbone of the network operating system. The bindery is a massive database of everything defined on the server: users, groups, workgroups, and printers. The bindery also keeps track of all information related to a bindery object, such as who has rights to a particular printer, the trustee directory rights for a particular group, or the member list for a particular group.

The bindery knows what is located where on the file server, who can access it, and when. The bindery keeps track of which groups you belong to and which rights you have in every directory on the server. The bindery even stores your password and knows when it will expire. Perhaps it would be better to say that the bindery is really the brains of the server because without it you wouldn't have a server.

Setting Up Groups and Users

Defining your groups and users is a breeze in a small network, and a small nightmare in a large network. Use SYSCON for adding a few users at a time. Use one of the command-line utilities, such as USERDEF or MAKEUSER, if you will create more than five users at a time. There is no shortcut to creating groups, but that's OK because, after the users are defined, setting up the groups is pretty easy stuff.

Usable user definitions

Log in as SUPERVISOR or supervisor-equivalent before attempting to define new users. In SYSCON, select User Information from the main menu. Press Insert and type the new user login name. (A login name can be as long as 47 characters, but we suggest that you keep them to 8 characters or fewer).

Most people cannot type 47, or even 15, characters in a row without mistyping a character or two. Your usernames should follow some simple rule that allows sufficient variation to account for duplicates or near-duplicates. Using the last name and first initial, for example, is an invitation for duplication in most medium to large networks.

One company we know of uses the first six letters of the last name plus the first letter of the first name. If there are duplicates under this system, a number is appended to the end of the login name to differentiate between similar IDs. MCDONAK is Kim McDonald's login name, for example, and MCDONAK1 is the login name for Ken McDonald.

As another approach, you can also try the first six letters of the last name plus the first and middle initials. Whatever system you use, plan ahead for the day when your network explodes in popularity and use. At that point, it is a major headache to change the naming standard for your login names, so why not beat your head against the wall right away?

Producing users in bulk

The USERDEF and MAKEUSER utilities are preferred over SYSCON for defining a large number of new users. MAKEUSER uses a batch technique and a sophisticated script language to automate user account creation. By using MAKEUSER, you can specify all the same options available in the SYSCON user-creation menus, including Account Expiration, Groups Belonged To, Concurrent Connections, and Home Directory.

USERDEF serves as both a front-end data-entry utility for the MAKEUSER text files and as an independent user-creation tool. USERDEF lets you define a default *template* that can be used to create a large number of users with identical setups. Both utilities can save you hours of repetitive, tedious work if you need to define lots of new users.

Chapter 20
File, Information, and Menu Utilities

. . . .

In This Chapter

▶ How to find which directories are yours and get to them fast

▶ How to find out how much or how little space you have on the server

▶ How to find that file you think you lost

▶ How to look at all the stuff you own and get rid of what you don't need

▶ What to do when you delete files and then wish that you hadn't

▶ How to copy files from one place on the network to another

▶ How to find out who you are, what everyone else is doing, and how LAN life is in general

▶ How to control your destiny on the LAN

▶ How to change your NetWare perspective by changing the colors you look at every day

▶ How to know what to buy if the NetWare utilities aren't enough

. . . .

*N*etWare has more utilities than you will probably ever need. Some of them are useful and you use them every day. Others you never touch because they aren't much good for anything. And then there are some that you won't touch, if you know what's good for you. We tell you only about the good ones and leave it to you adventurous types to test the rest.

NetWare utilities come in multiple forms, but most are based on the command line, or around menus. With some utilities, you type the utility's name at the command line (which looks like this: F:>). Other utilities have menus from which you choose selections you start from the command line. Just as in DOS, everything starts somewhere; in NetWare, it's at the command line.

There's not much difference in appearance between the DOS and NetWare command lines, except for the drive letters you see. In DOS, you don't ever get much beyond a C prompt; in NetWare, you see anything ranging from drive F to drive Z.

Command-line utilities take a little more practice to get used to, although the menu utilities are pretty easy to learn with a little less practice.

Utilities generally are divided by who can use them — whether it's the garden-variety user, a privileged network administrator, or someone called a console operator. If you read on, we tell you which utilities are which, after we tell you about some keyboard gotchas we urge you to learn about if you plan to tinker around with commands.

Common Keyboard Gotchas You Need to Know

When it comes to dealing with command - line utilities, a fair amount of background information scattered around the NetWare manuals could turn you into a power user, if you had time to read your way through the whole set. On the other hand, you could rely on the advice of a grizzled veteran and learn from her experience. If you are feeling bold, the following few rules will turn you into a master commander:

- If it's a command-line utility you're using, you can get help by typing the name alone or by adding a /H, /?, or /HELP after the utility's name, like this: SLIST /H.

- When you see "path," it means that you have to tell the network where to look for what you want.

- If you see square brackets, you can either enter information or not — it's optional.

- The brackets (< >) you see instruct you to hit a certain key. This key most likely is <Enter>. Do what it says or your command won't work. The term "hit" is used casually here. Hit is used for certain circumstances, and depress or press for others. Both work.

- The wildcard characters are the same in NetWare as they are in DOS. They mean that you can substitute something wherever the * or ? appears.

- The | character tells you to enter either what is before the | or after it, but not both (or all).

- The (ellipsis) . . . tells you that whatever precedes it can be repeated. For example, /option . . . means that it's valid to enter multiple options at this point in the command.

NetWare also uses keys that mean the same thing in any menu utility. These keys, shown in the following list, are the universal commands of choice for those in the NetWare know:

- **<F1>:** Means help in almost any language. It does in NetWare too.

- **<F5>:** Lets you mark items you want to modify, add, or delete.

- **<Esc>:** As we all know, takes you back to the preceding menu or lets you exit from the program. Depending on the utility, the use of Esc differs.

- **Arrow keys:** As in many other programs, let you get where you want to go. The up arrow takes you to the preceding line; the down arrow takes you to the next line. Obvious stuff, but essential.

- **First letter:** The first-letter rule, which applies to NetWare, states, "If a user enters the first letter of the menu option, she will be taken to that menu option." This rule makes sense, and it's also a great way to motor around a large selection list.

Getting Your Bearings: The File and Directory Utilities

Novell has a bunch of built-in utilities that give you information about the files you own on the LAN and the directories they are in. Just like DOS, these utilities let you snoop around and find out just how much information you know. You can sneak down back roads and into subdirectories you haven't been in before, or you can look for all the files you created yesterday (in case your short-term memory resembles ours).

Some of the more common utilities you will use are discussed in this section, with the syntax (the special commands you have to enter from the keyboard) for correct operation. Many times, if you need help in figuring out the syntax, you can simply type the command and see the options you have. We have split the information about utility use into four parts that tell you the utility name and its purpose, the syntax for using the command, who should use the utility, and any options you need to know to use it. Some utilities, such as NDIR (the *NetWare dir*ectory command), have a language unto themselves. We explain most of the more important ones. You can dig in to the NetWare manuals (and we mean *dig*) to unearth the rest of them. Happy keyboarding — now NetWare really gets fun!

CHKDIR (NDIR, if you're using 4.0)

CHKDIR lets you check out the directories on your system. If you simply type **CHKDIR**, you see a list of the maximum amount of space in your current directory, the amount in use, and the amount available.

Syntax: CHKDIR fileserver/volume:directory
CHKDIR drive:

For use by: Anyone

Options: None

CX (4.0)

Novell's newfangled CX command replaces the CD command, which took you around the directory tree. CX shows you where you are in the 4.0 directory tree. Your current location is called the *context,* and if you want to move somewhere else, you change the context. Just remember that CD = CX in 4.0.

Syntax: CX [context] *[/option ...]* | [new context] | *[/option ...]*

For use by: Anyone who wants to get around in 4.0

Options: To learn the intricate details of using CX, refer to your on-line documentation or type **CX /?**, Novell's universal help option.

NLIST (for 4.0 geeks only)

NLIST is 4.0's be-all and end-all utility. It lets you see objects (such as users, groups, and printers), search for objects, and find out whatever you need to know about them (their rights or whether they are logged in, for example). If you want to be a serious 4.0 user, NLIST should be in your repertoire.

Syntax: NLIST [object] [=object name] *[/option ...]*

For use by: Anyone who is anyone

Options: The options that NLIST uses are too numerous to talk about here; refer to 4.0's on-line documentation for the low-down.

NETUSER (4.0 and higher only)

NETUSER is one of those commands you can't live without. It replaces SESSION, parts of SYSCON and FILER, and parts of the printing utilities. Learn to use NETUSER and then don't leave home without it.

Syntax: NETUSER <Enter>

For use by: Anyone who thinks that he knows how to use 4.0

Options: NETUSER is a 4.0 menu utility; see the 4.0 on-line documentation for all the things you can do.

LISTDIR (NLIST in 4.0)

LISTDIR is the utility that draws you a map of your file and directory system.

Syntax: LISTDIR [fileserver/volume:directory I drive:]
         LISTDIR
         LISTDIR VOL1:

For use by: Anyone

Options: Refer to the NetWare *Utilities Reference* manual.

MAP

The MAP command is a command you cannot live without. You should learn everything you can about this command. It lets you assign network drives to different directories and subdirectories so that you can access them quickly when you need to get at the files within them.

MAPs can be of two kinds — search mappings or simple drive mappings. As many as 16 search mappings can exist, which automatically take you to a program located in the directory from any other directory.

Imagine that your default NetWare directory is F:\USERS\DENI and you want to bring up WordPerfect for Windows, located in Z:WINAPPS\WPWIN. From your default directory, you can simply type **WPWIN** and rely on the search mapping defined for Z:\WINAPPS\WPWIN to locate and start up the WordPerfect application. It sounds easier than it is, but it saves you unnecessary footwork in the NetWare directories.

Drive and search mappings you make on the fly when you are logged in to the network are lost when you log out. To prevent this loss, you should define search mappings (or drive mappings, if you prefer) for your most frequently used directories, in your NetWare login script. If you don't know how to do this, ask the supervisor.

Syntax: MAP F:=\USERS\DENI <Enter>
            MAP S1:servername\volume:directory\filename <Enter>

For use by: Anyone with a need for organization

Options: See the NetWare *Utilities Reference* manual for details.

NCOPY versus COPY

NCOPY, for — you guessed it — *Network COPY,* is faster than the DOS COPY command. You should use it, therefore, whenever you copy files across the network.

Syntax: NCOPY [drive: | directory\ ]filename [drive: | directory\ ]filename NCOPY F:*.* G: <Enter>

For use by: Any network speed demon

Options: See the NetWare *Utilities Reference* manual.

NDIR versus DIR

NDIR is another utility that bears a remarkable similarity to a DOS command. Short for *Network Dir*ectory (get it?), NDIR has some additional options. It shows you the size of files, when they last were changed, when they were created, their attributes, and who owns the file. It shows you more than you ever wanted to know about directories too — the inherited rights mask, the user's effective rights, the owner of the directory, and the creation dates for the directory and subdirectory names.

Just like DOS's DIR, you can get carried away with all the options for NDIR, but remember them. They're invaluable for finding that file you just know you created two weeks ago Thursday.

Syntax: NDIR [path] *[/option ...]*

For use by: Anyone

Options: See the NetWare *Utilities Reference* manual for details

Use the /HELP format option to let you know what arcane parameters NDIR uses.

NDIR can also sort files in many different and less common ways. It can sort by file and directory attributes. It can also search for files by owner, size, or files that were created, deleted, or modified before or after a certain date. The possibilities are endless and far too numerous to mention here. Refer to the NetWare *Utilities Reference* for details.

If you want to cause your administrator fits, slow your LAN down to a crawl, and generally irritate a lot of other users, type **NDIR *.*** and watch the LAN creep. You will wish that you hadn't, because you won't get any work done until it stops.

PURGE (FILER in 4.0)

PURGE does just what it says — it permanently erases files you have erased before.

Syntax: PURGE <Enter>

For use by: Anyone with a strong stomach

Options: Nada — not one

Use PURGE only if you don't ever, ever, ever want to get the file back. If you use the /all statement, you purge anything you have already erased.

RENDIR (just REN, for short)

For neat-freak LANkeepers, RENDIR lets you rename directories when you find that you don't like their names anymore.

Syntax: RENDIR [drive:] oldname to newname <Enter>
REN [drive:] oldname to newname <Enter>

For use by: Anyone who can't make up his mind

Options: None here

Information, Please

Some utilities give you information only. They show you a plethora of information — some useful, some not. If you're a trivia freak, these utilities are for you.

CHKVOL (NDIR in 4.0)

If you want to see how much of everything you have out there on the LAN, use the CHKVOL command. It's not much good for anything other than documenting what you already have, but when you're deciding what to name something, this information can be very useful.

Syntax: CHKVOL <Enter>
CHKVOL VOL1: <Enter>

For use by: Anyone

Options: Zip

FCONSOLE (MONITOR in 4.0)

FCONSOLE is your principal diagnostic tool for NetWare 2.x, and MONITOR does likewise for NetWare 3.x and 4.x. These utilities typically are run from the server console, to check on your server's health and well-being.

Syntax: FCONSOLE <Enter>

For use by: Supervisors or console operators

Options: See Chapter 19 for more details.

SLIST (NLIST in 4.0)

SLIST is NetWare's utility for calling all servers. File servers that respond to NetWare's roll call are listed here. If your LAN has only one file server, it is the only one listed. If you have one down the hall in accounting, however, DADDY_WARBUCKS may be listed.

Syntax: SLIST <Enter>
SLIST DAD*.* <Enter>
SLIST LAMBIE_PIE <Enter>

For use by: Any curious user

Options: ALL (Lists all the file servers it finds)

USERLIST (NLIST in 4.0)

Do you sometimes wonder whether you're the only one working at 10 p.m.? If you do, USERLIST helps you to find out.

Do you wonder whether your boss is in yet? Type **USERLIST BIG_CHEESE** to see (see Table 20-1).

Syntax: USERLIST ALL <Enter>
USERLIST BIG*.* <Enter>

For use by: Anyone

Options: See the NetWare *Utilities Reference* manual for details

Table 20-1	USERLIST Options
Option	**What it does**
/A	Shows everything, including network and node addresses.
/C	Use this option if you need to read fast. It doesn't stop at the end of the display.
/H	Help!
/O	This option tells you whether listed items are users, print servers, and so on.

VOLINFO (FILER in 4.0)

VOLINFO tells you how much information you have on a volume and how much disk space is available.

Syntax: VOLINFO <Enter>

For use by: Anyone

Options: Nada

WHOAMI

WHOAMI is the ultimate utility if you forget who you are. If short-term memory loss strikes late Friday afternoon, type **WHOAMI** at the command line and you will instantly remember. WHOAMI shows you other stuff too that's not as important as your username. It tells you which workstation you're logged in from (as though you care) and also the rights and attributes you have in the directory you're working in.

Syntax: WHOAMI <Enter>

For use by: Anyone in need of self-identification!

Options: Whoops! — before we forget — Table 20-2 shows the options you can use with WHOAMI.

Table 20-2	WHOAMI Options
Option	**What it does**
/A	Lists your effective rights, the groups you're in, your security equivalences, the people you manage, whether you're a workgroup manager, and other information
/G	Lists the groups you're in
/O	Shows the names of the users and groups you manage
/R	Lists your effective rights
/S	Shows your security equivalences
/SY	Shows other system information
/W	Shows who you manage

Order from the Menu — No Substitutions Allowed

Menu utilities offer lots of support in that they present each and every choice you can make at any given point in the menu tree. They also offer context-sensitive help, which means that all you have to do is press F1 at any point on a menu and the Help system explains what is currently highlighted. Even though it sounds easy, climbing around in menu trees all day can make you slightly daffy! This section covers the main NetWare menu utilities.

COLORPAL

You should avoid the COLORPAL utility unless you have a bachelor's degree in fine arts. This utility lets you change the colors of your soothing NetWare menus to colors you might see on a psychedelic acid trip. Even though COLORPAL is fun to use, NetWare's menus look pretty good considering what they had to work with when they were first created.

FILER

FILER does lots of stuff you can do from the command line. It shows you current directory information and displays the contents of the directory. You can choose a directory and change directories you are using. You can view information about volumes, attributes, and effective rights. FILER lets you copy files or move them around and set the attributes of a file. Its options are too numerous to cover here. Refer to the NetWare *Utilities Reference* manual for a blow-by-blow description.

Syntax: FILER <Enter>

For use by: Anyone who needs some menu-by-menu file help

MAKEUSER (UIMPORT or NetAdmin in 4.0)

MAKEUSER is an alternative to creating users with SYSCON. With MAKEUSER, you can create users in batches rather than one at a time. As a bonus, some of MAKEUSER's options make creating users easier than it is with SYSCON.

Syntax: MAKEUSER <Enter>

For use by: Supervisors

Options: See the NetWare *Utilities Reference* manual for more information.

MENU (NMENU in 4.0)

The MENU utility lets you create menus for your users to work from. A DOS-based interface, MENU helps you keep users where they should be in the NetWare file system. Given some time and effort, MENU can help with other tasks too. NMENU replaces MENU in 4.0; this licensed subset of the Saber Menu Utilities is much more powerful and easier to use than its MENU predecessor.

Syntax: <MENU>

For use by: Anyone

Options: See the NetWare *Utilities Reference* manual for more information.

NetAdmin (a 4.0 product only)

NetAdmin is NetWare 4.0's SYSCON replacement. You wonder why Novell changed the name, but NetAdmin actually replaces a number of other utilities in addition to SYSCON.

Syntax: <NetAdmin>

For use by: Administrators only

Options: See Chapter 19 for details.

NETUSER (for 4.0 only — don't try this utility at home)

NETUSER is 4.0's all-purpose user tool, which replaces a number of utilities in earlier versions of NetWare. If you're aching to start using 4.0, NETUSER is a good place to start.

Syntax: NETUSER <Enter>

For use by: Anyone

Options: See the 4.0 on-line documentation for details.

SALVAGE (FILER for those in the 4.0 know)

SALVAGE has much to do with salvation. It's the catch-all command you need to use whenever you have erased a file on a NetWare server that you really didn't want to erase. SALVAGE gives you several options: You can look at all the files you have deleted; recover files that have been deleted; or put files back in the directories they occupied before they were erased. SALVAGE also lets you PURGE files.

Syntax: SALVAGE <Enter>

For use by: Anyone who goofed

Options: None

Because files aren't biodegradable, you can get them back with the SALVAGE utility.

SESSION (NETUSER in 4.0)

SESSION lets users move around from directory to directory without requiring explicit DOS commands for manual directory changes. Personally, we have always found SESSION to be a pain in the neck. But if you have to jump around directories a lot, SESSION might be just the thing for you!

Syntax: SESSION <Enter>

For use by: Anyone with couch potato(e) tendencies

Options: If you really believe that you have to use SESSION, refer to the NetWare *Utilities Reference* manual for all the boring details.

SYSCON

SYSCON is the NetWare control center. If you're a user, you can see all the information about yourself, which groups you are in, and your effective rights. If you happen to be the supervisor, you control your LAN operations from SYSCON.

Syntax: SYSCON <Enter>

For use by: Everyone

Options: See Chapter 19 to learn more about SYSCON.

The 5th Wave By Rich Tennant

Chapter 21

Keyboard Practice: NetWare's Command-Line Utilities

● ●

In This Chapter

▶ What command-line utilities are and how to use them

▶ Which commands you can use if you're just a user

▶ Which commands you can use if you're the supervisor too

▶ What's different with each version of NetWare

● ●

*W*e have divided this chapter into several parts: some general, unrelated but very important utilities; some utilities that you need to know if you end up managing the LAN; and some utilities that only certain people can use from the file server console.

General Command-Line Utilities

Two utilities, ATTACH (MAP in NetWare 4.0) and HELP for v3.11, are important only if you meet one of two criteria:

✔ You have more than one file server on your network.

✔ You are hopelessly lost and don't know what to do next.

You use ATTACH to connect to other file servers after you have logged in to the server you always log in to. The following line shows the ATTACH syntax:

```
ATTACH fileservername/username
```

If you have an account on that file server, you may be asked for a password before you're let in. If you don't have an account, you're out of luck.

HELP is another utility that might come in handy. Personally, we don't use it because it's easier to type the command (ATTACH /?) and get help that way.

The rest of this chapter talks about utilities that only the SUPERVISOR can access. If you're not a SUPERVISOR or SUPERVISOR-equivalent, don't waste your time reading this chapter.

Management Utilities

Much of NetWare management begins at what people in the know call the *file server console,* which is the monitor attached to the file server. From the file server console, you can control normal life on the LAN. You can decide whether the network is working, get it into working condition, configure it to do different things, or disable it so that users cannot work on it. That's why, if you're a network administrator, you need to limit access to the file server console. Administering it can be a life-or-death responsibility.

In the lingo of the networking business, "bringing up" the file server means that you do two things:

✔ Boot the file server, just as you would do with a DOS machine. You either power the server on or give it a three-finger salute: Hold down the Ctrl and Alt keys simultaneously and then press the Del key.

✔ Enter the command SERVER from the DOS prompt.

Taking the file server down and bringing it up again is not something you do casually. It disturbs users because they no longer have a connection to the network, and it can disturb your boss because she no longer has a connection either. Bringing the file server down is something you do in only the most extreme cases.

If you take the server down, do it after normal business hours. Spend a night or part of it away from home to do it. You may think that you deserve "comp time" the next day, or you might just take off the following afternoon. Believe us — it just won't happen. When you're wed to the network, your wedding to anyone else might as well be postponed.

When you're at the file server console by way of either a local monitor or remotely from a monitor on your desk (we tell you briefly how to do that later), you should know about a number of important commands. We tick off the list in alphabetical order so that you can find them quickly, and we skip over anything you're not interested in.

CONFIG

The CONFIG utility does what it says, almost. Actually, it just shows you information. You can't use it to "configure your system."

CONFIG shows you the LAN drivers that are loaded in your file server, the file server's network number and name, the protocols that are "bound" to each network adapter, and the type of packet (frame type) being sent across the network. In addition, CONFIG tells you the node addresses of the network adapters in the server and all their hardware settings. If you ever have a question about your server's configuration, CONFIG is there to answer it. And you can bet your bottom dollar that the technical-support people will ask you to use it to tell them about your server profile.

Syntax: CONFIG <Enter>

Options: None

DISABLE LOGIN

This command is the ultimate meanie. Ever wonder why you couldn't log in when you did just minutes ago? DISABLE LOGIN probably happened. See your network manager. He is likely to be tinkering with the system. You will be told to stay out. Go back to your desk. Do not pass go. Do not collect $200.

If you're the network administrator, you should use this command before you back up or make any repairs to the system.

If users are already logged in to the file server, DISABLE LOGIN doesn't affect them. You have to kick them off in the conventional way or send them a message with the SEND command, "LOG OUT NOW OR LOSE IT!"

Syntax: DISABLE LOGIN <Enter>

Options: It's such a simple command that it doesn't have any options.

DOWN

Entering DOWN is similar to turning off the lights. Don't do it unless you really want to leave users in the dark. DOWN takes the file server "down" so that users cannot use it. It also makes sure that the data on your file server is safe by closing files, writing information in cache to disk, and updating all the tables it can.

Syntax: DOWN <Enter>

Options: None

Before you "down" the file server, use the BROADCAST command to send to all users a message that you will take the file server down in x minutes. It's just a courteous thing to do.

ENABLE LOGIN

This command is the opposite of DISABLE LOGIN, and you should use it when you want users to be able to log in to the network again.

Syntax: ENABLE LOGIN <Enter>

Options: None. Don't you wish that there were some? Imagine the statement ENABLE LOGIN EXCEPT FOR BERT AND ERNIE. Gosh, the power of the SUPERVISOR account (temporarily, it went to our heads).

EXIT

If you want to return to DOS before shutting off the file server for maintenance, you enter EXIT after DOWN. You can then rerun SERVER.EXE to operate with new parameters.

Syntax: EXIT <Enter>

Options: This command has no options, except that you have to press the Enter key to exit. Shouldn't keyboards have Exit keys too?

FIRE

This command tells you if your file server is on fire. It should be used only by people who have fewer brains than a three-toed paramecium.

Just kidding! There is no such command, but at least we know that you are reading this book. The closest thing NetWare offers, for those running 2.x, is FIRE PHASERS. It makes keen noises when you log in!

LOAD

This all-purpose command lets you do many essential things. LOAD lets you run the INSTALL program, which lets you diddle with LAN drivers and the STARTUP.NCF and AUTOEXEC.NCF files, and install all sorts of equipment on your file server. It lets you load MONITOR, which we talk about later, and lets you run VREPAIR, which you use if, for some reason, your volumes freak out.

Syntax: LOAD's syntax is easy. Just follow LOAD with a space and whatever program you need to run and then press the Enter key.

Options: LOAD has numerous options.

INSTALL

INSTALL lets you mirror or duplex drives, format your hard disk, load NetWare floppy disks during installation, configure devices you are adding to the file server, change or create volumes, and do other things too numerous to mention.

Syntax: LOAD INSTALL <Enter>

Options: Some

If you load INSTALL with the NH option, you save about 16 kilobytes of RAM but sacrifice any on-line help.

INSTALL tells you whether it is already loaded. See the *File Server Utilities* manual for the skinny on INSTALL.

MONITOR

MONITOR shows you file server utilization and what is happening on the file server. It's a command you should have loaded most of the time. Three options are available with MONITOR: /P, which gives you information about processor utilization, NS, which turns off the screen saver that MONITOR uses, and NH, which turns off any help you might receive with MONITOR and saves memory.

With MONITOR, you can find out who is connected to your network, get information about a server's disks and the utilization of its resources, and get information about the LAN adapters and drivers loaded on that server. Other than just provide information, you can lock the file server console from MONITOR, unlock it when you want back in, and clear workstation connections to the LAN if, for some reason, a workstation hangs and its files are left open.

You can mount or dismount storage devices, activate or deactivate a file server's hard disk, or cause the hard disk light on the front of the file server to flash. We know that you have been just aching to make this light flash (we think that it's weird).

For a detailed, play-by-play analysis of MONITOR, refer to the NetWare *System Administration* manual.

If file server RAM is at a premium, load MONITOR with the NH option. It saves you about 25 kilobytes of memory.

MIRROR STATUS (4.0)

MIRROR STATUS shows you all the disk's partitions that are mirrored and their status.

Syntax: MIRROR STATUS <Enter>

Options: None

MOUNT

You "mount" volumes on the file server so that users can see and use them.

Syntax: MOUNT *volumename* <Enter>
    MOUNT ALL

You may want to mount volumes that you don't use very often, such as histori-cal data or last year's financial records. Remember to DISMOUNT them when you finish.

Options: ALL

REMIRROR PARTITION (4.0)

REMIRROR PARTITION is pretty obvious: It lets you remirror partitions that have been unmirrored. You don't have to do this often, because the server automatically does it for you. If something hiccups and the server doesn't do its job, however, you can take over and force the remirroring operation to occur.

Syntax: REMIRROR PARTITION number <Enter>

Options: None — just the number of the partition

SECURE CONSOLE

The SECURE CONSOLE command is the electronic lock and key for NetWare — SECURE CONSOLE lets you lock the console and then unlock it when you're ready. If someone tries to break into the system with a debugger, SECURE CONSOLE prevents him from loading NetWare Loadable Modules and from changing the date and time. It's an eminently useful utility.

Syntax: SECURE CONSOLE <Enter>

Options: None of any intruder's business

SERVMAN (4.0 only)

SERVMAN, short for *Server Man*ager, lets you look at the operating system parameters and change them if you want. It also lets you view lots of stuff, such as the configuration of IPX and any devices in the server, and it lets you edit the

AUTOEXEC.NCF and STARTUP.NCF files. Like the INSTALL NLM, you must LOAD SERVMAN before you can use it.

Syntax: LOAD *[path]*SERVMAN <Enter>

Options: None

SET

SET is a common function that is far too complicated to explain in this book. It lets you see the parameters of the operating system and change them if you want. SET commands are placed in the STARTUP.NCF file and can improve file server performance. See the *File Server Utilities* manual for an extensive explanation.

Syntax: SET *[parameter]*

Options: Lots and lots

SET TIME

SET TIME lets you set the date and time of the file server. You should reset the time the first thing when you wake up at daylight savings time, or someone surely will remind you about it. (And they think that we aren't smart enough to figure it out.) As for the date, who can be trusted to always know what day it is?

Syntax: SET TIME newtime <Enter>
       SET TIME newdate newtime <Enter>
       SET TIME newdate

Options: None

TIME

See SET TIME in the preceding entry and then try to figure this one out.

Syntax: TIME <Enter>

Options: None

TRACK OFF

TRACK OFF is the opposite of TRACK ON — it turns off the router tracking screen. What's a router tracking screen? See TRACK ON for all the details!

Syntax: TRACK OFF <Enter>

Options: None

TRACK ON

TRACK ON is a useful troubleshooting utility. If you are installing a workstation and are having trouble getting a connection, use TRACK ON. It displays the Router Tracking Screen, which tells you all the data being transmitted or received at a workstation and file server. TRACK ON has lots of useful parameters. See the *File Server Utilities* manual for details.

Syntax: TRACK ON <Enter>

Options: Lots

UNLOAD

UNLOAD does the opposite of LOAD. It unloads NetWare Loadable Modules and the MONITOR program.

Syntax: UNLOAD *NLMname*

Options: None

VERSION

VERSION tells you (if you or a tech-support person wants to know) the version of the network operating system you are running and its copyright notice.

Syntax: VERSION <Enter>

Options: None — just the different versions of NetWare displayed: v2.15, v2.15c, v3.11, and 4.0.

VOLUMES

This command tells you how much bookshelf space you need for the NetWare manuals. It automatically calculates, based on the version number you are running, whether you need a full shelf or just a portion of it. If you're using 4.0, you don't need any shelf space — you need a CD-ROM.

An old joke in the networking industry asks, "What weighs more than your file server?" The answer is "The NetWare manuals." Seriously now, VOLUMES tells you the names of the volumes mounted on the file server.

Syntax: VOLUMES <Enter>

Options: None. Did you want some?

VREPAIR

VREPAIR can fix problems with volumes. It is used to fix damaged files or screwed-up directories. It's also recommended whenever an abnormal shutdown happens, on the off-chance that open files have been damaged.

Syntax: LOAD *[path]* VREPAIR

VREPAIR is on the System-2 disk. Because you may want to run VREPAIR on a damaged SYS: volume and cannot get to it if SYS: is damaged, make sure that you put VREPAIR in the DOS boot partition so that you have it if you need it.

Why you may need VREPAIR

VREPAIR comes in handy in these situations:

✔ If you cannot mount a volume or if you receive a disk read error

✔ If the power goes out and corrupts the volume or if you get an error on the file server console when it tries to mirror a volume

✔ If you get other miscellaneous memory errors

Chapter 22

The GUI Utilities:
They Stick to Your Mind,
Not to Your Hands

In This Chapter

▶ Making it with Windows on the NetWare scene

▶ Using the newfangled mouse

▶ Recognizing that the NetWare Administrator isn't always a person

▶ Using and abusing the NetWare Administrator

▶ Finding the other GUI stuff NetWare has in store

*W*ith NetWare 4.0, Novell came up with a bright idea, one that ranks right up there near the invention of NetWare. Novell decided to offer some utilities based on Microsoft Windows. It's called, in the lingo of the industry, a WIMP interface. You get the picture: *W*indows, *i*con, *m*ouse, *p*oint. (The real reason we call it WIMP is that real NetHeads use the command line!) You see, until the advent of 4.0, NetWare used a distinctive but rather staid menu system, called the C-Worthy interface (the default colors are blue, white, and yellow). You're already accustomed to it, if you have used NetWare v2.*x* or v3.1*x*, and you know that it's no great shakes. That's a fact, as you can see when you call up any of the menu utilities.

Let's Get GUI

Version 4.0 still has many menus like its predecessors, but with 4.0, Novell finally has moved into the "mouse age." In NetWare 4.0, the NetWare Administrator utility and a limited assortment of other utilities use Windows, which brings NetWare into the realm of the *graphical user interface* (*GUI*).

GUI is pronounced "goo-ee," for those of you running into it for the first time. Take the "goo" from Moo Goo Gai Pan and cross it with the fifth letter of the alphabet. GUI interfaces attract applications like flies, and if you're like us, you soon will prefer that all your applications have GUIs. Many of them already do.

NetWare's primo GUI utility is called the NetWare Administrator (also known as NetAdmin), which takes the place of more utilities from previous versions of NetWare than you can count on all your fingers and toes.

If you're working with 4.0, the NetWare Administrator (and its mouse sidekick) soon will become your best friend. It lets you organize your network, create users and manage their rights and attributes, perform file and directory management, and set up printing and manage it, all from within the same utility. In reality, NetAdmin replaces just four utilities — DSPACE, SECURITY, SYSCON, and USERDEF — but it also adds a sprinkling of printer controls for good measure.

After you catch up with some of the lingo 4.0 introduces, we take you on a walking tour of the NetWare Administrator to show you just how cool it really is.

What's a Directory?

Using the NetWare Administrator and the few other NetGUIs (short for NetWare GUI, not a strange new networking protocol) requires a certain knowledge of how NetWare 4.0 works.

When someone installs NetWare 4.0, a single account is created. This account, called ADMIN, has the heady responsibility of setting up the directory and file system for the NetWare users who some day will work on the LAN. The directory and file system in NetWare 4.0 differs from v2.x and v3.1x versions of NetWare because it organizes its directories around objects.

In NetWare 4.0, a database (creatively called the Directory) replaces the NetWare bindery. This directory is meant to service not only a single file server but also all the file servers connected by the internetwork. Terry's Cookie Company, which experienced explosive growth in 1992, bought a 4.0 LAN that arrived yesterday. Figure 22-1 shows the Directory for tcc, short for Terry's Cookie Company.

In Figure 24-1, the Directory window contains all the objects defined for tcc. If Terry is the ADMIN (which he isn't — it's a two-man and one-woman shop), he needs to do a little more work. He has to add the contract worker who comes in every day to stir macadamia nuts into his cookies, and the woman who comes in to measure the ingredients. Call them Chip and Deni.

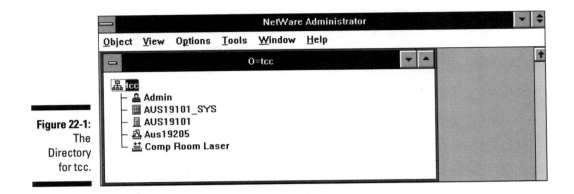

Figure 22-1:
The
Directory
for tcc.

These users are called *objects* in NetWare 4.0 (a somewhat desultory name when mere humans are reduced to objects, but that's the way it is in 4.0). A printer might also be an object; as you can see, two objects are printers — called Aus19205 and Comp Room Laser. A directory map object lets the network administrator define commands that point to an object, such as a printer or a user, rather than to a specific directory on the server. If the path to that object ever changes, you have to update only the object definition, not all your users' MAP commands. This feature gives the administrator the flexibility to change the definition of objects and their locations and not worry about breaking previous commands set up for each user.

An object can represent such real-world objects as users, printers, countries, and groups. We stop defining application directories and server paths, and instead define objects with certain characteristics. You can see that our volume on TCC, called AUS19101_SYS, contains all the directories from which NetWare works.

If you click on the volume, you can see the profile for the volume; if you select and then click on Statistics, you can see statistics about that volume.

After you have defined an object, you can refer to it anywhere else you want in the directory by defining an alias. (Like the alternate names criminals use to do their nefarious deeds, an alias is nothing more than another name for the same thing.) Whenever the original object changes, you won't have to go back and change the setup of every alias for that object in the file system. By changing the object itself, the other references to it are not affected, but the changes are made through the directory structure.

If you define a printer object as an HP LaserJet Series II, for example, you then can copy references to that object wherever a printer object is needed in your organization. If you later upgrade that printer to an HP IIIsi, you have to update only the original object definition. All other references to the printer remain unchanged. Make sense?

Using the NetWare 4.0 Administrator Utility

To use the NetWare Administrator, you have to have an 80386 or higher machine with a minimum of 6MB of RAM. No more 4MB Windows machines. In fact, with the NetWare Administrator, a healthy 8MB is recommended. You also must have Read and File Scan rights in the SYS:PUBLIC directory (it seems that some things always stay the same).

When NetWare 4.0 is installed, the files for the NetWare Administrator are automatically placed in PUBLIC.

Now, bring up Windows or OS/2 and select and choose the NWAdmin icon located on your desktop. A menu bar appears that has different options for working with the objects on your LAN.

Under the menu bar, the window in which Directory objects are displayed is called the Browser. This is the area in which you pick a particular object to inspect or browse.

The Browser displays all the Directory Services objects defined on the network. You can select one, such as Comp Room Laser, to see a profile of what it is; with the Options button, you can control what you do with it.

Suppose that you want to look at a printer. Select Comp Room Laser. Click on it with the left mouse button, and you will see its profile.

As you navigate through the directory, you see different objects, called *container objects,* that have a + sign in front of the object's name. These objects contain other objects. You can click on the container object to expand the tree and then click on it again to compress it.

Or, if you point to object ADMIN and select it so that you can get up close and personal, you can see that a profile exists for ADMIN too. In Figure 22-2, you can see that Terry trusts Deni, the ingredient measurer and book writer, to administer his LAN. In the center of the window, you can see that there are many things (all good, of course) to find out about her.

You can select and choose any of the boxes on the right side of the window or change any of the information in the main window. Whatever you do, you have to live with the changes you make. The information available through the right-hand size boxes includes selections that overlap considerably with the main SYSCON menu choices, right down to the names that choices are called (Login Restrictions and Password Restrictions, for example). The good news is, if you know how to use SYSCON, you already know a great deal about how to use NWAdmin.

```
┌─────────────────────────────────────────────────────────────────┐
│ ─                        NetWare Administrator              ▼  ▲▼ │
│ ┌───────┬────────────────────────────────────────────────────┐  │
│ Object│ ─               User : Admin                          │  │
│ ┌─────────────────────────────────────────────┬─────────────┐│  │
│ │ Identification                              │ Identification│ ↑││
│ │                                             │ ╶───────────╴ │  ││
│ │   Login Name:    Admin                      │  Environment  │  ││
│ │                                             │ ╶───────────╴ │  ││
│ │   Last Name:    │CONNOR│        █│ │...│    │    Login      │  ││
│ │                                             │  Restrictions │  ││
│ │   Other Name:   │DENI│          █│ │...│    │ ╶───────────╴ │  ││
│ │                                             │   Password    │  ││
│ │   Title:        │Co-Author│      █│ │...│   │  Restrictions │  ││
│ │                                             │ ╶───────────╴ │  ││
│ │   Description : │Writes DUMMIES books   ↑│  │  Login Time   │ ▲││
│ │                 │                       ↓│  │  Restrictions │  ││
│ │                                             │ ╶───────────╴ │  ││
│ │   Location:     │                │ █│ │...│ │   Network     │  ││
│ │                                             │   Address     │  ││
│ │   Department:   │Editorial│       █│ │...│  │ ╶───────────╴ │  ││
│ │                                             │   Print Job   │  ││
│ │   Telephone:    │512-794-8035│    █│ │...│  │ Configuration │  ││
│ │                                             │ ╶───────────╴ │  ││
│ │   Fax Number:   │                │ █│ │...│ │  Login Script │  ││
│ │                                             │ ╶───────────╴ │  ││
│ │   E-mail Address: │dconnor│       █│ │...│  │   Intruder    │  ││
│ │                                             │   Lockout     │  ││
│ │                                             │ ╶───────────╴ │ ↓││
│ │                                             │Rights to Files│  ││
│ │ ┌─────┐  ┌──────┐  ┌──────┐                 │     and       │  ││
│ │ │ OK  │  │Cancel│  │ Help │                 └───────────────┘  ││
│ │ └─────┘  └──────┘  └──────┘                                    ││
│ └───────────────────────────────────────────────────────────────┘│
└─────────────────────────────────────────────────────────────────┘
```

Figure 22-2:
The profile
for Deni.

Point to Password Restrictions and click on it. You see a screen much like the one shown in Figure 22-3. The ADMIN requires a password, but so far no minimum password length has been defined. Click on the box to set it to a minimum; a good rule of thumb is five characters. Then point to the OK box and click on it to close the window.

From the profile, you can also display and change login restrictions for the object, make changes to the user's login script, and show the object's rights to files and directories.

The NetWare Administrator is much like SYSCON and does many things in the same way.

The first option on the NWAdmin menu bar is called Object. Selecting Object lets you work with the directory tree and the NetWare 4.0 file system. From the Object menu, you can choose any particular Directory object such as ADMIN from the Browser window. From the Object menu, you can also create a new object (a user or printer, for example), assign it rights and grant trustee assignments, and rename or delete an object or display. The Directory is made of objects, so it should come as no surprise that working with objects is what working with the Directory is really all about.

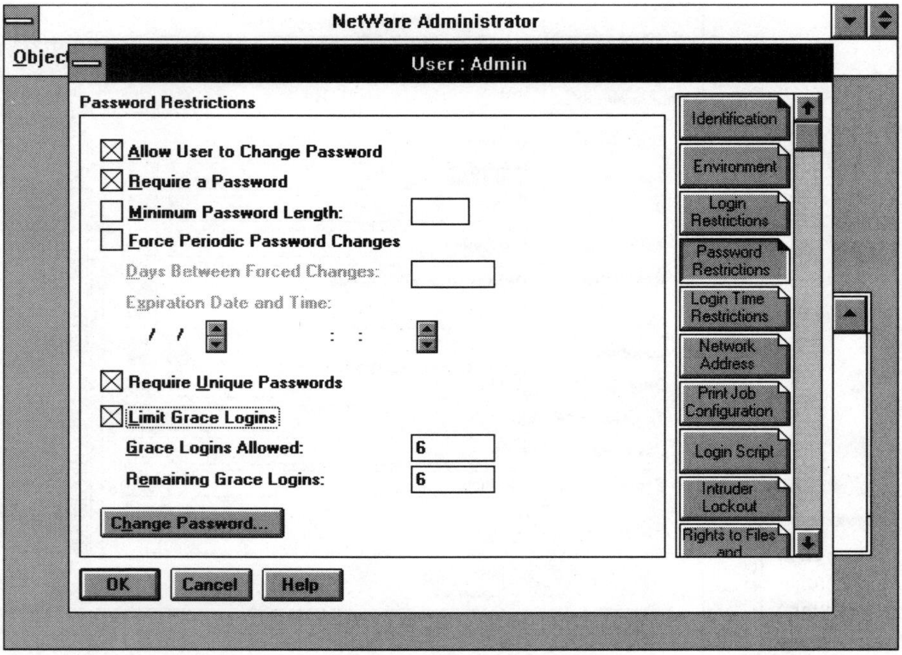

Figure 22-3:
Using
NWAdmin to
manage
password
restrictions.

The other windows are View, Options, Tools, Window, and Help (we all know what that means).

The View menu lets you choose the type of objects you want the Browser to display. You can also set the context of a container object.

The Options menu shows you a file's or directory's startup settings and also lets you assign files to certain name spaces.

On the Tools menu, you find another copy of the Browser, the heart of the Net-Ware Administrator. Here, you can do all sorts of tasks, including changing the context of an object; you can also see what is in the different containers, view bindery objects and queues, and perform printing operations.

The Window menu does just what you would expect if you're a Windows fanatic. If you're not but want to be, the Window menu is a standard Windows feature that lets you arrange the different windows on your desktop and switch between windows as you want.

Then there's the Help window. And, as we said, we all know what that means.

Creating Chip's Identity

To define a user in the Directory, you must create a user object and then select the container object you want the user object placed in. To create a user, first select the Object menu and then select the Create entry. When you see a list called the *class list,* select the "little guy" icon (it's red on our screen). Click on OK and then enter Chip's username and fill in the Last Name field.

Select the item named Use Default Settings. These settings are the ones you created for Chip's Organizational Unit, tcc. Confirm that everything you entered is OK and then return to the main menu bar. That's it — you have just created a user!

Learning the rest of NWAdmin requires experience with a good portion of the NetWare 4.0 documentation. Feel free to dive right in. This is your system, and only you can muck it up. Take a NetWare 4.0 class and complete it before doing any of this with real objects, or try it out for a "toy" company, just as we did. Buy the *NetWare 4.0 Quick Access Guide* if you plan to spend a great deal of time managing the LAN — it's a good investment.

Chapter 23

Troubleshooting Common Problems

. . . .

In This Chapter

▶ Troubleshooting step by step

▶ The `Disk Full` and `Access Denied` messages: Don't take 'em personally

▶ Why network printers don't print

▶ Why some DOS commands and applications don't work with netware

▶ Command-line utilities for getting things done

▶ Troubleshooting user PCs

▶ How to live through a file server crash

▶ What to do when the network goes on vacation

. . . .

*N*ow that your network has been up and running for a few hours or days or months, your first real problem rears its ugly head. What do you do? We have good news and bad news for you. The good news is, you get to use this chapter on troubleshooting a lot. The bad news is, you *have* to use this chapter on troubleshooting a lot.

Remember our network motto: "On all networks a little rain must fall." If the rain doesn't get you, surely the misbehaving applications, faulty wiring components, glitchy servers, and balking printers will.

The hardest part of network troubleshooting is that so many different variables and components can act up. The error messages you see only compound the problem. A malfunctioning network interface card can cause your spiffy new word processor to report a DOS 74.35c error. Doesn't help you to identify the problem much, does it?

This example shows you the quirky nature of network troubleshooting: The error messages rarely coincide with or identify the root problem. Quite the opposite, the error messages frequently point you in the wrong direction. That's when you don your Double-Naught Network Spy Sleuthing Hat with matching NetWare Error-Message Decoder Ring and hit the streets.

They Shoot Troubleshooters, Don't They?

The first step in troubleshooting network problems began when you first installed your servers and network cabling. The proper documentation of the network is the most important step toward successful troubleshooting.

If you don't know how things were, how do you know when things are fixed? You *did* document every step of the original installation, *didn't you?* You certainly know the interrupt setting of the server NIC and where your network hubs are physically located . . . right? Right?

Trust those of us with greater experience and who have endured many more all-night server rebuilding parties: Every hour you spend documenting your network before a big problem occurs saves you ten hours when the server croaks and you can't remember who manufactures the hard drive controller. Backups are almost as important as network documentation, and we think that backups are crucial to network survival.

Your LAN survival kit

Before the first problem strikes, put together a LAN Bugaboo Survival Kit. Your kit should include at least the following items:

- ✔ Documentation of the server, cabling layout and design, user PC setups, backups, and so on.

- ✔ A complete and recent set of server backups.

- ✔ As many spares as you can afford: NICs; network cables, connectors, and terminators; hard drives and controllers for vital machines; monitors; and so on.

- ✔ Someone to talk to when network travails strike. Someone to bounce ideas off and milk suggestions from. We use the many manufacturers' fora (as in the plural of *forum,* not as in flora and fauna) on CompuServe, and we recommend that you get a CompuServe account if you don't already have one. On CompuServe, you can ask questions directly to the manufacturer or, better yet, you can ask questions to other users who have experienced similar problems. If you don't have CompuServe access, you can ask for ideas from a friend who knows networking, the reseller who sold you your hardware or software, the geeky PC guy with the thick glasses and a pocket protector back in the corner cubicle, or one of the many books available that are dedicated to troubleshooting NetWare problems.

- ✔ Diagnostic gadgets and tools: an ohm-meter, soldering iron, wire-crimping tool, cable tester, protocol analyzer, and so on. A few tools — some very cheap, some not so cheap — can be a big help when you are looking for hardware problems and even some software problems. Just remember the First Rule of Network Troubleshooting: The more complex your network, the more expensive your diagnostics gadgets and tools tend to be.

The trouble with troubleshooting

The way you approach problem-solving is almost as important as fixing the problem. If you aren't careful, you might fix the problem but not be able to figure out how you fixed it. Here are a few tips:

- **Change only one thing at a time.** Changing more than one thing at a time might fix the problem, but you won't know exactly how you did it. Plus, you might unknowingly also cause other problems.

- **If possible, remove the misbehaving PC from the network and see whether the problem persists.** This step often tells you whether the problem is a result of network problems or stand-alone-itis.

- **Simplify things until it works.** If you have a PC with all nine expansion slots filled with everything from a fax-modem board to a two-port game card, try removing cards *one at a time* until you identify the problem.

  If you load 53 different terminate-and-stay resident programs in your AUTOEXEC.BAT file, remove them one at a time until you can identify the conflicting program (or programs).

- **Be suspicious.** You're a Double-Naught Spy, so start acting like one! Always be skeptical of error messages, particularly any message that is vague or offers no information about the cause of the error. A large number of simple-sounding DOS errors are caused by seemingly unrelated server and cabling problems.

- **Learn from your experiences and the experiences of others.** Don't let your network keep shooting you in the foot. Be diligent and try to not make the same mistake more than 10 or 20 times.

- **Cabling is *always* a prime suspect.** We have said it before and we will say it again: The network cabling is the most used, most abused, and most confused component of any network.

Now that your documents are in order (you did document everything, didn't you?), the next step for a network troublehound is to begin ruling out probable causes. After you have some idea of where to begin looking for the cause of the problem, you can look at possible solutions for a number of common troubleshooting problems.

Bogus, dude: Disk Full when it ain't

The DOS Disk Full error message is a common occurrence in today's LAN environment. That it usually is identified as a DOS error can be misleading because the underlying cause can very easily be the network file server.

Your first step in discovering the problem is to find out which disk is apparently full. Ask your user what she was doing at the time the error first occurred. Was she trying to save a document, create a file, or re-index a database file? If so, is the file in question located on the file server or on a local drive?

The `Disk Full` error message has two likely causes: The disk may be, of all things, full; or, in the case of a network drive, the user may be restricted from storing any more files on the file server. The crucial step, therefore, in solving this problem is identifying which disk appears to be full.

After you have narrowed down which hard disk is creating the problem, you have to check the available space on that disk. On a local disk, run the DOS command CHKDSK C: (or whichever drive letter is appropriate). On a network drive, run the NetWare CHKVOL command-line utility. Both of these utilities tell you the total size of the hard drive in question and the amount of available storage in bytes.

In the case of a local drive, whenever the available bytes get below 100,000, you have exceeded the capacity of the hard drive and either a larger drive or the deletion of unneeded files is in order. In the case of a network drive, there may be 12GB of free space on a network hard drive, but a `Disk Full` error message still is generated if the user's disk space allotment has been exceeded. Use the Account Restrictions option in SYSCON to increase the user's network disk allowance or else erase from the server disk unneeded files *belonging to that user.*

Access Denied: Your program is fried

The ubiquitous `Access Denied` message also makes appearances on network user screens all over the country. Just as with the `Disk Full` error message, your first goal is to try to determine exactly which file, program, or gremlin is denying you access. You also will find two primary culprits for this error: Either you are trying to lock a file already locked by another user, or you are trying to save a file to a network directory in which you do not have WRITE rights. Right?

If the user is trying to use a database file that uses file locking, you can check the File Locks option of FCONSOLE to see which other user currently has the file locked. You can keep retrying until the other user unlocks the file; you can identify which user has the file locked and ask her to exit the application; or you can be a mean and nasty network administrator and clear the other user's file lock. We are happy to report that this particular cause of the `Access Denied` error is fading fast. Most modern databases enable a user to lock only a record within a file, not the entire file. This feature is by far a better way to design your database systems and should be considered de rigueur for any successful implementation of a networked database.

The easiest way to test for the lack of WRITE rights is to get to a DOS prompt and change directories to the network directory in which you or your application is trying to write the file. Type the NetWare command-line utility RIGHTS and study the results. If you do not have WRITE rights, indicated by a W, you have every right to demand WRITE rights. Network administrators are traditionally very reluctant to grant application directory WRITE rights to users because it is one of the rights needed to delete files, and you don't want users deleting files at will.

The answer is probably that the application is not properly set up to store user-modifiable files in a directory separate from the application program files. Because most applications, such as databases and word processors, require some place to keep notes for their own use, a separate data or temporary directory is part of the setup options. This directory is WRITEable by all users of the application without the threat of erasing or modifying the application files themselves.

Balk like a dog: why network printers don't print

Printers don't print for as many different reasons as there are printers. The following is a partial list of what causes printer problems:

- Bad printer cable
- Printer cable too long
- Printer not turned on
- Printer not on-line
- Network print queue not set up properly
- User hold on printer queue
- Printer out of paper
- Printer memory error
- Printer hardware error
- PC port not configured correctly

As you can see, troubleshooting a network printer can be a long and trying process. So many things can go wrong that you're probably asking, "Where do I begin?"

Start at the printer and work your way back to the user's PC. Attempt to print a test page from the printer control panel. Check the printer cable for a secure connection. Make sure that the printer is set up for the same type of connection as the cable: parallel, serial, or some type of built-in network connection. If the printer is connected to a server or attached directly to the network, use a parallel cable to connect the machine to a DOS-based PC and try the following command from the DOS prompt:

```
C:\> COPY CONFIG.SYS LPT1:
```

If this command works, you can eliminate both the printer and the cable used for the test as problem suspects. Next, check the print queue setup and status in PCONSOLE and check the print job configuration in PRINTCON. If the user is running Windows, check the printer driver and Print Manager settings. Try to print to the network printer by using the following NPRINT command-line utility:

```
C:\> NPRINT C:\CONFIG.SYS Q=LASER1
```

You might also enter a CAPTURE statement to see whether the printer queue name is available on the network:

```
C:\> CAPTURE L=1 Q=LASER1
```

Send print jobs to the printer and check the print queue active job list in PCONSOLE to see whether the data gets to the queue. Make sure that there is no "hold" on the queue in PCONSOLE. Last, and most drastically, you might try using a protocol analyzer to decode the printer job packets bound for this printer.

Printer troubleshooting should be a systematic series of steps that begins at the network printer and ends with the user's PC. As we always say, change only one thing at a time. Examine every piece of hardware and software between the application and the printer paper output tray. Don't be afraid to call on experts and the manufacturer's technical-support personnel. You can persevere over any kind of printer problem with patience, knowledge, and an occasional bit of good luck.

Friend or foe: why some DOS commands and applications don't work with NetWare

DOS and many early DOS application programs were developed years before anyone had even heard the term "PC network." Some DOS commands and programs, therefore, don't know how to react to the LAN environment. Most of the conflicts between DOS and the network are a result of DOS thinking that it resides on a stand-alone PC with one or two hard drives physically installed.

If you try, for example, to execute the DOS command CHKDSK on a network drive, the command fails with the error message Cannot CHKDSK a network drive. CHKDSK was designed to detect and correct *file allocation table (FAT)* problems with local hard drives. If a user could CHKDSK a network drive, he could wreak havoc with all the files residing on the file server. You can see how some DOS commands would be either totally useless or very dangerous when run in a network environment.

Many old DOS applications (and even a few new ones) aren't written to run in a network environment. Those programs expect a standard DOS-based local hard drive on which to execute their computer code.

You have seen *lots* of early DOS programs that could be installed and run only from the C: drive. Even if you have a second hard drive or drive partition and want to install one of these old programs on the D: drive, you are out of luck. Most short-sighted programming like this is long gone, but many programs still are designed to run only as stand-alone programs. Computer programmers sometimes code their programs specifically so that they cannot be installed on a network to prevent copyright violations. Other programs cannot handle concurrent access of files from different users. Sharing is not in their nature.

We have some good news among all this doom and gloom. The majority of all current computer applications support network installation. All modern network database programs handle record locking, file sharing, and transaction tracking with ease. Even word processors and spreadsheet programs are now "network aware," so they can easily be run in a network environment. Always be careful to check for network compatibility when you purchase new software for your users.

Stop making nonsense: command-line utilities that get things done

Novell does not send you unarmed into the battle of the network trouble-shooters. All three versions of NetWare come with an extensive collection of command-line utilities, which are listed in the NetWare *Utilities Reference* manual. These utilities are a crucial part of your network tool chest. You can save many hours of troubleshooting if you know which tools to use to get the job done.

Troubleshooting Workstations: Brain Surgery for PCs

The most frequent call you receive as a network administrator is from a frantic user who asks, "Why can't I log in to the network?" Although the answer we think of first is usually "Must be a loose nut behind the keyboard," we don't suggest that you use it on your users. Try to be very analytical in your ap-

REMEMBER

Do unto others

Most PC users consider their PC and everything on it to be their personal property. Always be respectful of your users' privacy and personal preferences when you are making changes to their PC. We try not to change any CONFIG.SYS or AUTOEXEC.BAT options without discussing the implications with the user. This courtesy is par-ticularly important with the more sophisticated users in your organization: They may have spent months getting their PC set up to their liking. Remember that you are the network administra-tor, not the administrator of each individual PC. That title belongs to each user.

proach to all network troubleshooting. Are there any error messages to point you in the right direction? Is the cable connection to the back of the PC secure? Has the user changed his hardware setup lately? Has he moved the PC? Is the Caps Lock or Num Lock key on when it shouldn't be, or vice versa?

Most users cannot log in because they either mistype their passwords or their passwords have expired and they are locked out of the file server. You may come across an occasional user, however, who honestly cannot log in. Put on your Double Naught Spy hat and start sleuthing.

You may be surprised how ingenious users can be when it comes to their PC. Most users will tell you that nothing has changed on their PC in the past five years. A few hours under hot interrogation lights usually gets them to admit that they recently installed a different network card, changed the interrupts on their modem, revamped their AUTOEXEC.BAT, and swapped hard drives with the guy down the hall.

If IPX and NETX load successfully but a file server cannot be found, look at the cabling and hubs of your network. If either IPX or NETX does not load, you probably have a software configuration problem. If your user's PC locks up at either predictable or unpredictable times, you probably have a memory conflict in your hinterlands. After you look for cabling and connector problems, your next step is to boot the PC and check the network setup. If you don't already know the memory address, I/O address, and interrupt setting of the NIC in question, pull the cover off the PC and make a note of each setting. Then go to the directory in which the IPX.COM file resides and type the following line:

```
C:\NET> IPX I
```

You then see information that resembles the following:

```
Novell IPX/SNnPX  v3.10 (911121)

(C) Copyright 1985, 1991 Novell Inc.  All Rights Reserved._

LAN Option: SMC EtherCard PLUS V4.00EC (910924)_

Hardware Configuration: First Software Configured Adapter
```

Be sure that the correct driver is configured and that the IPX settings match the settings on the user's NIC. If the settings don't match, you must either change the jumpers on the NIC, use the DCONFIG utility, or regen the IPX program. If the wrong driver is configured, you must regen IPX with the driver for the NIC installed in that PC.

Never count out the luck factor when you are helping your users fix their network problems. Sometimes, you just walk up, and everything miraculously starts working flawlessly. Just smile and tell users that that's why they pay you the big bucks. Take the credit while you can 'cause there are more than enough times when nothing you do seems to help. That's one of the joys of networking.

Survival Techniques: How to Live Through a File Server Crash

Boom! Your file server just crashed and you don't know why. What do you do next? First, count to ten and take a deep breath (it may be the last one you get for a while). Write down any error messages from the server console screen or from any of your users' screens. The next obvious step is to turn the computer back on and see what happens. Nine times out of ten, the server comes back up successfully with no intervention from you. It's that tenth time that can be a bugger. This section provides a few suggestions about how to deal with a server that doesn't want to come right back up.

Poll your users to rebuild a portrait of what the server was doing at the time of the crash. Some crash causes are obvious: Lightning strikes the antenna on your AM/FM/8-track that sits on top of the server, for example. Other crash causes can be, shall we say, more subtle. We have had crashes in which the server was operating normally at the time of the crash and no errors were observed. We still don't know what caused some of the crashes on our network.

Airplane pilots are taught to undo the last thing they did when they are confronted with mechanical problems in the air. Likewise, we suggest that you look for any recent changes to the network cabling, server, or installed applications when you are trying to pinpoint the source of problems. If the server crashed right after you loaded the new version of MegaWord on your server, try unloading the MegaWord software and see whether the server returns to normal. If you connect a new segment of cabling just before the server locks up hard and fast, try removing the new cabling and rebooting the server.

Frequently, server crashes damage the server database, called the bindery, or other software files open at the time of the crash. The server displays messages on bootup that the bindery tables are corrupt. Or your database may display error messages after a server crash. Refer to your NetWare manuals regarding the BINDFIX program and when its use is warranted. Refer to the application manuals for any specific recovery techniques for database and other types of programs.

Gone to Jamaica, Mon: What to Do When the Network Goes on Vacation

Your phone begins to ring off the hook. Irate users want to know why the server is down in the middle of a busy day. You saunter nonchalantly over to the server console and everything appears to running normally, although no users are attached to the server. Your network cabling, hubs, bridges, and routers just went on vacation and you're left holding the proverbial bag. What to do, what to do?

Remembering our earlier advice, you should undo the last thing you did. As you begin to look for network problems, run diagnostics on any hubs or network "black boxes" that include diagnostics routines. Check all the cable connections in your wiring closet. In particular, check all connections between your server and the rest of the PCs on your network. Without the network card and cable between the server and the rest of the network, none of your users can connect to the file server, even though the file server remains "up" and running. You might also try bringing your server down and then restarting it. Run the diagnostics disk that came with the NIC installed in the server. Replace the NIC, if possible, but only with an identical NIC. This is no time to be changing your basic hardware setup.

If you have access to a cable scanner, check your cable plant for any shorts or open circuits. Remember that cable scanner anomaly distance reports are frequently inaccurate, but they can still point you in the right direction. An ohmmeter can come in handy on Ethernet cabling, but only if the entire network is down — its use tends to disrupt any network activity that is still going on. A protocol analyzer can also be a good tool for tracking down the source of the problem, although protocol analyzers cannot point you to a physical location the way a cable scanner can.

If all these steps fail to get your network back up, begin working with a small subset of your network workstations to isolate the problem. Connect your server directly to one other PC and see whether they can talk to each other. Then insert a network hub between the two to see whether communications continue. Then add additional cable segments and machines, one at a time, until you locate the offending PC or cable. From that point on, repairs are usually easy to concentrate on. Leave as much of the network operational as possible so that your users don't grab torches and chase you into an old castle. Your network eventually returns from Jamaica and then you can take that long-deserved vacation. On second thought, maybe you better call in every few hours, just in case.

The 5th Wave

By Rich Tennant

"BETTER CALL MIS AND TELL THEM ONE OF OUR NETWORKS HAS GONE BAD."

Part IV
The Part of Tens

The 5th Wave By Rich Tennant

ON A BET, HOWIE LENDELMAN, THE OFFICE TINKERER, TRIES LINKING HIS T.I. CALCULATOR INTO THE WORKGROUP'S DESKPRO 386/25 NETWORK FILE SERVER.

HE'S GETTING FILES! HE'S GETTING FILES!

In this part...

When Moses came down from the mount, how many commandments did he have? Ten.

Each chapter in this part is a list of commandments, guidelines, suggestions, ideas, and other stuff worth paying attention to when it comes to wrestling with NetWare. We would like to claim divine inspiration, but we're going to have to lean on brute experience.

Maybe that's why some of the chapters have more than ten items, some less, and some right on the magic number.

However many items there might actually be, you will find them calculated to help you save time, skip common gotchas, and deal with everyday mayhem on your NetWare network.

Chapter 24
Ten Tons of Trouble: The Network's Broken!

O K, so things aren't going like they're supposed to. In fact, they're not going well at all. Don't worry — everybody's network breaks every once in a while. Before you give way to a full-scale panic, first check out our rogues' gallery of common network gotchas. Chances are, one of these is the one whodunit; if not, though, you may still get inspired enough to figure things out anyway!

Is Anybody Out There?

The most disconcerting problem for anybody on the network is when the whole thing goes away. Nobody can even access the network, let alone log in. You will *hate* when this happens, and so will your users, but what can you do?

The most common cause of *network interruptus* is a break somewhere in the cable. This problem is far more likely to happen on a bus topology than on a star topology. If it does happen on a star, go immediately to the hub that services the users affected and, most likely, you will go to the source of the problem.

When a bus topology fails, the most common cause is a break in the cable. Look for someone who is changing offices or for people messing around near where the cable runs. If you're lucky, somebody disconnected something he shouldn't have; if you're unlucky, you have to splice a broken cable. If you're *really* unlucky, the break is in a trench in the ground where a backhoe has used its unique ability to find and break cable on your network.

File Server not Found

This is a typical symptom for a user who has been mucking with her machine. If things were working yesterday but have mysteriously quit working today, the first thing to check is what has changed between now and then. It might be anything from changes to the AUTOEXEC.BAT or CONFIG.SYS files to forgetting to reconnect the PC to the network. Start with the wires and work your way up to the software: Check the connection to the network, the NIC, and the network software configuration, in that order. Sooner or later, the cause of the disconnection jumps out and bites you. Again, cable problems are the most likely cause.

Networking in Geological Time

Under some circumstances, a network begins to run really s-l-o-o-o-w-l-y. Even if you don't notice it yourself, don't worry — your users will, and they will rush to let you know. Curiously, nothing stimulates hurry like a slow network. Can this be a case of opposites attracting?

The most common culprits for excessively slow networks are shown in this list:

- Cable shorts that cause the network to work only intermittently
- Server problems that constrain resources, such as running out of disk space or running low on available memory
- Excessive user demands on the server

Your best diagnostic tool is to go to the server that has slowed down and check the MONITOR or NETADMIN utilities. If you look through the various displays, especially those related to network utilization, the file system, and server memory, you typically get enlightened right away. The intermittent-short problem is much trickier to catch, but it typically shows up in the form of lots of transmit-and-receive errors in the network utilization display. Anything over 2 percent of total traffic for errors is abnormal and should clue you in to potential cable troubles.

Help! I Can't Get There from Here

On networks in which there is more than one server, especially when long-distance connections might be involved, the day will come when you cannot get there from here. The obvious thing to check first is the link between "here" and "there." In most cases, the link is down or the router that ships traffic between the two locations is on the fritz. Checking the link is the first step; making sure that traffic can flow across the link is the second. Our experience has been that a reset of the link most often does the trick — especially if a modem is involved — and that checking the router may require it to be reset, too (especially if you're using the NetWare external router).

Oh, No! The Network Has Gone Away

When the network goes away, the first thing to check is who is affected. If it's a single workstation, proceed as with the `File Server Not Found` message from earlier in this chapter; if multiple workstations are affected, get out the network map and see how they're related to each other. Chances are, they're all on the same cable segment or connected to the same hub. If that's the case, you have to look for cable or hub problems in the affected neighborhood. If everybody's out of commission, proceed as in the first section in this chapter, "Is Anybody Out There?"

The Server's Out of Disk Space

Running out of disk space on your server is an unassailable argument for good housekeeping, as we advocated in Chapter 14. After you have rooted around on the disk that's full and have thrown out the stale stuff and removed the not-so-necessary files that build up over time, go back and reread Chapter 14. Then, you can practice prevention in the future rather than have to clean up full disks.

The key is to make some space. You should survey your file system, find out who the big consumers are, and tell them to clean up their act. Another approach is to check out electronic-mail files and clean them up yourself. NetWare keeps deleted files around until you PURGE them, so you should clean up right away. Look around for bogus temporary files created by applications (Microsoft Word is especially good at this); deleting all files with a .BAK or .TMP extension is also a good idea.

By going through these motions, you can make some much needed room. As a follow-up, consider tightening disk allocations for individual users or adding more disk space.

It's dangerous to run a NetWare server without at least 10 percent disk space free. Why, you ask? NetWare needs room to breathe — for such things as print queue files, temporary working files, and so on — and room in which to work. Without some empty space, things can really slow down. Double this number if you have turned on transaction tracking or auditing, because they both consume appreciable amounts of disk space.

NetWare 4.0 includes an option to compress files stored on disk. Using this option can effectively double your file storage space and may justify the upgrade costs all by itself. If you have done everything you can to prune your file collection and still are nearly full, price the cost of adding disk space versus the 4.0 upgrade. It may just be worthwhile to do it with software for a while.

Coming Back from Power Outages

OK, the power has gone away, and it has just come back. NetWare servers would rather be shut down gracefully than have their plugs unceremoniously pulled. Unfortunately, that's the effect of a power outage.

You have to restart the file server and perform any necessary file system repair. If you're lucky, that's all you have to do. If the server has been hosed, however, you have to restore from a recent backup and break the news to your users that their work has been lost. Be prepared to be unpopular.

It's worth considering an Uninterruptible Power Supply (UPS) for your servers. If a power outage occurs, it gives you enough time to shut down the server gracefully and avoid file system damage. The right UPS even lets you run for a while without A/C. (If you don't have UPSes on your workstations, however, nobody will be up and running to care!) At a minimum, install a high-quality surge suppressor and spike arrester on your server; this device should protect you from outright damage if lightning gets up close and personal.

If losing a server means losing business, consider NetWare SFT III as a possible alternative. It greatly improves the odds against server failure, but you must balance that benefit against the increased hardware and software costs. Run the numbers for yourself. If it's cheaper to double up on server hardware and buy SFT III than it is to be down for 30 minutes to an hour, you will know.

Breaking the Rules

There are many creative ways to break the rules of networking, ranging from excessive cable lengths or connection violations to having more users trying to log in than your NetWare license allows. Rules were made to be broken, but you have to be prepared to suffer the consequences.

The closer to the wire these violations occur, typically the more dire the consequences. For instance, the sixth user who tries to log in to a NetWare server that has a five-user limit is politely rejected with an informative error message which indicates that no additional user connections are available. On the other hand, exceeding cable limitations can cause intermittent failures if the violations aren't too extreme or outright, and total network failure if they are way over the line.

Again, prevention beats cure every time. If you know the rules and stay inside them, you are completely safe. If you don't, you have to begin troubleshooting. Unless the problem is completely obvious, begin at the cable and work your way up to the software. Persistence and thought pay off, and practice helps improve your response time.

Intermittent Failures

Patterns of errors that come and go are the trickiest kind to nail down. Intermittent problems are far more likely to be caused by hardware, especially cable shorts or loose connections, than by anything else, but that's more of a tendency than a hard and fast rule.

The first thing to do when you are faced with an intermittent problem is to determine its scope; figure out who's affected and where they are, and catalog the symptoms. Pay attention to everything, no matter how unrelated it may seem.

As an example, the weirdest intermittent problem we have ever encountered resulted from running an unshielded cable through an elevator shaft. The only time trouble occurred was when the elevator was in the immediate neighborhood (within one floor of the cable). At those times, it would interfere with the signals running through the cable. At all other times, everything worked fine. The solution was to reattach that section with a new, heavily shielded cable in a metal conduit.

We have also heard stories about similar problems caused by industrial vacuum cleaners, servers being moved to mop underneath them, and other strange and wonderful tales. If you're lucky, you won't have one to tell yourself. Just keep your eyes peeled for the out-of-the-ordinary situation and, as always, round up the usual suspects.

I Can't Log In

Not being able to log in covers a multitude of causes but typically is limited to a single workstation. Again, the cabling is the most common culprit, so start at the cable and work your way through the NIC to the software. Users who have made recent changes to their environments may have inadvertently redefined their DOS PATH to leave out the directory with the network drivers, or AUTOEXEC.BAT simply may not be loading the network software.

When you are troubleshooting user workstations, it's a good idea to bring with you a set of bootup disks that include appropriate network software (IPX, NETX, ODI drivers, or VLM.EXE, and necessary VLMs). You can fire up the workstation with your own environment that way and boot from the disks. This process makes it immediately clear if something's out of whack with the workstation's software.

If you have a portable or laptop with a network connection, you can bring that with you and connect it to the network in place of the suspect machine. That too lets you know right away whether the network's working. The biggest difference between this and the disk approach is size and weight. You decide.

When it comes to troubleshooting, the key ingredients are a positive attitude and persistence to see your problem-solving through to its inevitable conclusion. If things seem hopelessly screwed up, take a break: Go for a walk, call a friend, go have a cup of coffee. Often, you get so wound up in decoding the symptoms that clues right in front of your nose elude you. If you get too wound up, you miss them. A little relaxation gets your creative juices flowing and restores your deductive abilities. If Edison's best hours were spent daydreaming, why not yours?

Chapter 25

Keeping Track:
Ten Things to Know (and Write Down) About Your Network

Chapter 6 makes an eloquent argument for the virtues of a network map and a database of configurations to go with it. This chapter is a checklist that serves as a reminder of what you want them to include.

Where Are the Cables?

The most important thing to indicate is where the ends are and how they might be color-coded or labeled (this is especially critical for twisted-pair wiring, in which cables run in packs and tend to look alike). For complete reference, record the code on the outside of the cable (typically printed on the insulation) and the name of the vendor, if available.

Where Are the Connections?

For wiring schemes, such as coax, that involve taps, knowing where (and how many) connections are out there is important for staying on the right side of the rules.

How Long Is Each Cable?

You can get this information in two ways — the easy way and the expensive way. By measuring as you go, you can accurately keep track of how long each cable is as you lay it out. If you're dealing with already installed cable or if you didn't keep track along the way, rent a Time-Domain Reflectometer and use it to measure each cable. Especially with twisted-pair, don't be surprised when you find some scary length limitations: Cabling folklore is full of stories about finding a cable that has a whole spool of wiring hidden in the ceiling. Because you often cannot see the wires, the only way to tell how long they are is by measuring them.

Where's the Networking Gear, and What Kind Is It?

When you keep track of the locations of any hubs, routers, concentrators, or other pure networking gear, you know where to look when you need to find it again. It's also a good idea to keep track of network addresses, used and unused ports, and other configuration information about these devices.

Know Your NICs

Make sure that you keep at least one manual from each kind of NIC you use and that you have a source for the latest and greatest drivers for each one. The manual's best feature, typically, is that it includes the number of the manufacturer's technical-support hotline. They can tell you everything you need to know about the NIC and its software.

Also, for each NIC installed, write down any and all of its current settings (IRQ, memory base, I/O port, and DMA channel, for example). If you don't mind gumming up the back of your PCs, write down this information on a small label on the outside of the case. That way, you don't have to open the case and pull out the NIC just to check its settings. It's an even better idea to record this information in a configuration database.

Know Your Nodes

Each machine on a network is called a *node* (borrowing from mathematical terminology), which refers to each point on a connected collection of lines as a node. For each machine, you should keep track of its hardware configuration and software configuration, and keep an inventory of the software it contains. This information, too, has a rightful place in your configuration database.

The Vendor File

Inevitably, you will buy pieces and parts of your network from all kinds of sources: mail order, local computer stores, and maybe even a direct sales representative. You also will buy stuff from different vendors. It's a wonderful idea to build a vendor file that includes the following information for each one:

- Name and model number of the item
- Date and price of purchase (a copy of the invoice or purchase order is a good idea)
- Serial number or other identification information
- Vendor's address and phone numbers for sales and technical support

By keeping all this information in one place, you are ready to call for help at a moment's notice, and you have all the information you need to convince whomever's on the other end of the phone that you have a legitimate reason to be asking for help.

The Contact Log

Every time you call a vendor (or a reseller or a professional support organization or anything else of importance to your network), make a log of the call. Record the date, time, and the name of the people you speak to. If they promise you anything or advise you to do anything, write that down too.

This log has two kinds of value: If things get really weird, you have a record to support your side of the story. On a more positive note, you can use it to figure out who's worth talking to on the other end of the line and to be able to ask for them by name the next time.

The Plans, the Layout, the Map!

Get a set of engineering or architect's plans for your building or office or barn or whatever. Use it to record cable placement and length and machine placement. This map becomes the key to finding things and to figuring out just how big a problem might be if you suspect that the cause is a cable or hub. It's a simple thing, really, but incredibly valuable.

Don't mark up the original plans — check your local Yellow Pages for a drafting or architectural supply store. Most of them can copy blue lines or other architectural drawings for you. Then, when you have created your network map, make a few working copies of it so that you can mark up a working copy and not mess up the original. You probably will want to supply a copy to your building management or to the facilities people — they can use it to forewarn outside contractors before they start messing with your network. It's easier to avoid trouble than to fix it when something happens.

Spare Change . . . or Spare Parts?

Over time, you build a stockpile of spare parts and unused cable. Keep a list of what you have and where it's stored. That way, if you get hit by a beer truck, the person who replaces you will be able to find stuff when she needs it. Consider it an exercise in following the golden rule — if you had to take over from someone else, you would want the same thing, wouldn't you?

As the eminent cyberneticist and mathematician Alfred Korzybski so poignantly remarked, "The map is not the territory." True though that statement may be, it's the best tool we know of for finding your way around the territory. All the best networks have one — why not yours?

Chapter 26

The Ten Things You Have to Know Before Anyone Else Can Help You

- -

In This Chapter

▶ Gather all necessary information about problems before calling technical support

▶ Assemble a complete description of the hardware and software

▶ Describe a problem completely and accurately

▶ Make a special note of any recent changes or additions to the system

▶ Keep your story short and be as polite as you can

▶ Offer to fax or send files by modem

▶ Make sure that you have covered all the bases

- -

*T*here will be times when you get stuck on a networking problem and just cannot get past it. A good rule of thumb is to guess how long a particular job will take before you begin. If you find that half your original estimate has expired and you're not as far along as you think you should be, maybe it's time to bring out the heavy artillery.

To deal effectively with another person, whether it's somebody from tech support or just plain old Fred, the NetWare guru from next door or down the hall, you should address the concerns in this chapter to get things moving again.

For Tech-Support Calls Only: Assemble the Facts

Technical-support operations require that you identify yourself as a legitimate owner of the product or system being supported. It's much like checking in to the hospital: Before they admit you, you must identify yourself and provide proof of insurance (or at least an ability to pay).

For tech support, you have to know the name of the product in question and its serial number, or be able to provide proof of purchase. If you have built the purchase records file we suggested as a part of the network map and configuration database, you have this material right at hand. If not, start digging — some technical-support operations won't talk to you until you can provide this information, so it's best to be prepared to rattle it off when you are asked.

What's the Situation?

Write down everything you can think of about the system that is involved.

If the system is a workstation, write down each and every interface with settings information for each one, the kind of CPU, the amount of memory, the type of disk drive and controller, the version of DOS, and copies of the AUTOEXEC.BAT and CONFIG.SYS files.

If the system is a server, write down everything we already mentioned plus the version of NetWare and the copies of the AUTOEXEC.NCF and STARTUP.NCF files, if applicable.

The idea is to be able to completely document what you're dealing with.

What's the Problem?

Give as accurate a description of the problem as you can, including any error messages that crop up. (It's important to copy them down verbatim, especially if numeric codes or crash dumps are involved.)

What's New or Different?

If your system has been running until you made a recent change or addition, it's very important to describe what has changed and why you cannot get back to where you started.

Which Avenues Have You Already Explored?

If you have tried to fix the problem on your own, it's important to recount whatever you tried and what the results were. By doing this, you may be able to save the other party to your conversation some time and energy. Ask whether they're interested in knowing about the blind alleys you already explored.

What Happened?

If a power outage has occurred or if someone has accidentally pulled the plug on your server, please tell your support contact about it. Make sure that you test the A/C outlet to be sure that there's power in that receptacle, and make sure that the PC is capable of powering up. If there's no power or the unit is dead, the response is different than if you can at least turn it on.

Does the Problem Have a History?

Sometimes a badly damaged file system or a failing disk drive starts off with small, occasional faults and then gets worse and worse over time until the system fails altogether. If the problem you're having has been in the making for a while, let the other person know how long it has been happening, how it began, and how the symptoms have progressed.

Be Clear, Concise, and Polite

It's upsetting to have your system or network go down in flames, but the people trying to help you cannot deal with your emotions. They can deal only with your problem. Take a deep breath and do your best to calm down.

If you can be clear and direct in describing your problem and the other information they need, things go much faster. If you have done your homework and you have built the configuration database and files we have suggested, you should be able to tell them everything they want to know as soon as they ask.

Offer to Send Information By Modem or Fax to Speed Up the Process

If the help you seek isn't in the neighborhood, you should tell the technical-support people what information you have gathered and ask whether you can upload or fax it to them (assuming that you still have the capability). Especially when the contents of configuration files or other computer information gets called into question, a copy for the person on the other end of the conversation can be a real time-saver.

Ask Whether There's Anything Else You Can Do or Say

It's easy to get carried away with worry when things are broken. If you can focus on how well you're communicating and keep checking in to see how you're doing, it helps you to be more objective and to focus on getting the information across. The more good information you can give, the better (and faster) the results should flow. A positive attitude works wonders, too.

Getting help requires going through the painstaking process of re-creating the environment and the causes of whatever problem prompted your pleas for help. The more you can do to depict the circumstances accurately and objectively, the better your support person can function. Just remember that you both share the same goal — to get things working as quickly as possible.

Chapter 27
Remain in Lite: Ten Tips to Keep It Shining Bright

. . . .

In This Chapter

▶ Let your Lite users know that what they do to "their" machines can have a profound effect on fellow users

▶ Make the naming scheme simple and understandable

▶ Dedicate a machine to ensure server availability

▶ Try not to be a "file hog"

▶ Establish rules for your Lite network

▶ Check your error log

▶ Realize that anything worth sharing is worth backing up

▶ Set up and use accounts and passwords

▶ Get to know the Lite status and error messages

▶ Keep multiple servers time-synchronized

. . . .

*N*etWare Lite's middle name is Simplicity. Even so, it's not a maintenance-free environment. By following a few simple rules of prudent networking practice, you can keep things up and running — and available to those who need them. Peer to peer means that everybody's a network administrator, whether or not she cares to admit it.

Make Users Feel Responsible to Each Other

In the world of Lite, PCs can be either clients or servers. Anybody whose machine is a server has to be educated about what that means — namely, that fellow users will depend on some of the things their machine can do for them. This means that they cannot reboot their machines whenever they feel like it; it also means that they shouldn't power their machines down over a lunch break. A shared resource has to remain available to all who want to share it!

If you can succeed in making your users understand that they have to depend on each other, and on their machines, you can help them feel responsible to each other. This responsibility makes for safer computing and a more workable Lite network.

Pick a Naming Scheme and Use the Heck Out of It

If users can access drives or printers on multiple machines around the network, try to organize the way things are named to make them make sense.

Let LASERP be the name of the laser printer, and DOTP be the name of the dot matrix. Make the directory in which shared applications live reflect that use. Call the spreadsheet drive SPREADS, for example, and the word processing drive WORDS.

If the names communicate what the resources are or what they contain, users can find their way around without too much help. Even so, build a map of the Lite network's shared resources, name the file LITE.MAP, and put a copy on every network drive. Tell your users that they can count on it to be there when they want to find something, and keep it up to date. After users get the hang of it, you spend less time explaining things than you did before.

If It's Really a Shared Resource, Consider Dedicating a Server

For heavily used network drives or printers, the poor slob whose machine plays host will suffer from the traffic. If you have a heavily used resource, beg, borrow, or invent a separate machine to put it on. The poor slob will thank you, and the rest of the users will get better service.

Don't Be a File Hog

Just because there's space out there on a network drive doesn't mean that it *must* be filled up. Exercise restraint and store on the network drives only things that have to be shared or that require public access. Anything more is just plain piggish.

Make Some Policies and Make 'Em Stick!

Bring your users together and tell them what to expect from the network and what role they all play in it. Make it clear that users whose machines host network drives or printers must respect others' needs to access those resources. Make it clear that some machines must be left on all the time, if that's what's necessary, or what the normal hours of operation should be. Make it clear that calling in sick or taking vacation means that someone else has to know how to boot up your machine and get the network resources loaded. As we have said, make some policies, make 'em clear and make 'em stick!

Check the Error Log Regularly

NetWare Lite maintains an error log for each machine that runs SERVER.EXE. As a network supervisor, it's your job to check it regularly and see that it doesn't grow too large.

The contents of the file can be a helpful troubleshooting tool and should be checked at least once a week (and immediately, when problems get reported). It's your key to the pulse of the network and your best diagnostic tool. Use it and then lose it (erase it so that it doesn't wax prolific).

Keep Backing Up, No Matter What

Anything that's worth sharing is worth keeping around. Establish a backup routine for all network servers and perform regular backups at least once a week. The more valuable the data, the more often it should be backed up. Don't forget that, come hell or high water, if either one hits, a backup may be all that stands between you and perdition.

Train Your Users for Smart Security

NetWare Lite supports user accounts and passwords. If any of the data on the network is sensitive, or if the network is exposed to visits from the outside world, it's a good idea to make accounts and passwords mandatory. That way, you can protect the good stuff, even if a single machine can get compromised. If you have serious security requirements, maybe NetWare Lite is too lightweight of a solution for your needs.

Stay on Top of Server Status

NetWare Lite is very good about providing server status information, ranging from messages about startup and activity to errors and problems as they occur. As a supervisor, it's vital that you stay informed about the status of the Lite servers on your network.

Familiarize yourself with Lite's status messages from the manuals and check in on them frequently. Because these messages are what you work from if you have to troubleshoot any problems, it's best if you are able to recognize them and are ready to interpret what they might mean.

If It Makes a Difference, Stay in Synch

NetWare Lite makes it possible to synchronize the clocks on multiple servers on the network. If you're doing development work or have to worry about using the time/date stamp on files to tell them apart, make a habit of synchronizing your servers at least once a week (more often, if their clocks drift apart quickly).

The reason that this process is important is that two out-of-synch clocks can create a situation in which a later version of a file gets mistaken for an earlier version (such as when you compare a file from your local drive to one from a network drive to determine which is the most current) and might be mistakenly overwritten or deleted. Don't let this happen to you!

Keeping Lite burning bright really isn't that much work. It requires developing some good habits and practices and then sticking with them day after day. Anything less is simply unacceptable.

Chapter 28

Ten Things to Know Before Making Changes to a NetWare Server

● ●

In This Chapter

▶ Make two complete backups before changing your server

▶ Get acquainted with the server's file system layout and contents

▶ Fully document the server's hardware configuration

▶ Know what the server is running and document all VAPs and NLMs

▶ Document special network addresses for all network cables and for internal server use

▶ If your server is part of an internet, map out the routers and where your server fits

▶ Find and map out all print servers, print queues, and network printers

▶ Survey your server's situation

▶ Get to know the server's user accounts and defined groups and find out who has supervisory rights

▶ Document your server's NetWare version number and research how up-to-date the installation is (or isn't)

● ●

*T*he power of common practice is strong, and the power of common expectations is even stronger. Although most servers tend to have similarities in their setups, each has its own unique quirks and kinks. These things must be thoroughly understood when you take over a NetWare server, especially before you bring your own individual perspective and personality to bear and begin changing things to fit your own ideas of good structure and organization. In case you miss or forget something, this chapter presents a checklist so that you can become familiar with what you have — and get back to where you began if you need to reverse all engines. . . .

Make Two Complete Backups

A complete backup means that you copy everything. Why, then, do you want two of them? For insurance — if anything is wrong with one of them, the other one should still be OK. If you are going to make changes, the backups are your lifeline back to a known working system configuration.

Map Out and Inspect the File System

Print directory structures of the SYS:SYSTEM volume and other NetWare volumes. Try to understand how the pieces fit together: Does the file system follow conventional NetWare structures, or does it do its own thing completely? The answer to that question lets you find your way around this server and figure out what, if anything, must change.

While you're looking around, inspect the files to see whether the system has been cleaned up. Look for lots of outdated files, unnecessary duplicates, and .TMP or .BAK files in mass profusion, and check the contents of the e-mail directories in SYS:MAIL and its user subdirectories. Avoid the temptation to clean up as you go — you're making a survey, remember?

Map Out the Hardware Configuration

Unless you're lucky enough to inherit a server from someone who already has made a network map, with the configuration database to go with it, you have to do some sleuthing. Print copies of the AUTOEXEC.NCF and STARTUP.NCF files, and check the various LOAD statements at the operator's console as the server boots up. This information is a good start for most of what you need to know.

Make a List of Add-Ons That Are in Place

Regardless of the version of NetWare in use, you will want to make a list of the VAPs or NLMs that are in use. Unless you're manually loading some after startup, you should be able to get this information from the startup configuration files (STARTUP.NCF for NetWare 3.11, for example). This information tells you which services are available to users and who cannot load and unload NLMs or VAPs anyway. You can also check this information in the Modules section of the NetWare MONITOR or NETADMIN utilities.

Map Out the Network Addresses and Configuration

You have to get the network number for the internal IPX network inside the server, plus the network numbers for any of the networks to which the server is attached (typically, one additional network address per NIC installed). You also have to get network addresses or address ranges for other protocols in use, including TCP/IP, AppleTalk, OSI, SNA, or whatever else might be installed.

Understand How Routing Works on Your Network

If you're running NetWare 3.x or higher, the server can act as a router. Check to see whether routing for protocols other than IPX is enabled. If an external router is in use, map out the networks it services. Build a routing map of the network that shows the network addresses involved and the routers that link individual networks together. This map shows you how data moves around on your internetwork.

Map Out the Print Services and the Role the Server Plays in Them

Create a list of the printers, print queues, and print servers on the network. Add locations for print servers (including RPRINTER workstations) and printers to your network map so that they are easier to locate when you need to find them. Try to determine which kinds of forms or special service queues have been set up and how users are directed to use the currently available print services. If everybody's pretty happy with the way printing works, you probably should leave things alone until you fully understand them.

Check the Environment: Power, A/C, and Physical Security

Check out the physical situation of the server. Is it in a secure area or out in the open? Does it have a UPS, or a surge/lightning suppressor, or is it just plugged straight in to the wall? Does it have adequate cooling and ventilation? Negative answers to any of these questions should spur you to consider improving conditions, at the very least. If everything is satisfactory, you can move on to other concerns.

Learn the Users and Groups and Who Else Has SUPERVISOR Rights

Check to see who has accounts defined and what their patterns of use might be. You should work backups and system maintenance around normal working hours, so it's a good idea to determine what they are. See who the heavy users are so that you can provide the services they need.

If you're working on a 4.0 server, familiarize yourself with the directory structure for this environment. Is the server the sole occupant of a stand-alone directory tree, or is it a part of a larger directory services environment? What's the structure of the tree, and how are users and groups defined within it? You can use the directory services Browser to climb around the directory tree and become familiar with it. The more you know, the better prepared you are to deal with whatever comes your way.

Check the NetWare Version and Inspect the Patches and Fixes That Are in Place

The final check is on the currency of your NetWare version. The first thing you have to find out is the version number (and revision, if applicable). The next thing you have to look into is which patches and fixes are being applied during the loading process.

Here's where investigation of the startup or configuration files pays off again. These files tell you — or someone who knows more than you do — how up-to-date your server is. If you can't tell, try to find someone who can so that you both can decide whether new changes and enhancements should be installed on your system.

The whole idea when you take over an existing server is to become as familiar with its design and layout as you would be if you had built it yourself. If you're lucky, it is laid out along familiar lines — the well-worn defaults that most folks use — and you can begin to feel at home right away. If not, you have to do a formal investigation. This takes time, but the effort is always rewarded.

Chapter 29

Ten Paths to Perfect Printing

In This Chapter

▶ Keep print configurations simple

▶ Build CAPTURE into the login script to avoid user-induced printing problems

▶ Don't leave NPRINT to your users

▶ Set up separate queues for envelopes, special paper, or print forms

▶ Keep your Macintosh and UNIX print users separate from DOS and Windows users

▶ Dedicate a machine for print services

▶ Use remote printing only when nothing else will do

▶ Don't use the PSERVER.VAP unless there's no other choice for print services

▶ Train your users to kill print jobs

▶ Listen closely to PCONSOLE

*D*espite NetWare's importance as a print service provider, printing is not a perfectly transparent thing in the NetWare environment. Maybe that's because thousands of different kinds of printers are out there, each with its own eccentricities. Maybe that's because print services require many more bells and whistles for occasional special use than normal, everyday printing ever requires. Maybe it's because providing perfection for print services is a difficult thing to do.

Whatever the case, printing seems about as clear as mud until you really get the hang of it — and even then, it's a dirty job! In the meantime, our ten nuggets of wisdom should keep you out of unnecessary trouble and help you stay on the beaten track to provide print services that work. Our advice: Worry about perfection later; just get your printers printing!

Don't Get Fancy Unless You're Forced into It

Basic printing requires one printer, one queue, and one print server. Why do any more, unless you have to? And, if you do, take it slow and careful.

Make sure that what you provide (whether it's special queues, print forms, or additional services) works before you give it to your users. The only thing worse than not having what you need is being told that you have it and then finding out that it doesn't work.

Handle CAPTURE for Users Yourself

Write a good system login script that defines basic capture capability, test it thoroughly — particularly with DOS applications from inside Windows — and then put it where users cannot escape from it. If special CAPTURE definitions are needed, write batch files for each one and build them into user access to the applications that need them. If you do it yourself and test it well, you can get it right.

If special needs exist, consider spending some time with PRINTDEF to service them. It pays off by hiding some of the tricky details from your users.

Set Up NPRINT Batch Files for Applications That Need It

The same thing is true for NPRINT as for CAPTURE — it's best to embed access to the applications that need special treatment in batch files that can deliver working NPRINT services. If you set your users loose with enough knowledge to try but perhaps not enough to succeed as do-it-themselfers, you will have only yourself to blame when they come crying for help.

What's in a Name? One Form Per Queue

If you have to set up print services to handle envelopes, letterhead, preprinted forms, labels, and more on your printers, set up special print queues for the most heavily used ones. LABELQ is a good name, for example, for where label-printing jobs can be queued up, and ENVQ is good for envelope-printing. You get the idea.

Special Services for Macintosh, UNIX, and More

If you have to service AppleTalk- and/or TCP/IP-based printing on your server, set up separate queues for those special users. It lets them access their print jobs more directly, and it lets you more easily troubleshoot the special kinds of problems they're prone to have.

Dedication Is a Wonderful Thing

If you have an extra, unused PC lying around, consider setting up a dedicated print server using PSERVER.EXE. This approach has the following advantages:

- ✔ Lets you keep your NetWare server locked up
- ✔ Lets you separate print services from other services and provides better response time for all of them
- ✔ Lets you locate printers (and the dedicated print server) sensibly — close to their users — rather than as dictated by restrictions on the length of the printer cable

Use RPRINTER Sparingly

RPRINTER, the remote print server DOS TSR, can be a real godsend, especially for small, isolated groups of users who otherwise must trudge halfway around the world to pick up print jobs.

If that's not the case, don't use RPRINTER just because it sounds like a neat idea. The use of RPRINTER on machines that users employ as their everyday desktops means putting print services at their mercy. If the users reboot often or turn their machine off while print jobs are in process, they can make life miserable for other users, which makes it equally miserable for you.

Stay Away from PSERVER.VAP

For NetWare 3.x and higher, NLMs are efficient, useful ways to extend the functionality of the server. For NetWare 2.15 and higher, VAPs are a crude attempt that tries to do something similar but doesn't quite make it. VAPs are balky, kludgy, and inflexible. Don't run PSERVER.VAP unless you have absolutely no other choice.

Be Quick on the Kill!

Teach your users how to kill their own print jobs. This job takes some time and effort, but it is well worth the time (and interruptions) it saves you. It also saves at least one tree, if not a small forest!

The Status Apparatus

The information provided by PCONSOLE's Printer Status menu provides information that tells you most of what you need to know to keep your printers up and running, and to find out why they're down when they're not running. Use it regularly and, if you have a dedicated Print Server, keep the status window on display at all times.

The secret to print services that work is not to get too fancy and not to rely too much on the kindness or perspicacity of your users. Doing it right typically means doing it yourself and making sure that it's right before giving it to users. If you live by these rules, you stay out of the printer problem zone.

Chapter 30
Ten Unbeatable Backup Benefits

*I*t's a frightening but totally predictable statistic that only 40 percent of all NetWare servers are backed up regularly. It makes you wonder how the majority manages to rationalize living on the brink of unrecoverable disaster. This statistic proves what we have always believed — that there's absolutely no guarantee that the majority is always right!

If you want to risk everything against the chance of failure and loss, we cannot stop you. If you're smart, however, you will get into the backup habit and be ready to fend off Murphy when he eventually does show up (Murphy's Law: What can go wrong will go wrong). If you're prepared, you can laugh him off; if you're not, it's time to play the crying game! Follow the ten prescriptions in this chapter, and you'll never have to play.

Buy a Big Enough Backup System

The biggest problem with the backup process is that it must happen regularly to be any good. The more data you have to back up, the longer it takes (and the more media is required to accommodate it).

Don't cut corners by buying a cheap, low-capacity backup system when you have an expensive, high-capacity network. If you can back up everything to a single tape or magneto-optical disk, that's good. If you can back up to that medium a multiple number of times, that's even better.

The idea is to be able to fit everything you need on your backup system so that you don't have to be on hand to shuffle cartridges or disks or whatever. Because backup usually happens on weekends and in the wee hours, this approach helps you get your beauty sleep.

Completely Automate the Backup

The best way to ensure that backup happens is to let the computer handle it. The only good backup is a fresh one, and you can make the computer do it every day — no excuses accepted. If you make yourself responsible, the inevitable excuse doesn't make up for the data lost as a consequence.

What You Miss Is What You Lose!

When you are selecting backup intervals, you have to make a trade-off in frequency against time and expense. The key is to figure out how much data you can afford to lose before it really begins to hurt.

Most businesses that make this decision rationally decide that a day's work is about all that they can afford to lose. That amount has as much to do with the fact that they can back up only at night as it does with damage control. Think long and hard before you stretch that interval. Think about what the loss of several days' or a weeks' worth of work will cost you and your company.

Set Up Off-Site Storage

If you're going to go through the trouble of backing up, take the next step and make arrangements to store a set of backups off-site. In many areas, you can even make a provision to store backups in underground bunkers that will get your data through most catastrophes. This method may be overkill, but the idea is to have a backup somewhere else so that if your building goes up in flames, your backup doesn't get barbecued along with it.

Plan for Disaster

The next step after off-site backup storage is to arrange for a backup site on which to install your off-site backup. If your company cannot do business without your network, it's worth the money to arrange access to an equivalent system if your main system ever gets put completely out of service. This process, called disaster recovery, may seem completely unreasonable, but, if you need it, you have no other choice.

Practice Makes Perfect

The best backup system in the world, and a completely fresh backup in hand, doesn't do you any good unless you know what to do with it. And, if your backup system doesn't work, your backup is worthless.

The only way to find out whether things work is to try them and see what happens. The only way to get good at restoring from a backup is to practice, practice, practice.

A good approach to staying in top backup shape is to do a restoration drill once every three months or so. Then, when a real crisis happens, you can concentrate on getting back to work, instead of learning how to restore first, and then deal with the problem at hand!

The Pros and Cons of Workstation Backups

After you get into the backup habit for your servers, the next hurdle to jump is deciding what to do about workstations. If your users can be trained to keep their important stuff on a server, there's no need to back up workstations. If not, you must decide whether it's worth the additional time, expense, and effort.

Typically, the only employees who routinely merit this kind of consideration are your bosses. Sometimes, covering your assets means covering theirs too!

Rules for Rotation Mean Equal Wear and Tear

As you get your backup scheme going, remember to introduce new media from time to time. Chapter 18 discusses a variety of rotation schemes in some detail, but the important thing is to keep from completely wearing out the tapes, cartridges, or whatever. Worn media can render a backup unreadable and therefore worthless. Pick a rotation scheme and schedule, and stick with it.

How to Deal with Upgrades and Changes

Another occasion for backing up is easy to overlook: Whenever a server changes, whether it's hardware or software, there's some danger that a failure might result. If you cannot time your upgrades or changes to follow your regular full system backup, you have to time a backup to follow the upgrades or changes. It's much safer, though, to back up first and make changes second.

The Backup Desiderata: What to Look For

When you are buying a backup package, you should consider many factors (see Chapter 18); the following list, however, shows the top three considerations:

- ✓ **File-by-file restore:** Users lose files, and sometimes the SALVAGE utility just cannot get them back. A file-by-file restoration lets you restore only what you need, which saves a great deal of time and frustration.

- ✓ **Automatic backup scheduling:** If the package you're looking at doesn't let you automatically order up regular, full, and incremental backups, move on to the next candidate.

- ✓ **SMS compliance:** If you're backing up NetWare, pick a solution that supports Novell's Storage Management System. This step insulates you from the impact of potential file system changes and ensures that similar media can be read on backup systems from multiple vendors.

The bottom line is to get the most effective backup package you can find that meets your needs.

Backing up is the cheapest form of insurance for your company's investment in the systems it uses. Even though the majority of companies don't take advantage of this potential lifesaver, try to stay ahead of the herd!

Chapter 31
Ten Symptoms of Growing Pains

. . . .

In This Chapter

▶ Erratic network performance

▶ Really s-l-o-o-o-o-w network response

▶ You have more users than NetWare connections

▶ You're always short on disk space

▶ The traffic is excessive because the wires are getting too crowded

▶ Your users have growing pains

▶ The network is growing by itself

▶ Servers crash or lock up regularly

▶ Your backup system has gotten too small to accommodate all the data that needs to be backed up

▶ You or your server gets burned in effigy

. . . .

So your network is up and running and things are going well. Was there ever a more tempting invitation to the Lords of Chaos to come and shower trouble all over your head?

They say that nothing succeeds like success, and growing pains are the inevitable reward for doing your job well and pushing networking to boldly go where it's never gone before. Just as your pants legs got a little too short when you were outgrowing them as a youth, you can tell when the fabric of your network begins to stretch. This time, though, your ankles are showing because you're running around like a madman, putting out fires.

If you keep your eyes open for some of the symptoms we describe in this chapter, you can begin measuring for the next expansion before things start busting out at the seams.

Erratic Performance Begins

If everybody gets to work at about the same time and fires off his workstations right after that, and if the network falls to its knees immediately thereafter, it might be the case that you're nearing the limits of your server or network capacity.

If you have only one NIC in the server, you can get a boost by splitting the cable layout in two and attaching half the users to one of a pair of NICs instead.

If your server's getting short on running room, the cure is a little more drastic. Maybe it's time to buy a second server (and a second NetWare license, and more disk drives, NICs, and all the other stuff...) and split up your user community.

Living in Geological Time

If the server starts out slow and then speeds up, that's one thing. If it starts out slow and stays that way, that's entirely another. The most common cause of server slowdown is cramped RAM, and the first thing to try is adding some more.

As this book is being written, 16MB of RAM costs between $480 and $640 (depending on speed). This price is about as cheap a performance fix for NetWare as you're ever likely to find.

You Have More Users Than Slots

The temptation always exists to save money by scrimping on the number of users provided by a NetWare license. Even though it may start out that not everybody wants to be logged in all the time, one of the major consequences of a successful network is that this will change.

If you don't have enough slots — which is to say, if more users want to use the server than the number provided by the license — there's a pretty easy cure. You can upgrade a NetWare license from a lower number to a higher number of users at any time, for about 65 percent of the difference between what you paid and the cost of an entirely new license for the higher number. If you don't have to do a major hardware upgrade along with it, this approach can be downright reasonable.

Constant Messages Tell You That You're Out of Disk Space

Disk capacity is usually the first resource to be stretched on a server, and it's one of the easiest to fix. All it takes is money — to pay for more disk drives and possibly a controller to go along with them.

Because of the disk compression that 4.0 provides, try pricing a 4.0 upgrade rather than the disk purchase and buy whichever one is cheapest. Don't worry — the time always comes when you need more disk space, but you may want to wait and buy a whole new server with newer, faster disk technology rather than expand what you already have.

Excessive Traffic Exists on the Wire

If MONITOR or SYSCON or NetAdmin keeps telling you about excessive transmission errors on the network, it may be a sign that you're overloading the carrying capacity of the network medium. This means that you're asking the wire to carry more traffic than it can really handle.

This is another case in which you may want to think about adding more NICs to the server and splitting the wiring into subsets, to reduce the traffic that any particular cable segment has to handle. You can tell that this technique will help if your server utilization stays below 30 percent but the wire gets congested anyway.

You Get Dirty Looks in the Hallway

Users may not always tell you how they feel about network performance, but if you start catching lots of dirty looks, consider it a warning that things are getting out of hand. If you're smart, this situation will never happen to you.

Things You Never Knew Existed Show Up on the Network

When mystery printers, workstations, and more — even mystery servers — begin to show up on your network, it's a clear indication that more stuff is out there and that more resources are needed. The first thing you should do is up your capacity; the second thing is to go out and resurvey your network to get a new handle on it.

Regular Server Crashes or Lockups Occur

Server failures or hangs are a clear indication that all is not well in Mudville. If this problem begins to happen regularly — like maybe at the end of the month, when the folks in accounting are running the numbers, or at other peak load times — it's pretty clear that the server is being stretched beyond its capacity. Again, the rule is divide, duplicate, and conquer.

Your Backup Capacity Is Insufficient

One clear signal of growing pains is suddenly discovering that your backup system cannot accommodate all the hard disk storage on your server anymore. Think about upping your coverage — or think about the impact that staying up to hand-feed the existing system will have on your life. (You *do* have a life, don't you?)

A Server Gets Burned in Effigy on Your Desk

You must have missed those dirty looks in the hallway but — hey, now you know! Get cracking on increasing resources, or they may burn *you!*

Growing pains are good because they mean increasing demand for the services the network provides. If you can stay ahead of them and add capacity before things get out of hand, you will be a hero. Watch for the warning signs and head 'em off at the pass.

Appendix A
Glossary:
Everyday Explanations of
Techno-Babble Networking Terms

10BASE-2   On the Ethernet freak's sanity scale, falls somewhere between 10BASE-T and 10BASE-5. It doesn't weigh as heavily as 10BASE-T, has the same properties as 10BASE-5, and is what most Ethernet networks are composed of. Try it — if you don't mind the problems a bus topology can cause.

10BASE-5   The cabling that many old buildings have. Definitely antiquated Ethernet stuff, this type of cabling is rapidly being replaced by 10BASE-T. If you use 10BASE-5, expect derision from those in the know about LANs, but at least you will work with bulky, heavy, copper media.

10BASE-T   A cabling option for the Ethernet access method that uses unshielded twisted-pair (not telephone wire) to make its connections. This stuff is cheaper than Cheapernet (10BASE-2) and more versatile. If you want to be part of the "in crowd," this is the media to use.

abend   Means *ab*normal *end*. Simply, this process happens when the server crashes, and it sounds better than the unsavory term "abort."

access privileges   Similar to having the keys to the candy store, these privileges tell you what you can do with files or directories.

account   Have you ever opened a checking account at the bank? Certain restrictions exist and a variety of plans are available, all aimed at making you "accountable." The account each user has on the LAN works in the same way.

account manager   This guy is two rungs down the management ladder. Account managers have less authority to manage the LAN than do Supervisor or Workgroup managers, but definitely more authority than simple users do.

active hub   The carbo-loading, lowfat device of the networking access methods. An active hub is used only in ARCNET, and then only to congregate and distribute data to workstations on the LAN in a star or distributed-star topology.

adapter   Like the ignition switch on a car, the adapter gets workstations talking on the LAN. Placed in the workstation's bus, the adapter communicates requests between the workstation and the physical media that connects the LAN.

ADMIN   Like SUPERVISOR, ADMIN is the big kahuna of networking. ADMIN has access to the "root" of the directory tree. ADMIN can therefore create the network's initial directory structure and create administrators to manage segments of the directory tree called partitions. Or ADMIN can create a portion of the initial structure and let partition managers create the rest.

AppleTalk   The name of the set of protocols developed by Apple Computer, whose Macintosh was one of the first mass-market computers to offer built-in networking capabilities. In most cases, where there's a Mac, there's also AppleTalk.

applications   You cannot have one application without the other. Networks need applications like you need air to breathe. Being without applications is similar to having a car with nowhere to go. Word processing programs, spreadsheets, and e-mail are examples of applications.

archiving   The process of removing old files from the server so that there's room for vibrant and fresh new files. If you ever want any of the old dogs back, you unarchive them. Archive media can be CD-ROM, WORM, or — simply — tape.

ARCNET   The economy car of network access methods, ARCNET transmits data at 2.5 Mbps. Like token ring, ARCNET uses a token to make sure that each workstation gets its fair share.

attach   What you do to connect to a server other than the one you are logged in to.

attributes   The characteristics that define what users can do to the files and directories managed by NetWare. Attributes vary by user or group and affect whether a file can be copied, deleted, executed, modified, and so on.

AUDIT   Available only at the DOS prompt in NetWare Lite. In order to work, auditing must be turned on in the NET menus. This command sends the characters following the command to a special file, called an audit file, that keeps track of network activity. The AUDIT command is used primarily in batch files to make note of network operations.

AUI   The AUI (for *a*ttachment *u*nit *i*nterface) applies to Ethernet NICs. It is the connector that lets the card be cross-wired with a different media such as unshielded twisted-pair or thin Ethernet.

AUTOEXEC.BAT   The file that contains the commands which enable you to start your computer in the manner you want. You load the NIC driver in this file, and you can put the LOGIN command in it.

AUTOEXEC.NCF   Like the AUTOEXEC.BAT file, this file is used to boot the server. It lets you load the server drivers and any NLMs the network operating system will use.

backbone   If your network gets a slipped disk, it's just as incapacitating as when it happens to your back. A network backbone connects file servers in a single, unified internetwork.

back door   The secret entrance that network administrators use to get into the network in case something happens to the SUPERVISOR account.

backup   This term has nothing to do with raising your hackles, but it can cause you to do so. Refers to the procedure you should perform on your LAN every night: Save the files on the network to some form of off-line storage.

bad sector   An area on a hard disk that for some reason doesn't play back what's recorded. It might be the result of a manufacturing defect, damage to the drive's platters during shipment, or the wrong phase of the moon. The fact is, that area cannot be used. By marking bad sectors in the drive's manufacturing process, manufacturers now save you the time spent having to find them yourself. It may not sound like much, but Novell's disk-analysis program, called COMPSURF, has been known to take three or four days to finish.

base I/O address   Many devices have an I/O address that identifies them to the system, just as your address lets you get junk mail. See also *I/O address*.

baseline   Gives you a snapshot of the network to establish what normal activity patterns look like. It involves capturing statistics that describe how the network is being used throughout the course of a normal working day.

base memory   Like the IRQs and DMA, the base memory setting on an NIC must be unique. You have to watch for potential address conflicts and steer around them, and you will typically use jumpers to set the base memory address. Common settings for network cards include C000h, D000h, and D800h.

bindery   A database which NetWare v2.*x* and v3.*x* use that contains information about the users, groups, and other devices on the LAN, such as printers. Like some people and their Day-Timers, if they lose them, they just cannot cope.

BNC   The BNC connector, which has a great deal of weird lore behind it, is simply the type of connector that thin Ethernet networks use to attach the media to the NIC.

boot   What you do to your workstation when you turn it on or to the server when you load SERVER.EXE.

buffer space   NICs contain their own RAM to provide working space for information coming on and off the network. Called buffer space because it provides room for incoming and outgoing data to be stored.

bus   A network topology type in which all computers are attached to a single, shared cable. A bus topology is most commonly used for Ethernet networks or other contention-based networking schemes.

CAPTURE   A NetWare print utility that redirects local printer ports to network printers.

CD-ROM   A device similar to the one at home that plays Sinead O'Connor, but it's less inflammatory. It just stores data you think is important enough to save.

cache   Squirrels cache nuts so that they can eat them in the winter. Like the expansive pouches in a squirrel's mouth, NetWare stores data in caches so that it can get to it quickly later. Ick!

client   A desktop machine is called a client on the network, or simply a client. Calling it a desktop focuses on its role in supporting an individual, who typically is working at a desk; calling it a client focuses on its connectedness to the network. Whatever you call it, it's still the same thing: the machine you sit in front of when you're working.

coaxial cable   A two-element cable, with a center conductor wrapped by an insulator, which is wrapped by an outer conductor that is typically a wire braid covered by still more insulation. Coaxial cable (or coax, as it prefers to be known) is used for cable TV. Even if you don't think that you know what it is, you probably can relate to cable TV.

compression A mathematical technique for analyzing computer files to squeeze them down to a smaller size. A feature of most backup systems, compression is also available in NetWare 4.0, which can compress files stored on the file server. According to Novell, this kind of file compression can result in an increase in storage capacity that is better than two to one.

COMPSURF A Novell disk-analysis program that takes an unbelievably long time to complete its job. For more information about what it does, see *bad sector*.

communications Communications establish the rules for the way computers talk to each other or what things mean.

concentrator Applies directly to Ethernet, where it concentrates a number of workstations so that they share the same path to the file server. A concentrator is typically composed of 8 or 12 ports into which workstations attach along their own media segments.

CONFIG.SYS See your DOS manual for an explanation (this is a NetWare book).

connections Include the physical pieces of gear needed to hook up a computer to the network and the wires or other materials — known as the networking medium — used to carry messages from one computer to another or among multiple computers.

connection number When a device logs in to the file server, it is given a connection number, which is then used to identify that device's ongoing network session, as a way of directing replies back to satisfy its requests for network services.

console The monitor attached to the file server. You can access the console remotely with RCONSOLE or across a modem line with ACONSOLE. Either way, you get to it,

and if you're the only SUPERVISOR, no one else can. Special NetWare commands called console commands are run from the server keyboard.

console operator This dude has the authority to use the file server console.

conventional memory The memory below 640K. Normally, your LAN drivers are loaded in this space if you have room.

crash See *abend,* not the Highway Patrol.

DAT Stands for *d*igital *a*udio *t*ape; a special kind of 4mm-wide recording tape used in some computer backup systems. **Note:** Even though they're the same format and size, computer backup tape is usually quite different from audio recording tape. This means that you should not use an audiotape to back up your network. (Even though you can use a computer tape to record Bon Jovi, computer-grade tape costs so much more than audio-grade, you probably can't afford it.)

dedicated server A PC you cannot use to type a letter, play a computer game, or run any programs directly on the keyboard and monitor. In other words, a PC at which you cannot sit down and perform useful work directly. Most network operating systems require their servers to be dedicated PCs. NetWare 3.11 and 4.0 require dedicated servers. Under NetWare 2.2, a dedicated server is optional but questionable — among the cognoscenti, it's definitely not recommended.

default drive The drive in which you are placed when you log in to the network. The drive letter most commonly used for the login drive is F:, and it probably maps to something like SERVER\SYS:\USERS\HORACE — that is, if your name is Horace (although the server's name is probably not SERVER).

default server If the default drive is the one you log in to, what do you think the default server is? If your file server is the only file server on the LAN, it is also the default server. More tough questions to come.

directory Similar to the Yellow Pages. Even though directories are not alphabetical, they organize the files on a file server volume. Not to be confused with the NetWare Directory maintained by NetWare Directory Services on 4.x-numbered versions of NetWare.

directory entry Every file on the system has a directory entry. If your system gets clobbered, NetWare uses the Directory Entry Table to reconstruct it.

disk duplexing Not only mirrors the drives but also provides the capability to use totally backed up and redundant disk controllers. Disk controllers are the adapter cards that make the drive go round. With disk duplexing, you have redundancy of most of the critical moving parts inside your server. We always use disk duplexing and strongly suggest that you do too, whenever your budget permits. Duplexing beats having spare controllers and hard drives in stock because it doesn't require you to bring the server down immediately to make repairs. You have the luxury of postponing repairs until a more convenient time for both you and your users.

disk mirroring A process in which you can install duplicate hard drives, one active and one backup, which NetWare then writes to simultaneously. If a crash or other problem occurs on the active drive, NetWare automatically begins to use the backup drive and notifies you of the switch.

disk subsystem A fancy name for some extra storage on your file server.

distributed-star A topology that looks like a cross between a bus and a star. It's used by ARCNET.

DMA DMA (*d*irect *m*emory *a*ddressing) works by matching up two areas of memory, one on the computer and the other on the NIC. Writing to the memory area on the computer automatically causes that data to get copied to the NIC, and vice versa. To set a DMA address means to find an unoccupied DMA memory block to assign to your NIC.

drive mapping When you map a drive, you give the system instructions so that you can find it fast. Most users have mappings to their default directories, to their MAIL directories, and to the PUBLIC directory.

driver The guy behind the wheel of a LAN adapter.

EISA A type of PC bus with a 32-bit wheelbase — er, make that data path. (We're writing a car-repair manual on the side.)

Ethernet Everyone's all-time favorite network-access method.

EVERYONE A group created automatically when NetWare is installed. EVERYONE is a good catch-all group in which you can put "everyone" who should have the same access to all the same applications.

FAT An abbreviation for *f*ile *a*llocation *t*able; a list of all the pieces of disk storage space that make up a file, for each and every file on the NetWare server. For what it's worth, DOS also uses a FAT-based file system, but it's considerably less sophisticated and powerful than NetWare's.

FDDI The Fiber Distributed Data Interface, a 100-Mbps network-access method. It's very fast, but very expensive, so you probably won't see it on your desktop any time soon.

fiber-optic cable   This type of cable is built around conductive elements that move light, not electricity. For most fiber-optic cables, the conductive element is most likely a form of special glass fiber rather than copper or some other conductive metal. Even though plastic-based fiber-optic cable is available, it's not as light-conductive as glass and cannot cover the long distances that glass can. The beauty of fiber-optic cable is that it's immune to electronic and magnetic interference and has tons more bandwidth than do most electrical cable types.

FILER   FILER is NetWare's built-in file- and directory-management tool, available to both end users and administrators. You can use it to move, delete, or rename files and directories, to review attributes and rights, and to navigate around the file structures on NetWare servers.

file server   The device on a network that services requests from the workstations.

file system   The way in which the network operating system handles and stores files.

FLAG or FLAGDIR   FLAGDIR does for directories what FLAG does for files: lets their owners change access and trustee rights for particular files and directories without having to change inherited rights. You use this command to make a single file available to other users, for example, without giving access to all files or directories in any portion of your directory structure.

FTP   The TCP/IP protocol suite includes a file-transfer program named FTP (for File Transfer Protocol), which can copy files between any two TCP/IP-equipped computers.

gateway   An electronic or software device that connects two or more dissimilar computer systems. For example, a NetWare-to-IBM-mainframe gateway takes the IPX from one side of the gateway and translates it to the SNA protocol required for some IBM mainframe communications. Gateways are becoming more and more common as vendors figure out how to make this computer talk to that computer.

grandfather-father-son   This term does have something to do with inheritance. In GFS, a tape-rotation method for network backup, 20 tapes are used. Four of those tapes are used to back up daily work (Monday through Thursday). Three tapes back up work done on the first three Fridays of the month. The fourth week, you use one of the 13 "grandfathers" (monthly tapes). There are 13 four-week intervals in the year, which keeps tapes circulating regularly and ensures that none of them gets too much wear.

GUEST   You know what this term means — you have to be polite and follow the rules because your visit to the network is only temporary.

HCSS   Stands for High-Capacity Storage System. Part of NetWare 4.*x*, HCSS lets NetWare administrators "migrate" less frequently accessed data from a server's hard drive to some kind of alternative storage medium, typically a rewritable magneto-optical drive. Because these types of media are removable and have large capacities but can retrieve data nearly as fast as conventional disk drives, we call this type of storage "near-line." By contrast, the server hard drives contain on-line files that are available almost instantly. When a user requests a file that is stored on the near-line system, it first must be copied back from that system to the server's hard drive before it can be accessed (a "reverse migration" process). Like file compression, the least active server files can be migrated automatically to optical disk according to a selectable "age" threshold, based on the date of most recent access.

HELP What you call for when you cannot find the explanation in this book. It's also a NetWare Lite command which displays the built-in text that explains the syntax of each of the Lite commands.

INFO A NetWare Lite command that displays information about servers and clients.

intruder Anyone trying to break in to the LAN, no matter what his intentions. An intruder may be your boss who's trying to break in to your directories to read your latest invective against him, or someone from outside who's trying to steal company secrets. Most of the time, these people are just plain stupid — in NetWare, there's usually a way to catch them.

intruder detection The series of measures you can put in place by way of SYSCON that let you find the people who are trying to break into the LANs or put their paws on information to which they don't have access.

I/O address Every card in a system has its own I/O address, where certain addresses are reserved for some interfaces, especially video cards. NICs aren't quite that picky and can typically get an I/O port address assigned from a reserved range of addresses. An I/O port gets set up to let the computer read from or write to memory that belongs to an interface. When an interrupt gets signaled, it tells the computer to read from the I/O port address, indicating incoming data. When the computer wants to send data, it signals the NIC to get ready to receive, and it writes to that address.

IP Called the Internet Protocol in the TCP/IP protocol suite, IP does what IPX does in NetWare — it sets up the mechanism for transferring data across the network.

IPX NetWare's transport protocol.

IPX.COM The file *is* IPX.

ISA A bus of the 16-bit kind used in AT-class computers.

ISO/OSI Not a cruel technician's idea of a nifty palindrome — it stands for the International Standards Organization's Open Systems Interconnect family of networking protocols. Although it was highly touted as the successor to TCP/IP and the next big "networking thing," OSI has yet to live up to its promise. Because most governments — including Uncle Sam — require systems to be OSI-compliant, a good bit of it is still out there in industry, government, business, and academia. Like TCP/IP, ISO/OSI is available for a broad range of systems, from PCs to supercomputers.

LAN A *local area network*. See also *network*.

LAN driver Like gas to a car, the LAN driver supplies the get-up-and-go and the brains for the NIC.

LARCHIVE A DOS command-line backup utility that backs up network drives to local drives or disks.

LRESTORE LARCHIVE is a DOS command-line backup utility that restores data on local drives or disks to network drives that were backed up with the LARCHIVE command.

loopback test Often a part of a vendor's board diagnostics. Running a loopback test tells an NIC to talk to itself to see whether it's working. From an electronic standpoint, this test exercises circuitry on the card all the way up to the actual network medium interface to the login.

LOGIN The LOGIN command, well, logs you in.

login script A file that can exist either individually for each user or that can serve all users. It contains commands that control the way a user views her desktop. Users can create and edit their own login scripts. Only the supervisor can create and edit the System Login script.

log out What you do when you check out from the LAN.

LOGOUT The logout command orders your breakfast and a newspaper from room service. Oops! Sorry, that's the CHECKOUT command. Actually, LOGOUT just logs you out of the network.

media filter Used with the token-ring access method to change the type of media used from Type 1 (shielded twisted-pair) to Type 3 (unshielded twisted-pair) or vice versa.

Micro Channel Another 32-bit bus used most commonly in IBM PS/2s and IBM-controlled workplaces.

MSD.EXE Microsoft includes with Windows a peachy utility called the Microsoft Diagnostics (also called MSD.EXE, which gets installed in the root Windows directory). If you run this utility from DOS, it tells you all kinds of useful things about your PC's configuration that will steer you toward the clear spots needed to install an NIC. Plenty of third-party configuration-management tools can do the same thing too.

name space Each time you want to add a different type of machine, such as a Macintosh, an OS/2-based machine, or a UNIX-based machine, you have to provide for file compatibility with NetWare. You do this through name spaces loaded on the file server as NLMs that regulate the cross-network conversion that has to take place.

NARCHIVE A NetWare command-line backup utility that backs up network drives to other network drives.

NCP See *NetWare Core Protocol.*

NDLIST A NetWare Lite command that displays a list of available network directories.

NET The NetWare Lite NET command is used for all supervisory actions in NetWare Lite. NET lets you change passwords, set up printers, and define and delete users.

NetBEUI Stands for *NetBIOS Extended User Interface* and was designed as a second-generation protocol especially to support NetBIOS-based communications. You can call NetBIOS and NetBEUI a matched set — that's what Microsoft and IBM use for their networking products.

NetBIOS Stands for *Networked Basic Input-Output System* and was designed by IBM as a networked extension to PC BIOS. NetBIOS is a higher-level protocol that runs on top of lots of lower-level protocols, including IPX and TCP/IP as well as others. Even though NetBIOS is pretty old, it's very easy to program with and consequently is used in lots of different networked applications on a broad range of computers and operating systems.

NetWare Core Protocol An NCP is the service protocol for NetWare. Virtually every service that NetWare can provide has an NCP used to let users send requests for that service and to start the process of delivering in response to that request. The services provided by the NetWare NCPs range from file transfer to directory services lookups.

NetWare Lite The opposite of NetWare Heavy. NetWare Lite is Novell's peer-to-peer LAN incarnation.

NetWare Loadable Module A program loaded at the file server. NLMs can be LAN drivers, backup applications, or utilities.

NetWire   Doves communicate by billing and cooing. NetWare geeks communicate with each other by way of NetWire, Novell's on-line service on CompuServe.

network   A collection of at least two computers linked together so that they can communicate with each other. Imagine — such a simple concept.

network interface card   The gear that hooks up a computer to a network and acts as an intermediary between the computer and the network is called the network interface. (For PCs, it typically comes in the form of an add-in board called a network interface card, or NIC).

network operating system   The network's main control program is called its operating system because it's the program that lets the network operate.

node   Any device on the network. It can be a workstation, a printer, or the file server.

nondedicated   Both NetWare v2.2 and NetWare Lite can use nondedicated machines as file servers. While you are running a program from your local hard drive, therefore, someone else can access a file or program on your hard drive from across the room by way of the network. Nondedicated means "ready to work whenever you are." It also means "as cheap as it gets."

A nondedicated server is a PC you use as both a client and a server.

Novell-certified   Novell's program that says "Yes, it undoubtedly works with NetWare." It costs money for a vendor to get its devices certified, but many vendors do it to keep their users happy. Neat, huh? Someone's watching out for you!

NPLIST   In NetWare Lite, this command displays a list of available network printers.

NRESTORE   A NetWare command-line backup utility that restores data from network drives that were originally backed up using the NARCHIVE command.

object   A directory map object enables the network administrator to define map commands that point to an object rather than to a specific directory on the server. If the path to that object ever changes, you have to update only the object definition, not all of your user's MAP commands.

ODI   The Open Data Link Interface specification. Novell prefers that you say "oh-dee-eye," not "Odie," like the dog in the Garfield comic strip. Originally, the specification's moniker was ODLI, but it sounded strange ("odd-ly") when you said it that way. ODI is a specification for writing LAN drivers that saves vendors from work and gives users a certain comfort level that their ODI drivers will work in a predictable way.

passive hub   The couch potato of network devices. Used in ARCNET as a device that joins segments, but it does not amplify the signals; it simply passes them along.

password   The LAN's equivalent to "open sesame." NetWare lets users have passwords that range in length from 1 to 127 alphanumeric characters. Passwords aren't mandatory, but you use them to log on to most networks. We don't recommend the use of overly long passwords (more than 12 to 15 characters is too difficult to remember).

peer to peer   A method of networking NetWare Lite uses to share local resources across the network. A server-based network requires all shared resources to reside on a centralized server. A peer-to-peer network gives everyone on the network the opportunity to share her local stuff with others on the network.

PRINT   This NetWare Lite command lets users print files directly to a network printer without capturing a local port.

print queue   NetWare uses print queues to store pending print jobs, in the form of print-image files, while they wait their turn to be printed. The queue is the mechanism that handles requests for printing from users and that supplies the print-image files to the printer in the proper order. See also *queue.*

print server   The device or software that controls network printing and services printing requests.

protocol   In diplomacy, refers to the rules for behavior that let representatives from sovereign governments communicate with each other in a way calculated to keep things peaceful, or at least under control. For that reason, diplomats refer to heated screaming matches as "frank and earnest discussions" or to insoluble disagreements as "exploratory dialogue." Double-talk aside, the word *protocol* captures the flavor of what these sets of rules have to do for networks. Most networking protocols consist of a named collection of specific message formats and rules for interaction rather than a single set of formats and rules. For this reason, protocols are also called protocol suites, not because they like to lounge around on matched collections of furniture, but because they travel in packs.

QIC   Stands for Quarter-Inch Cartridge, a common format for backup tapes.

queue   The British word for *line.* When you share a printer, NetWare creates a queue to store print jobs waiting for that printer. Each printer has its own print queue. As the server sends print jobs to the printer, Lite lines them up in a manner similar to a queue forming outside a British privy. Jobs print in the order in which the queue receives them.

This system means that the printer doesn't have to be available at the time you ask to print something. The print queues accept any and all print requests as they occur and then lines up all print jobs for printing as the printer becomes available.

RECEIVE   This NetWare Lite command enables your client to receive messages from other network users.

redirector   A piece of software that looks at each request for service from a user. If the request can be satisfied locally, it passes that request on to the local PC's operating system for it to be handled. If it cannot be handled locally, the request is assumed to be directed to the network, and the redirector then passes the request on to a service provider (also known as a server) on the network. Using a redirector is a pretty common way to handle network access from a desktop.

ring   Token ring uses the ring or star-wired ring topology. Real rings seldom get built because they're too sensitive to failure, but the idea of a ring often gets implemented over a bus or a star, or in the form of a redundant ring with multiple cables and pathways to improve the odds that it will keep running. It sounds strange, but mapping a ring onto a star or a bus is the way some networking technologies work.

RIP   The Routing Information Protocol is a broadcast protocol (it's addressed to everyone who's listening on a network) that gets used one time per minute by every IPX router on a network to declare what it knows about how to get around on the network. (For NetWare 3.11 or higher, any server can be a router.) Routers exchange RIP packets to keep the common knowledge of how a collection of individual networks — called an internetwork — is laid out. This information is used to move packets around, which is why the servers that do it are called routers.

SAP   Service Advertisement Protocols advertise the services that are available on the network. SAP is a broadcast protocol, and each server sends out its collection of SAPs one time per minute in versions of NetWare before 4.0. NetWare version 4.0 and higher use directory services to deliver and advertise services, so the only services that have to be advertised in that environment are the directory services themselves.

SBACKUP   SBACKUP works with both NetWare 4.0 and 3.11. As a server-based backup system, it can handle DOS, Macintosh, OS/2, and NFS files on workstations or on the server's hard disk. SBACKUP works with a NetWare Loadable Module (NLM) called the TSA.NLM to see that data on a "target" is backed up. The target can be another file server or workstation on the LAN. In case you haven't guessed already, SBACKUP beats the pants off NBACKUP. To run the program, the SUPERVISOR starts SBACKUP from the file server console.

SCSI   SCSI, pronounced "scuzzy," isn't an alternative form of grunge. It's an interface in the computer to which you can attach almost anything, but mostly you attach disk drives.

search drive   Not a charity drive for misplaced things, but rather a drive mapping you set so that you can find files from any drive you are in. Typically, users have search drives mapped to the PUBLIC directory and to any other directories in which applications might be stored. That way, they're always able to run their applications and the NetWare commands and utilities, no matter what their current default drive.

security-equivalent   Means that one account has the same trustee and access rights as another. Although users can confer security-equivalence on each other, this technique is most commonly used as a way for the SUPERVISOR to temporarily turn another account into a SUPERVISOR-equivalent. This capability lets other users function as SUPERVISOR without letting them learn the supervisor's password.

SEND   This command sends the included text to a user or to everyone on your network. Use the ALL option with discretion because it does what it says — sends it to everyone.

server   You don't leave tips for servers. They serve lowfat, no-calorie requests to clients, and the only weight they cause you to gain is the amount of information you save in your user directory. Sometimes, when it gets to be too much, you must purge the information from the server.

SERVER.EXE   Everything has to start from somewhere. The SERVER.EXE file loads the network operating system software on the file server. Naturally.

SETPASS   Enables you to set a new password for yourself but for no one else.

SFT III   This product is Novell's latest development in server redundancy (Novell calls it fault tolerance). SFT III is a copy of version 3.11 that mirrors the entire server PC to another PC. Server mirroring gives you the ultimate backup plan — if any hardware component in the active server fails, the other machine automatically takes over without any interruption of service. A dedicated network connects the two servers, usually over fiber-optics, and keeps both servers in sync. Granted, this solution can be expensive but is well worth the cost for truly mission-critical environments.

shell   Sometimes you use this type of special program so that you can get the network going and run the programs you're really interested in using. The shell handles all service requests and, rather than pass along things that aren't local to the network, the way a redirector does, it separates what's networked from what's not and hands things off accordingly. It too is a pretty common way to handle network access from a desktop.

shielded twisted-pair   Not an armored couple into heavy-metal music, but rather a type of twisted-pair cable used in Ethernet networks that has a cladding around the conductive copper core.

SMS   Stands for Storage Management Services, which is Novell's backup system interface. SMS automatically handles all the details that make up the NetWare file system, including name spaces, so that Novell can change its file system; yet SMS hides the impact so that SMS-compliant backup systems can keep right on working. For this reason, we recommend that you consider purchasing only those NetWare backup systems that are SMS-compliant.

SNA   Systems Network Architecture is IBM's basic protocol suite. Where there's a mainframe or an AS/400, you also typically find SNA. Because SNA was one of the pioneering protocols, companies that invested heavily in mainframe technology in the 1960s and 1970s also invested in building large-scale SNA networks.

SPX   A guaranteed-delivery protocol that NetWare occasionally uses.

star   A type of networking topology; consists of separate wires that run from a central point (called a hub 'cause it's in the middle) to devices — typically, computers — on the other end of each wire.

STARTUP.NCF   This file resides on the file server and is integral to bringing up the file server.

station   Short for workstation.

SUPERVISOR   The big kahuna. This guy is in charge.

SYS:LOGIN   The directory you use to log in to the network.

SYS:MAIL   The directory that serves the same purpose as the circular file in your office. Mail is stored here after it's sent. Even though most of the stuff in this directory is ancient history, don't delete it — it's where your login script is kept.

SYS:PUBLIC   The directory in NetWare Heavy that contains all the programs which are "public" (any user can get his hands on it).

SYS:SYSTEM   The directory in which the server stores files necessary for server upkeep and administration as well as some utilities intended for use by only the network supervisor and supervisor equivalents.

sysop   An abbreviation for *system operator*, who is typically the person responsible for coordinating traffic and for answering questions on an on-line bulletin-board or electronic information system. The ladies and gentleman who field NetWare questions on CompuServe's Novell-related forums — known collectively as NetWire — are the people we mean when we talk about sysops in this book.

system administrator   The big kahuna in NetWare. This guy wins and controls all the marbles, but he's also responsible for keeping the servers and the network up and running.

T-connector   Not a coffee-and-tea exchange — this device lets you connect a BNC connector to the media for a workstation in the middle of an Ethernet bus.

TCP/IP   The real name of this protocol suite is the Transmission Control Protocol and the Internet Protocol. Because the Internet is composed of more than 30,000 sites worldwide and TCP/IP claims more than 15 million users, it's another major player in the protocol world. TCP/IP has deep roots in the UNIX community and is also widely used to link computers of different kinds.

TELNET   The name of a standard TCP/IP network service, which lets one computer pretend that it's a terminal attached to another computer over the network. Telnet is the way TCP/IP users typically work on other computers over the network, when they're not working directly on their own machines.

thick Ethernet   See *10BASE-5*.

thin Ethernet   See *10BASE-2*.

throughput   A measure of the speed of a network-access method, typically stated in bps (bits per second).

TIME   This NetWare Lite command doesn't mean what you think that it does, and it isn't the same as the DOS TIME command. The TIME command synchronizes the internal clock in your PC with the clock in the network server. Why didn't Novell call it TIMESYNC?

token   Similar to a marker on a poker table, it indicates who has the deal or which workstation can send data on a token ring, ARCNET, or FDDI network.

token ring   Another one of the access methods, token ring is a networking technology that tells a workstation when it can send data over the network, by using a circulating token to grant permission. Token ring communicates at either 4 Mbps or 16 Mbps.

topology   The lay of the LAN, or how workstations are laid out and connected with the file server by way of the media. See also *bus, star,* and *ring* if you want the details.

transaction tracking   Databases use transaction tracking in NetWare to guarantee the integrity of the data. If someone trips over the server's power cord, transaction tracking "rolls back" individual transactions to the state they were in before the system crash occurred.

transceiver   Using a transceiver is similar to pouring water from a pitcher into a soda bottle. It enables you to connect a network adapter for one type of media to another type of media. Commonly, you use a transceiver in Ethernet to translate from thin Ethernet to unshielded twisted-pair. In token ring, a media filter replaces the transceiver.

twisted-pair   TP comes in two flavors: shielded and unshielded. It sometimes is abbreviated as STP for shielded twisted-pair and UTP for unshielded twisted-pair. The difference between the two, of course, is that one has a foil or wire braid wrap around the individual wires that are twisted around each other in pairs, and the other does not.

ULIST   Displays a list of all users logged in to NetWare Lite; resembles USERLIST in NetWare Heavy.

unshielded twisted-pair   Same as twisted-pair except that it has no shielding element between the conducting stands and the outer insulator.

UPS   Contains a rechargeable battery that provides your server with a backup power source in case its A/C power fails. The UPS senses that A/C power has gone away, and it kicks in automatically to supply power to your server on a few milliseconds' notice.

user You guessed it — this is you. It could be someone else too, but you get the idea.

user account Keeps you in control or lets you get in trouble on your LAN, depending on whether the supervisor has it in for you.

username This is you, or you, or you. It's your name on the system. Ours are DCONNOR and ETITTEL. See also *user*.

workstation Where you sit whether you're just a lowly user or the big cheese.

WORM This thing isn't segmented, long, narrow, and slimy. It stands for *w*rite *o*nce, *r*ead *m*any, and describes a type of optical-storage technology.

volume NetWare divides the file server disks into areas called *volumes*, which are logical, or nonphysical, divisions of hard disk space.

XNS NetWare's protocols are derived from a similar protocol set developed at Xerox, called the Xerox Networking System and abbreviated as XNS. There are lots of XNS-derived protocols out there in the networking world, but IPX/SPX is the most prevalent.

Appendix B

Screaming for Help: When and How to Get It

*W*hen you need help with the network or the software running on it, you can get it if you know the right steps to take. Getting the support that most vendors supply shouldn't be like pulling teeth — if you know how to ask for and get the answers you need, it can be considerably more pleasant.

This appendix focuses on how best to interact with technical-support organizations. It tells you how to be effective when you work with these groups, from the standpoint of how to prepare to meet their needs and how to work with them to help them answer your questions. It also helps you to understand just what kind of help you can expect to get from these groups and how to handle the situation if your expectations aren't met.

Building a List and Checking It Twice

When you are organizing any network or the applications running on it, keep a list of the equipment you own (build a map and configuration database, as outlined in Chapter 6). You can do this with a variety of inventory packages, but often, just plain paper and pencil are enough. It's a boring, repetitive task, but it's critically important. It's similar to trying to collect insurance after your house burns down, without having a list of what was in it.

Record each of the network adapters on your LAN, the type of file server you use, information about each workstation, and which applications each user is running.

The following list shows the equipment and software you should inventory:

- ✔ File server
- ✔ Workstations
- ✔ Software running on each workstation
- ✔ Tape-backup unit
- ✔ Disk storage

Know Your Vital Stats

For your file server, you have to know its vital statistics. You have to know how much RAM it has, how much disk space, the type of network adapters it contains, which type of disk controller it uses, and which type of display. Record this information for your file server. Fill in the following blanks and save the information somewhere where you can find it when you need it.

File server

File server manufacturer: _____

File server model: _____

Processor (286, 386, 486)

Processor speed (12 MHz, 33 MHz, 50 MHz): _

Bus type (ISA, EISA, MCA): _____

Type of disk controller
(SCSI, IDE, MFM): _____

Drive manufacturer: _____

Drive model: _____

Drive capacity (in megabytes): _____

Disk drives: _____

Other stuff: _____

_____

Display

Display manufacturer: _____

Display type (monochrome, CGA, VGA,
SVGA): _____

Display resolution: _____

Interrupt set at: _____

Storage and RAM

Base memory address: _____

Amount of RAM (in megabytes): _____

Amount of disk storage (in megabytes):

_____

Network adapter

Network adapter manufacturer: _____

Type of adapter (Ethernet, token ring, and so
on): _____

Model number: _____

Interrupt set at: _____

DMA set at: _____

Speed set at (if token ring): _____

Base memory address: _____

Network adapter (for more than one)

Network adapter manufacturer: _____

Type of adapter (Ethernet, token ring, and so
on): _____

Model number: _____

Interrupt set at: _____

DMA set at: _____

Speed set at (if token ring): _____

Base memory address: _____

_____

Network adapter (for more than two)

Network adapter manufacturer: _____

Type of adapter (Ethernet, token ring, and so
on): _____

Model number: _____

Interrupt set at: _____

DMA set at: _____

Speed set at (if token ring): _____

Base memory address: _____

_____

Tape backup manufacturer: _____

Tape backup model: _____

Tape backup type (QIC, DAT, 8mm): _____

Tape backup capacity: _____

Location of off-site storage: _____

Location of on-site storage: _____

_____

Version of DOS: _____

Version of NetWare: _____

_____

Applications _____

Version _____

_____

Applications _____

Version _____

_____

Applications _____

Version _____

_____

NLMs loaded _____

Other stuff _____

Other stuff _____

Now you have to record the same kind of record for each workstation on the LAN. While you're at it, add to the list the contents of the workstation's AUTOEXEC.BAT and CONFIG.SYS files. Are you getting tired yet?

After you finish these lists, you will want to know more about the software configuration of the LAN. You need a listing of your server's AUTOEXEC.NCF and STARTUP.NCF files, and you have to put together lists of the following items too:

✔ Usernames on the LAN and their network addresses

✔ Groups on the LAN

✔ File and directory attributes and rights for each user and group

✔ Directory structure of the file server

✔ Drive mappings

✔ System login script

What to Write Down Before Making the Call

When you encounter a problem, document what happened before the problem occurred. List any changes you have made to files or any hardware changes you have made. Write down any error messages you have received. Know what you were doing when the problem occurred. Trust us: When you call the technical-support number, you will be asked for this information.

Talk the Talk, Walk the Walk

Now that you have all this information written down, when something goes wrong, you're ready to combat the vendor's technical-support line. When you make the call, have your ammunition ready, but be prepared for one of four things to happen:

✔ You are told that it is an operator error. "Operator error" is a catch-all term technical-support people use when they don't want to deal with the question or when they don't have the answer.

✔ You are told that no one in anyone's lifetime has ever done anything this stupid. Hold your ground. Someone has done this before, and it's the responsibility of the technical-support person to help you out of it.

✔ A nice person on the telephone helps you work through the problem.

✔ The person you talk to doesn't have the answer to the problem but has someone else get back to you to solve the problem.

Be prepared to answer all the technical-support person's questions, no matter how stupid they may sound. Tech-support people don't read minds. If they did, they would make big bucks.

Before you call, gather your lists together. Better yet, get close to the PC that is having problems so that you can lead the person through the problem by telling him about error messages you have received, by trying to duplicate the problem, for example.

Escalation: It's Not Just for Department Stores

If you get someone on the phone who doesn't want to help, act just as you do when you have a problem with your electric bill. Ask to speak to a supervisor — in the lingo of the business, this is called escalating the call. After all, you paid good money for the product and you should get satisfaction.

The same rule applies to technical-support people who don't call you back in a timely manner — 24 hours after your call should be the absolute drop-dead time for a return call. Call again and leave a message. Record the time you first called. Record how long it took someone to call you back and keep good records. This is one time when a little documentation can come in handy.

Some vendors are starting to offer technical support 24 hours a day, seven days a week. When you buy products, find out about the technical-support line. It may be worth it to pay a little more initially in order to have good support afterward.

Twenty-four-hour support is critical for network hardware. No one in her right mind takes down the LAN during working hours to insert a new network adapter in the server. Think about it. If you're required to miss dinner, the person on the other end of the phone should be expected to miss it too.

800-NETWARE and 900-SUPPORT

We just hate companies with cute phone numbers, but at least we remember them — they're just a pain to dial. These two numbers are for Novell's customer service department and its 900 Support (that's their name, too). Novell can help you with questions about NetWare directly, but you must be ready with a credit-card number or a support contract; 900 Support takes questions of any kind. Both cost a pretty penny, so have your checkbook handy.

One-Stop Shopping: the TSA

In 1992, Novell organized the Technical Support Alliance to provide better support for users. The TSA, a group of 42 vendors, cross-train each other in the use of their products. When you call a TSA member about a problem that may involve several vendors' products, you can get an answer from that vendor with just one phone call. Sounds neat, huh?

It's Good to Take Notes

One of the best sources for deciphering what the NetWare manuals don't tell you is Novell's *NetWare Application Notes*. These notes provide in-depth information about a variety of topics for computer geeks who are heavily into NetWare. Call 800-NETWARE to find out more information about them. Have your checkbook ready, too. These notes cost about $150 a year for a subscription, but they're really worth it.

Lookee Louie, I'm with NUI

If you're really getting into this NetWare stuff, look into joining a NetWare user group. Organized under NetWare User's International, a group affiliated with Novell, you can find out about a group in your area by calling the universal NetWare number, 800-NETWARE.

User groups meet monthly and may have subgroups on different topics for users who get into networking hot and heavy. Several NUI trade shows are also held each year in different parts of the country.

Let Your Fingers Do the Walking

Other places exist to get help when you're really out on a limb. One of these is NetWire, Novell's on-line information service on CompuServe, which we talk about later. Others are forums that vendors run on CompuServe.

Leaving these forums out of the list, many companies also operate their own bulletin board systems, on which you can leave questions or get copies of new adapter drivers, bug fixes, and other stuff.

Booking in the Fast Lane

Books that explain much of this stuff are also available, as are classes in which you learn more about NetWare than you ever wanted to know. Look in networking magazines for the NetWare training education centers in your city.

The Masters Program

Having gone through training classes, you may also decide that you want to be a Certified NetWare Administrator (CNA) or a Certified NetWare Engineer (CNE). If you're just a simple user on the LAN, neither of these certifications is for you. If you're responsible for the LAN, however, you should consider either one. The CNA covers the administration of the LAN and involves taking several courses and passing tests of your knowledge. The CNE is for people who not only will cope with the software (creating users, for example) but also work with the network hardware. It's for those types who consider NetWare system management a career. Strike that thought.

An Incredibly Concise Guide to CompuServe and NetWire

*O*ur goal in providing this appendix is not to tell you how to use CompuServe in general or NetWire in particular. Rather, we just want to tell you what NetWire is, what it's made up of, and why you might find it interesting.

This appendix focuses, therefore, on what's up on NetWire, how best to interact with it, and what kinds of things you can and cannot find up there. It tells you how to be effective when you work with NetWire, from the standpoint of knowing what to look for, which kinds of questions you can ask, and the answers you're likely to get. It also helps you to understand just what kind of help you can expect to get from the NetWire community and what to do if you can't get the help you need.

Welcome to CompuServe

The CompuServe Information Service (CIS) is an electronic information service that offers a selection of thousands of topics for your perusal.

CompuServe, a for-a-fee service, requires an individual account (called a membership number) with an accompanying password to be accessed. There are many ways to obtain trial access at no charge, but if you want to play on CompuServe, sooner or later you have to pay for the privilege. CompuServe charges a monthly membership fee, in addition to a fee for connection time. Some of the services available on CompuServe have additional charges as well. Be warned! It's easy to spend time — and money — on CompuServe.

Forums for conversation and investigation

When you access CompuServe, it's necessary to select an area of interest to focus your exploration of the information treasures available. On CompuServe, information is organized into forums. A *forum* is an area dedicated to a particular subject or a collection of related subjects, and each forum contains one or more of the following:

- **Message board:** Features electronic conversations organized by specific subjects into sections related to particular topics (Ethernet issues, for instance, are a topic, as are token-ring issues; in the Ethernet section, you would expect to find discussions of frame types, drivers for particular NICs, and the like). A given sequence of messages, chained together by a common subject or by replies to an original message, is called a *thread*. It's important to notice that threads may read like conversations but that messages in a thread can be separated from one another by hours or days. Following threads is a favorite pastime for those who spend time on CompuServe.

- **Conference room:** An electronic analog to the real thing, it brings individuals together to exchange ideas and information in real time. It's much like a conference telephone call except that, rather than talk to each other, the participants communicate by typing on their keyboards. Conference rooms are not for the faint of heart, and they can be frustrating for those with limited touch-typing skills.

- **File library:** A collection of files organized by subject that can be copied ("downloaded" is the CompuServe term) for further perusal and use. Examples of file types found in CompuServe libraries include archived collections of interesting threads, documents of all kinds, and a variety of software ranging from patches and fixes for programs to entire programs.

In all, many, many worlds of information are available on CompuServe, any or all of which can by themselves be a completely absorbing source of information, gossip, software, and activity. With all its elements taken together, CompuServe is a perfect example of what might be called an "electronic information warehouse."

Getting a CompuServe membership

You can obtain an account over the telephone or by writing to CompuServe and requesting a membership. For telephone inquiries, ask for Representative 200. Here are the numbers to use:

- Within the U.S. (except Ohio), including Alaska, Hawaii, Puerto Rico, and the American Virgin Islands, call toll free at 800-848-8199.

- Outside the U.S., in Canada, and in Ohio, call 614-457-8650.

Telephone hours are from 8 a.m. to 10 p.m. Eastern time Monday through Friday, and from noon to 5 p.m. on Saturday. Written inquiries for a CompuServe account should be directed to:

CompuServe, Inc.
Attn: Customer Service
P.O. Box 20212
5000 Arlington Centre Boulevard
Columbus, OH 43220
U.S.A.

Accessing CompuServe

To get access to CompuServe, you must equip your computer with a modem and attach that modem to a telephone line. You also need some kind of communications program, to let your computer "talk" to CompuServe by using the modem and to help you find your way around its on-line universe. Finally, you have to obtain a telephone number for CompuServe — most of them are local numbers, especially in the U.S. — that's appropriate for the type and speed of modem you're using.

Connection-time charges are based on how fast your modem is — faster modems cost more — but the higher charges are typically offset by even faster transfer speeds. If your CompuServe bill is $40 a month or higher, most high-speed modems will pay for themselves in six months or less based on the reductions in fees you realize by using one.

After you are connected to CompuServe, you enter your membership number and your password. First-time users should follow the instructions provided by your CompuServe representative or in the *CompuServe Starter Kit* that's available from CompuServe (for an additional fee). After you're logged in, getting to NetWire is easy. When you simply type **GO NETWIRE** from the CompuServe prompt, you are presented with a menu of additional choices for Novell and NetWare information.

What Is NetWire?

NetWire is a collection of CompuServe forums, all dedicated to networking topics and all focused on Novell products or related information. NetWire is a great alternative to using Novell's telephone hotline for technical support. Because of the large number of everyday users — NetWire is the busiest collection of forums on CompuServe — and the wide range of Novell products and related topics, Novell uses (at the time this overview was written) nine CompuServe forums, and it's growing all the time.

The benefits of using NetWire

The benefits of using NetWire are hard to overstate but easy to understand. First and foremost, there's the help that's available: NetWire is staffed by volunteer system operators (sysops), most of whom are not Novell employees, but all of whom are extremely knowledgeable about Novell and NetWare topics. The busiest sysop has set a record of 900 messages answered in one week; most sysops average at least four hours a day of connect time, when they upload and download information to their colleagues and to you — the curious and, sometimes, the desperate.

Together with other power users, the sysops and their colleagues are an invaluable source of information, help, and advice about networking topics. As a bonus, almost all questions are answered within 24 hours of being posted. You will want to log in at least once a day, in fact, when you are waiting for replies to questions. The *scroll rate,* the speed at which messages age and get deleted from the NetWire forums, is about two to three days, depending on message volume.

When technical problems cannot be solved by the sysops or other power users on NetWire, sysops can escalate these thornier issues directly to the Novell engineers responsible for dealing with those topics in Novell's Technical Support Division. This process uses the same channels that services Novell's hotline but does not incur the typical fees. Calling the hotline directly can cost upward of $100 per incident, or $20 for a Novell DOS incident, unless you are covered by some other preexisting arrangement. (Get out your credit cards, please!)

NetWire is also the place to go for the latest and greatest patches and fixes for NetWare and other Novell products. The libraries that contain the files available for downloading are uploaded daily and documented extensively in catalogs of information available on-line. These files include the most recent patches, fixes, drivers, and tips for tuning your NetWare server for maximum effect. Lots of third-party applications and utilities are available for your perusal, as well as a collection of *shareware* (software that can be downloaded for free and used for a trial period, but that must be paid for in order to be legitimately used).

NetWire is also the place where NetWare users of the world congregate. It puts you in touch with thousands of other users, most of whom are eager to share what they have learned — and the mistakes they have made — with others. Messages are posted in public forums so that all who access NetWire can see and add to the growing collection of information. As a side effect, NetWire is also the premier source of contacts for consulting, sales, and business opportunities for the NetWare community. If you need something that's NetWare-related, there's no better place to start looking than on NetWire.

Posting messages on NetWire

To request answers to your technical questions or get guidance about which resources are available from NetWire, simply choose the most appropriate section for the subject of your question. (To make this all-important decision, please consult the Forum/Section Directory that appears later in this appendix.)

The NetWire sysops request that you review the Forum/Section list carefully and that you post your questions in the most appropriate area. Good manners dictate posting a question only once. Even if you are asking about a topic that might legitimately appear in two sections, it's a waste of electronic space to post the same message a multiple number of times.

If you have a question about printing, for example, that involves a NetWare 3.12 Print Server, it's conceivable that the question could appear in NETW3X Section 1 (Printing) or in NOVB Section 3 (Printing). The fact is, it doesn't matter — the same people end up responding to the question no matter where you post it. If you're not sure, send a message to a sysop and ask for advice. Even though this process may take time, it probably will get you an answer faster than relying on the sysops to forward messages to each other before you get to the right source of information for the answer.

The NetWire forums

As of January 4, 1993, there were nine forums for NetWire, of which eight are publicly available. The ninth is a special forum, called NOVDEV, for software developers who are building applications by using Novell tools and development kits; this forum can be accessed only by requesting permission to join. If you're interested in joining NOVDEV, send a CompuServe e-mail message to user ID 76711,111 and state briefly why you want to get involved. (**Hint:** If you don't mention something about using Novell tools to develop code, the odds of being invited are not high!)

In the following sections, we present the remaining eight NetWire forums. The name of the subsection is the name of the forum, which is followed by a brief description of what you can find there. After that, we repeat the list of sections available. This setup should help you figure out where to look for information and to get help when you need it!

Folks who read the threads on CompuServe but who don't participate in the chatter themselves are called "lurkers." Even if you never graduate from lurking to expressing an opinion or answering a question, there's much to be learned by lurking in the right forums. Don't be afraid to lurk — or to learn!

NETW2X

The NETW2X forum is dedicated to NetWare 2.x versions, typically ranging from 2.12 to 2.2, with all points in between covered daily. If you're running a 2.x network, look here first for information and for help when you need it.

1. **Printing:** Information about printing, print servers, and print utilities

2. **NetWare Utilities:** Information about NetWare utilities and third-party programs

3. **Disk Drives/Cntrls:** Information about disk drivers and hard disk controllers

4. **Client/Shells:** Information about workstation client software, including protocol stacks, shells, and more

5. **LAN Driver/Cards:** Information about server drivers for NICs and about NICs themselves

14. **2.1x and Below/OS:** Look here if you're running a version of NetWare 2.x older than 2.2

15. **Operating System:** Information about the NetWare 2.2 operating system

NETW3X

This forum is dedicated to NetWare 3.x versions, typically ranging from 3.11 to 3.12, with all points between covered daily. If you're running a 3.x network, look here first for information and for help when you need it.

1. **Printing:** Information about printing, print servers, and print utilities

2. **NetWare Utilities:** Information about NetWare Utilities and third-party programs

3. **Disk Drives/Cntrls:** Information about disk drivers and hard disk controllers

4. **Client/Shells:** Information about workstation client software, including protocol stacks, shells, and more

5. **LAN Driver/Cards:** Information about server drivers for NICs and about NICs

14. **Operating System:** Information about the NetWare 3.x operating system

NDSG

The NDSG forum is dedicated to products from Novell's Desktop Systems Group, which include DR-DOS (now known as Novell-DOS), Multi-User DOS, Dataclub, NetWare Lite, and Personal NetWare.

1. **DRDOS/Applications**

2. **DRDOS/Disk**

3. **DRDOS/Memory**

4. **DRDOS/Utilities**

5. **Customer Service:** Direct contact with the Novell-DOS customer service group

6. Programming ?'s

7. Multi-User DOS

8. Dataclub

9. NetWare Lite

NOVA

The NOVA forum is dedicated to a variety of networking topics ranging from communications to wide-area networking (LAN/LAN Links) and dedicated also to a variety of Novell products ranging from ELS NetWare to Novell's LANalyzer for Windows. Read carefully — there may be something here for you.

1. **ELS NetWare**

2. **Async Communic'tns:** Dial-in and dial-out NetWare connections, remote access, and more

3. **IBM HostConnections:** NetWare for SAA, 3270 terminal emulation for NetWare, and more

4. **LAN/LAN Links:** WAN connectivity for NetWare and the NetWare Multiprotocol Router

5. **NetWare Macintosh**

6. **NetWare VMS**

7. **Portable NetWare:** NetWare for UNIX and other special OEM versions of NetWare for non-Intel computers

8. **NW NFS - TCP/IP:** NetWare for NFS, NetWare TCP/IP protocols, routing, and more

9. **CLOSED:** Means what it says!

10. **NW Support Encyclopedia:** Information and questions about Novell's CD-ROM-based support database (available by yearly subscription)

11. **LANalyzer/LANtern:** Information about Novell's network monitoring and protocol analyzer products

12. **Appnotes:** Information about Novell's Application Notes, a monthly technical publication

13. **UK Topics**

14. **CLOSED**

NOVB

The NOVB forum covers a wide range of server-specific topics, including backups, disk drives and controllers, networking technologies, and more. Look in this forum for workstation software information, and for information about using Windows and NetWare together.

1. **Server & Workstn**

2. **Backups**

3. **Printing**

4. **Disk Drives/Cntr'lrs**

5. **K-12 Networking:** Information for networkers in the primary education world

6. **Product Information:** Press releases, spec sheets, and other Novell product information, on-line

7. **CLOSED**

8. **Power Monitoring**

9. **Ethernet**

10. **ARCnet**

11. **Token Ring**

12. **Other LAN types**

13. **Cabling/Media**

14. **New Shells**

15. **MS-Windows**

NOVC

The NOVC forum covers an equally wide range of topics as does NOVB, but it includes topics related to third parties, such as Novell's resellers and dealers, and to general interests, such as NetWare education, software developers, and more. NOVC is the place to go to check out The Lighter Side, where the zany aspect of networking makes itself felt regularly and thoroughly.

1. **General Info/Misc:** If you're not sure where to post something, this is probably the place!

2. **Upgrades/Migration:** Moving from one version of NetWare to another? Check here!

3. **Application/Utils:** Information about NetWare-specific applications and utilities (not just from Novell, either)

4. **Btrieve/XQL/SQL:** Information about NetWare's record manager and database tools

5. **Email/MHS:** Information about electronic mail, messaging formats, and message-based applications

6. **P'gramming/N'Ware:** Basic information for would-be NetWare developers

7. **Network Management**

8. **Suggestion Box**

9. **User Groups/Train'g:** Information about NetWare Users International and NetWare Users Group; also, information about NetWare training courses

10. **OS/2 Requestor:** Information about using NetWare with OS/2 clients

11. **VAR/Dealertalk:** Traffic between Novell and its dealers

12. **CNEs:** Information exchange among Novell-certified NetWare engineers

13. **Developers:** Information exchange between Novell and its software developers

14. **CNEPA:** CNE Professional Association information, events, and activities

15. **The Lighter Side:** In this forum, you can get as carried away as you want to and on any topic. Often hilarious, never boring.

NOVVEN

Novell's vendor affiliates hang out in the NOVVEN forum — typically including the folks who offer NetWare preinstalled on their hardware or systems, or who offer NetWare-specific applications or services. It's a good place to get help from specific vendors.

1. **Folio:** The folks who developed the information-retrieval system used in the NetWare Support Encyclopedia

2. **LAN Support Group:** A consulting, training, and support organization for NetWare and Novell products

3. **Computer Tyme:** Authors of several outstanding NetWare utilities

4. **Infinite Tech.:** More NetWare software and services

5. **Dell Computer Corp.:** The source for Dell information on NetWare. Michael Dell himself drops in here regularly.

NOVLIB

All the Novell-related file libraries are kept in the NOVLIB forum. It offers only one section — 1) LIB Questions Only!! — which is meant to be used solely to get library access and usage questions answered. The real action is in the libraries, each of which typically includes a detailed and abbreviated catalog of its contents. This list shows the libraries available in NOVLIB:

1. **Novell New UPLOADS:** Files uploaded recently by Novell, Inc.

2. **General Information:** General information, Novell Education information, and official Novell press releases

3. **NetWare 2.X Specific:** Files pertaining only to NetWare 2.x

4. **NetWare 3.X Specific:** Files pertaining only to NetWare 3.x

5. **Client/Shell Drivers:** Workstation shells, drivers, Windows files, and more

6. **NetWare Utilities:** Utilities specific to NetWare 2.x and 3.x

7. **Btrieve/XQL:** Novell Development Division Products' Btrieve/XQL/SQL files and information

8. **Mac/UNIX/LANalyzer:** Files for Macintosh, UNIX, LANalyzer

9. **Communications Product:** Files related to Novell's Communications Products (NetWare for SAA, NAS, NACS, NetWare 3270 clients, and more)

10. **NetWare Lite:** NetWare Lite-specific files

11. **Techinfo/IMSP's:** Technical bulletins, FYIs, IMSP certification bulletins, and uploads mentioned in the Novell AppNotes

12. **NDSG/DRDOS:** Files for Novell's Desktop Systems Group products and for Novell-DOS (also known as DR-DOS)

13. **Other Patches/Drivers:** Third-party patches and drivers, typically for NICs, disk controllers, tape-backup units, and so on

14. **Independent Development:** Third-party code samples including code referenced in the *NetWare Technical Journal*

15. **Shareware/Demo:** Shareware/demo files

16. **Public Domain/Text:** Public-domain software and archived message threads

17. **Other NEW UPLOADS:** Third-party new uploads

After familiarizing yourself with the libraries, you probably will most often end up checking out libraries 1 and 17 (Novell's and third-party uploads, respectively). The new stuff hits here first, and these areas seldom require as much reading to find what you need as the others can.

A Concluding Cruel Caveat

What you have read in this appendix is true as it's being written, but, alas, the CompuServe forums and libraries change with changes to Novell and its products. Novell's acquisition of Unix Systems Laboratories seems to argue that it's just a matter of time before significant UNIX coverage gets added to the NetWire forums. Likewise, as new products get introduced and old ones phased out, the name and contents of the NetWire forums, their subsidiary sections, and the libraries all will change.

Our advice is to check out the New User Information, available on-line from NetWire from time to time. You should not only familiarize yourself with it to get oriented but also keep checking in to stay informed about what's changed and what's new and interesting. One thing's for sure: You will never run out of messages to read on NetWire. Just hope that you never have to plumb the full depths of its libraries, either.

Whatever your level of interest, we're sure that a trip to NetWire will be well worth it. If you want to be a real NetWare professional, it's the only place to visit!

Index

• D •

NetWare Notes

NetWare Notes

NetWare Notes

NetWare Notes

NetWare Notes

NetWare Notes

NetWare Notes

NetWare Notes

NetWare Notes

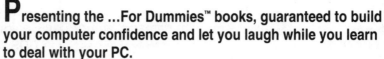

Order Form

Order Center: (800) 762-2974 (8 a.m.-5 p.m., PST, weekdays) or (415) 312-0650

For Fastest Service: Photocopy This Order Form and FAX it to : (415) 358-1260

Quantity	ISBN	Title	Price	Total

Shipping & Handling Charges

Subtotal	U.S.	Canada & International	International Air Mail
Up to $20.00	Add $3.00	Add $4.00	Add $10.00
$20.01-40.00	$4.00	$5.00	$20.00
$40.01-60.00	$5.00	$6.00	$25.00
$60.01-80.00	$6.00	$8.00	$35.00
Over $80.00	$7.00	$10.00	$50.00

In U.S. and Canada, shipping is UPS ground or equivalent.
For Rush shipping call (800) 762-2974.

Subtotal _____

CA residents add
applicable sales tax _____

IN residents add
5% sales tax _____

Canadian residents
add 7% GST tax _____

Shipping _____

TOTAL _____

Ship to:

Name _____

Company_____

Address_____

City/State/Zip _____

Daytime Phone _____

Payment: ❑ Check to IDG Books (US Funds Only)   ❑ Visa   ❑ MasterCard   ❑ American Express

Card # _____   Exp. _____   Signature _____

Please send this order form to: IDG Books, 155 Bovet Road, Suite 310, San Mateo, CA 94402.
Allow up to 3 weeks for delivery. Thank you!

BOBFD

IDG BOOKS WORLDWIDE REGISTRATION CARD

RETURN THIS REGISTRATION CARD FOR FREE CATALOG

Title of this book: Netware For Dummies

My overall rating of this book: ❑ Very good [1] ❑ Good [2] ❑ Satisfactory [3] ❑ Fair [4] ❑ Poor [5]

How I first heard about this book:

❑ Found in bookstore; name: [6] _____

❑ Advertisement: [8]

❑ Word of mouth; heard about book from friend, co-worker, etc.: [10]

❑ Book review: [7]

❑ Catalog: [9]

❑ Other: [11]

What I liked most about this book:

_____

_____

_____

What I would change, add, delete, etc., in future editions of this book:

_____

_____

_____

Other comments:

_____

_____

Number of computer books I purchase in a year: ❑ 1 [12] ❑ 2-5 [13] ❑ 6-10 [14] ❑ More than 10 [15]

I would characterize my computer skills as: ❑ Beginner [16] ❑ Intermediate [17] ❑ Advanced [18] ❑ Professional [19]

I use ❑ DOS [20] ❑ Windows [21] ❑ OS/2 [22] ❑ Unix [23] ❑ Macintosh [24] ❑ Other: [25]_____
(please specify)

I would be interested in new books on the following subjects:
(please check all that apply, and use the spaces provided to identify specific software)

❑ Word processing: [26] _____

❑ Data bases: [28] _____

❑ File Utilities: [30] _____

❑ Networking: [32] _____

❑ Other: [34] _____

❑ Spreadsheets: [27] _____

❑ Desktop publishing: [29] _____

❑ Money management: [31] _____

❑ Programming languages: [33] _____

I use a PC at (please check all that apply): ❑ home [35] ❑ work [36] ❑ school [37] ❑ other: [38] _____

The disks I prefer to use are ❑ 5.25 [39] ❑ 3.5 [40] ❑ other: [41]_____

I have a CD ROM: ❑ yes [42] ❑ no [43]

I plan to buy or upgrade computer hardware this year: ❑ yes [44] ❑ no [45]

I plan to buy or upgrade computer software this year: ❑ yes [46] ❑ no [47]

Name: _____ Business title: [48] _____ Type of Business: [49] _____

Address (❑ home [50] ❑ work [51]/Company name: _____)

Street/Suite# _____

City [52]/State [53]/Zipcode [54]: _____ Country [55] _____

❑ **I liked this book!** You may quote me by name in future IDG Books Worldwide promotional materials.

My daytime phone number is _____

IDG BOOKS

THE WORLD OF COMPUTER KNOWLEDGE

❏ **YES!**

Please keep me informed about IDG's World of Computer Knowledge.
Send me the latest IDG Books catalog.